REGULATION OF CONSUMER FINANCIAL SERVICES, ed. by Arnold A. Heggestad. Abt Associates, 1981. 275p index 81-66569. 24.00. ISBN 0-89011-562-1. CIP

Based on research by Abt Associates for the National Science Foundation, these articles deal with the effects of regulation of demand deposits, time deposits, and consumer loans. Unfortunately, the summarizing introduction and chapter on competition by the editor and principal investigator draw conclusions not justified by references or subsequent articles. Most of the articles are by academic economists who were on the research team. Charles Hayward (Kentucky) wrote the longest and shortest chapters while Shay and Brandt (Columbia) did analyses of the Truth in Lending and Equal Credit Opportunity acts. A lawyer and central banker cover their specialities and consumer representative Batko wrote an excellent review of reform proposals. The nine chapters range from descriptions to research reports but are not consistent or conclusive in their findings. No bibliography but extensive chapter references and several excellent tables of data. Limited index. Usable in both academic and public libraries.

Regulation of Consumer Financial Services

Research Team

Arnold A. Heggestad—Principal Investigator; Chairman of the Department of Finance, University of Florida

John J. Mingo—Federal Reserve Board

Willian Batko—Consumer Representative, Vermont Public Interest Research Group

William Brandt—Associate Professor, Graduate School of Business, Columbia University

Dwight Ebaugh—Attorney, MacLean, Seaman, Laing and Gulford; Lansing, Michigan

Franklin Edwards—Professor of Economics, Graduate School of Business, Columbia University

Charles F. Haywood—Professor of Economics, University of Kentucky

John M. Marshall—Associate Professor of Economics, University of California, Santa Barbara

Anthony M. Santomero—Professor of Finance, The Wharton School, University of Pennsylvania

Donald E. Sexton, Jr.—Associate Professor, Graduate School of Business, Columbia University

Robert P. Shay—Professor of Banking and Finance, Graduate School of Business, Columbia University

James Vitarello—Community Development Specialist, Office of the Comptroller of the Currency

Advisory Group

Kenneth Arrow—Professor of Economics, Harvard University

S. Lees Booth—Vice-President, National Consumer Finance Association

Jonathan Brown—Public Interest Research Group, Washington, D.C.

D. Dale Browning—Senior Vice-President, Colorado National Bank

Robert Dorfman—Professor of Economics, Harvard University

Allen Ferguson—President, Public Interest Economics Center

Zvi Griliches—Professor of Economics, Harvard University

Lewis Goldfarb—Acting Assistant Director, Division of Special Statutes, Federal Trade Commission

Leonard Lapidus—Special Assistant to the Chairman, Federal Deposit Insurance Corporation

P. Michael Laub—Director of Financial Research, American Bankers Association

John Lintner—Professor of Business, Harvard University

Peter Livingston—Director of Research, Credit Union National Association

Donald J. Melvin—Counsel, Credit Union National Association

Kathleen O'Reilly—Former Executive Director, Consumer Federation of America

Laurence C. Rosenberg—Program Manager, Division of Applied Research, National Science Foundation

Robert Solow—Professor of Economics, Massachusetts Institute of Technology

Regulation of

Consumer

Financial Services

Edited by Arnold A. Heggestad

348254

Abt Books/Cambridge, Massachusetts

*Based upon a report prepared for the National Science
Foundation under NSF/RANN Grant NSF-C76-18548.
Any opinions, findings, conclusions, or recommendations
expressed in this publication are those of the author(s) and do
not necessarily reflect the views of the National Science
Foundation.*

Library of Congress Cataloging in Publication Data
Main entry under title:

Regulation of consumer financial services.

  "Based upon a report prepared for the National
Science Foundation under NSF/RANN"—T. p. verso.
  Includes index
  1. Banking law—Economic aspects—United States.
2. Bank accounts—United States. 3. Consumer credit—
United States. I. Heggestad, Arnold A., 1943-
II. National Science Foundation (U.S.) III. Title:
Consumer financial services.
HG1778.U5R43   332.1'0973   81-66569
ISBN 0-89011-562-1   AACR2

CONTENTS

PREFACE

Under the auspices of the National Science Foundation, Abt Associates Inc. analyzed the costs and benefits to consumers of regulations affecting consumer financial services. The study focused on three types of consumer services—demand deposits, time and savings deposits, and consumer loans—one or more of which are offered by most financial institutions.

During the first phase of the study, the Abt Associates research team completed a descriptive analysis of the consumer financial services industry and its legal and regulatory environment, chose specific regulations to study, and developed the appropriate methodology and data bases for their evaluation. In addition, a comprehensive bibliography of relevant research in the area was compiled. In the second phase the empirical research was carried out and the effects of several key regulations estimated.

Regulation of consumer financial services has far-reaching consequences in many sectors of American society. Regulations that seem innocuous when viewed from one perspective may be particularly burdensome from other perspectives. Furthermore, benefits may accrue to one group while the costs are borne by others. In an effort to guarantee that all major perspectives were represented in the choice of regulations for study, the methodology used to evaluate the regulations, and interpretations of the results, the research team and the project's advisory group included representatives of three groups—consumer activists, industry members, and regulators.

ONE
Introduction

Consumers require numerous financial services, including deposit services, investment services, and provision of credit for a variety of uses. These services are provided by a heterogeneous group of firms. Some, such as consumer finance companies, specialize in a few specific services. Others, such as commercial banks, provide a wide range of depository and credit services.

The industry structure is constantly changing. New technology and regulatory reform have led to the development of different types of institutions and to fundamental changes in the conditions of local markets. For example, computer technology has made possible the use of credit cards for many types of consumer loans that previously had been available on an installment loan basis only from local financial institutions. In effect, the use of retail credit cards has increased the number of options available to locally limited borrowers, who now can choose among revolving credit plans offered by retailers, nonlocal banks, or other types of financial institutions. The future adoption of electronic funds transfer systems is likely to have a similar effect on deposit markets.

In addition to technological change, regulatory reform has also had an impact on the structure of these markets. For example, as states have modified their branching laws, the number of options available to local customers has increased. Many institutions have been given new powers that increase their competitiveness in areas outside their traditional domain.

Commercial banks, which number over 14,000 in the United States, are the dominant type of firm providing consumer financial services. They are the least regulated and are able to handle all major types of consumer deposits and most major forms of consumer credit. Historically, banks were the only institutions permitted to offer demand deposits, perhaps the most widely used consumer financial service. However, restrictions on geographic expansion and the local nature of the markets for consumer financial services substantially limit the options that commercial banks can offer consumers.

Credit unions are becoming an increasingly strong force in consumer credit and savings markets. Their growth rates have far exceeded the growth rates of other suppliers of consumer financial services. Credit unions are formed as voluntary cooperative institutions designed to facilitate low-cost credit and to encourage savings among their members. They are nonprofit, mutually owned associations and typically are managed by volunteer officers. Membership is limited in credit unions to a common bond, which is generally based upon occupation or place of employment. Other examples of possible common bonds are fraternal associations and homogeneous residential groups. This common bond is an important element of the credit union structure, because it effectively limits the potential growth of the credit union and ensures a cohesiveness among the members that helps minimize losses on credit transactions. Furthermore, the cooperative spirit and favorable rate ceilings encourage members to save through their credit unions.

In recent years the powers of credit unions have been drastically increased. They are now permitted to offer all forms of consumer credit to their members with very few limitations. They can offer demand deposit accounts with interest (NOW accounts), as well as savings deposits. Thus, credit unions will probably continue to be a growing force in the consumer financial services industry.

The third major group involved in the provision of consumer financial services consists of savings and loan associations. Traditionally, they were mutual associations that offered savings deposits and used the proceeds to make mortgage loans. Legislative and regulatory reform has widened their powers as well. In addition to mortgage loans, they now offer all types of consumer credit, including credit cards. Thus, savings and loan associations are also likely to become an increasingly important force in the provision of all consumer financial services.

Mutual savings banks are structured quite similarly to savings and loan associations and are particularly important in a few eastern states. They also compete for savings funds. Their aggressive behavior in creating NOW accounts has led to fundamental changes in the nature of demand deposits in the United States. As a result of their actions, interest is now allowed on these accounts, and all depository institutions are permitted to offer demand deposits. Thus, commercial banks have lost their advantage as the only type of institution able to offer demand deposits. Although mutual savings banks have the power to offer consumer loans in most states, they seldom exercise it. Instead, they concentrate their loan portfolios in mortgages and do not actively compete for consumer loans.

The final major category in the deposit and credit markets consists of finance companies and specialized providers of consumer credit. These firms have traditionally specialized in small loans and have operated under the small loan laws in the states. They generate funds not through deposits, but through the commercial paper markets and by borrowing from other depository intermediaries.

Regulation of Consumer Financial Services

The consumer financial services industry is extensively regulated. There are several different objectives behind the regulations. One major group of regulations is designed to limit competition in financial markets. Restricted competition is expected to reduce the incidence of failure that may result from excessive competition. Another group of regulations promotes soundness by limiting the risk exposure of firms in the industry. Still other groups of regulations are designed to protect consumers from potential abuse, such as discrimination and usurious interest rates. Finally, certain regulations are designed to affect the flow of credit. Regulations have been promulgated to increase credit availability for housing and for other purposes that may be in the mutual interest.

The effects of regulation are both direct and indirect. Direct benefits generally accrue to customers; for example, in the form of reduced discrimination or more credit for housing. The direct benefit of soundness regulations is a reduction in the number of failures of depository institutions and in the concomitant costs of failure to depositors. Thus, the benefits of regulations, at least the direct benefits, are relatively easy to delineate, although they are not necessarily easy to measure.

Direct costs are the resources required for compliance, for example, redesigning forms to comply with the Truth in Lending Act or the Equal Credit Opportunity Act (ECOA) or maintaining internal auditing programs to monitor insider transactions. In general, the direct costs of compliance with regulations are not great, and they are likely to be exceeded by the direct benefits. The heuristic cost-benefit analysis undertaken by legislatures often leads to the passage of regulations based on a comparison of *direct* costs with *direct* benefits.

However, the indirect consequences of regulating consumer financial services may well be considerably greater than the direct consequences. In general, indirect costs exceed indirect benefits. The indirect costs are the additional resources required to carry out the process of deposit gathering and credit granting when the regulation is in place. These costs arise from at least three sources. First, regulations may reduce economic efficiency by not allowing the financial firm to produce services in the least costly manner so as to maximize profits. Structural laws, such as the prohibition of branching, may not allow the firm to achieve minimal optimal size. Estimates of the cost function for financial intermediaries suggest that many banks are already too small, as are most credit unions. In addition, the intermediation process itself is disturbed by regulation as restrictions on investments and on the types of deposits a firm can offer prevent them from optimizing their portfolios.

A second source of indirect costs is the expenditure of resources to evade the burdensome effects of regulations. Competition may force firms to attempt to evade regulations. This is most evident in the case of regulations that limit the interest rates financial institutions may pay for deposits. It would be most efficient to generate deposits by increasing the interest rates paid on them. This would give management the flexibility to vary deposit rates as the bank requires funds or as loan demand conditions change. Currently, Regulation Q limits the amount of interest that financial institutions can pay to increase deposit levels. Since regulations prohibit the strategy of changing rates to attract new deposits, management is forced to rely upon nonprice methods of competition. These nonprice devices, such as advertising or the maintenance of an extensive branching network, which are a means of evading rate ceilings, increase the costs to firms of providing the services of financial intermediation. That is, to duplicate the impact on consumers of changing prices (deposit rates), the firms may have to spend more on nonprice devices.

Finally, regulations concerning entry, such as limitations on new charters and prohibition of interstate banking, as well as restrictions on competition between various types of institutions, often reduce economic competition. Markets that are not competitive in structure and that are protected from new entry tend to perform poorly. In general, prices will be higher relative to costs in noncompetitive markets. Furthermore, without competitive market pressure, it is less likely that credit will be allocated according to social priorities.

Two issues often arise in the analysis of consumer financial services regulation. The first is the diversion between the original intent of a regulation and its actual effects. Often, this is the result of improper specification. Regulations intended to achieve a particular objective may be poorly designed, may have no effect, or may have the opposite effect of that which is intended. For example, it is now evident that usury laws actually hurt the low-income, poorly educated people they are intended to help by foreclosing them from credit. Also, many financial regulations have been in effect for so long that evasion by participants in the markets has become commonplace, completely circumventing the intended effects. Thus, an analysis of regulations requires examination of the original intent of the regulation, as well as its actual impact.

A second issue is the strong interaction among regulations. There are two basic forms of such interaction. The first, and more common, way in which regulations interact is by overlapping. Where one regulation would be sufficient to meet a particular social objective, there may be several, each focusing on a different aspect of the firm or its market. For example, many regulations are intended to achieve soundness by preventing excessive failures in the industry. If one set of regulations, such as a capital restriction, is adequate to obtain the required soundness levels, the remaining regulations, which have a similar intent, may well be redundant. The second form of interaction is conflict among the various regulations. For example, reduction of competition to improve soundness may lead to monopoly and to business practices that violate consumer rights. The lack of competition then requires new regulations to protect consumers against these forms of abuses. These new regulations may in turn lead to other practices that, for example, endanger institutional soundness. Specific types of interrelations will be provided in the discussion of specific regulations that follows.

The possible social costs and benefits of several regulations of consumer financial services and the empirical evidence of their effects are discussed below. These regulations include deposit rate ceilings, competitive structure, management restrictions, usury ceilings, and consumer protection regulations. Many of the effects were determined in the study conducted by Abt Associates. The discussion of the effects of soundness regulations reflects the results of other studies funded concurrently with this study by the National Science Foundation.

Deposit Rate Ceilings

The traditional view of deposit rate ceilings for both banks and thrift institutions, including the prohibition of interest on demand deposits, is that such ceilings bestow monopoly power on financial institutions, allowing them to pay less for deposits than would otherwise be the case. While ceilings discriminate against consumers, the accompanying increase in monopoly power and profitability of financial institutions improves their soundness. According to this view, any regulatory reform that includes the repeal of deposit rate ceilings will lead to increased costs for financial institutions and lowered earnings. In addition, the direct risk exposure of financial firms may be increased if managers attempt to rely on higher yielding, riskier assets to offset increased deposit costs. Thus, failure rates may increase due to lower profits and to a shift in the riskiness of asset portfolios. Any benefit to consumers from repealing deposit rate ceilings in the form of higher savings rates must be weighed against the impact on institutional soundness.

The alternative view is that deposit rate ceilings are a classic example of regulations that do not satisfy their original intent. Managers will not take unnecessary asset risks to compensate for more expensive liabilities. In addition, managers have attempted to circumvent rate ceilings by using noninterest devices, such as advertising; extensive branching networks; and remission of fees for checking services, including "free" checking. Thus, ceilings represent a type of regulation that has been in place for a long time and that has been, to an important extent, evaded by most firms. But this attempt at evasion has induced increased costs in the industry.

The use of noninterest devices is less efficient than paying higher interest on deposits. That is, at the margin, the value to consumers of noninterest devices may not be as high as the cost to the bank of producing such devices. Also, financial institutions cannot always take full advantage of investment opportunities that arise because they cannot bid for more deposits with higher rates. Individual banks, of course, can bid for federal funds or large denomination certificates of deposit from nonhousehold customers; however, neither individual banks nor the system as a whole can bid for more household deposits, even when it is profitable to do so.

In periods of rising interest rates, as in late 1979, rate ceilings actually lead to increased risk of failure rather than greater soundness. As savers become dissatisfied with low ceiling rates on deposits, they place their funds in instruments that offer more attractive rates, such as Treasury bills or money market funds. This "disintermediation" places tremendous pressure on the depository institutions, which do not have sufficient liquid assets to meet the deposit withdrawals.

In summary, the two alternative views of rate ceilings are quite different in their assessment of the usefulness and consequences of imposing ceilings. Determining which view is correct is an empirical issue. The empirical evidence has to be studied to determine (1) how discriminatory rate ceilings are, (2) how they affect management behavior, and (3) to what extent they have been evaded.

In Chapter Five, "The Economic Impact of Deposit Rate Ceilings," John Mingo questions the assumption that imposing ceilings on liabilities leads to greater stability. Those institutions that relied as heavily as possible on interest rates as a competitive device in the 1970s were significantly safer and their income patterns more stable than institutions that relied upon nonprice means of competition. Mingo's results corroborate studies of institutions that paid interest on demand deposits in the 1930s. Their failure rate was actually less than the failure rate of institutions that did not pay interest. Thus, there is little evidence to suggest that the benefits accruing from these ceilings are substantial.

Studies by Mingo and others suggest that rate ceilings reduce savers' income. The victims of this discriminatory effect are low-income savers unable to invest in the larger denomination securities that pay higher rates of interest.

The prohibition of interest on demand deposits may not have had a similar effect on low-income depositors. An important finding of the Mingo study is that NOW draft ("check") usage is not very sensitive to the draft fee being charged, and as income rises this sensitivity disappears altogether. This result, together with the observation that check usage increases slowly as income rises, suggests that repeal of the interest prohibition, resulting in nationwide use of NOW accounts with explicit pricing of checks, may benefit higher balance (higher income) persons most. That is, high-balance customers will earn substantially more interest income on their balance than will low-balance (low-income customers) but will be charged only slightly more per month for explicitly priced checks.

Liability rate ceilings are closely related to other regulations of financial institutions. Rate ceilings restrict the degree of price competition, increase nonprice competition, and increase the liquidity risks of disintermediation. The first effect requires that other regulations stress procompetitive policies to overcome the restrictions on competition imposed by the ceilings. Thus, there is an interaction between regulations concerning competition and rate ceilings. With respect to their effects on nonprice competition and liquidity risks, rate ceilings interact strongly with soundness regulations, because they tend to increase the risk exposure of financial institutions. For example, increased nonprice competition, with concomitant higher fixed costs, will require greater soundness regulations, such as a capital requirement and restrictions on investments, than would have been required in the absence of the ceiling when competition would have taken a different form. Similarly, increasing the risk of disintermediation requires limitation of investments and restrictions on other forms of liquidity to compensate for this risk.

Entry and Branching Restrictions

The regulations and laws that fall under the general category of entry restrictions are designed to increase soundness and to promote interfirm competition. These include chartering requirements, state branching laws, the McFadden Act, the Bank Merger Act of 1960, and the Bank Holding Company Act as amended in 1970. In the case of chartering requirements, the main concern is with overbanking. Branching laws restrict concentration of resources—for example, preventing large banks from branching statewide and competing against the resources of small banks—and the destructive competition resulting from overbranching. The Bank Merger Act and the Bank Holding Company Act are aimed at maintaining or improving competition (that is, they require regulatory agencies to guard against the anticompetitive effects of proposed mergers and acquisitions).

Whatever the intent of entry restrictions, branching laws, and the like, the result has been highly concentrated local financial markets in which consumers have few options. Studies have found that most banking markets exhibit high concentration and reduced price competition, and that entry has brought substantial benefits to consumers in the form of lower rates and greater credit availability. Thus, chartering and banking laws that restrict entry are not in the interest of consumers. Studies of commercial banking have demonstrated that chartering laws restrict entry by as much as 50 percent over what would have been achieved in the absence of such laws.

Restriction of competition among the various types of firms offering consumer financial services has been used primarily as a device to allocate credit, with a secondary goal of increasing soundness by reducing excessive competition. A primary credit allocation goal of these regulations is to generate more mortgage funds by isolating savings and loan institutions and then restricting their portfolios to the holding of real estate mortgages. Most studies of the supply of mortgages have concluded that programs such as these do not increase the overall supply of funds. Increased mortgages from the thrift institutions are generated at the expense of a reduced supply of mortgage funds from commercial banks and other lenders. Thus, these regulations have not accomplished their primary goal of generating more mortgage funds; moreover, they have imposed substantial costs on consumers in the form of higher loan rates, lower deposit rates, and reduced consumer services, as Heggestad observes in Chapter Six.

Heggestad finds that the restrictions on interinstitutional competition have been effective at the local level in segmenting the markets of the various types of firms. Although the evidence is weak, it suggests that in 1977 commercial banks were, on the average, able to price their consumer products without taking into account other nonbank competition. In the consumer credit area there appears to be some breakdown in the restrictions on interinstitutional competition, but not at the expense of commerical banks. In local markets the Heggestad study finds some sensitivity to interinstitutional competition in rates of charge for consumer loans at credit unions and consumer finance companies. These institutions charge lower rates when they face strong bank competition. The opposite is not true, however: banks do not appear to adjust prices to reflect differences in the strength of alternative credit sources.

In Chapter Seven ("Regulation, Structure, and Technological Change in the Consumer Financial Services Industry"), Haywood examines yet another facet of the impact of market structure on financial services—the relation between competitive restrictions and the diffusion of new technology, such as computer-based bank operation and bank credit cards. He finds that computer use and dissemination of credit cards are positively related with bank size and with the degree of permanence in state branching restrictions. The Haywood results are noteworthy because no previous formal analysis of banking behavior has concentrated on the specific determinants of investment in new technologies and services.

Entry and branching regulations may interact with other restrictions on financial intermediaries. Limiting competition in this manner increases the need for consumer protection, for example, preventing discrimination through such laws as the Equal Credit Opportunity Act. The least costly and most efficient way to eliminate credit abuses would be to provide for competitive markets. Similarly, branching regulations may restrict the financial institution's ability to diversify its sources of deposits. Concentration of deposits in one or a few geographic areas could lead to greater deposit instability, which would (in turn) require stricter soundness regulations. Finally, differing degrees of competition among the various types of institutions, combined with prohibitions on interinstitutional competition and flows of funds between institutions, may lead to undesirable credit allocations to geographic areas. For example, because of restrictions on branching or entry, a market with a competitive and aggressive banking sector and a limited thrift sector may suffer from an insufficient supply of mortgages as compared to markets with greater competition in both sectors.

Asset Restrictions and Loan Rate Ceilings

Most types of financial institutions are subject to well-defined restrictions on the types and amounts of assets they can purchase and on the rates they can charge for loans. For example, commercial banks generally cannot purchase corporate stock or underwrite nongovernment bond issues; thrift institutions in most states cannot make commercial loans and banks cannot make loans exceeding 10 percent of their capital to one borrower; most financial institutions must keep some minimum portion of their assets in cash or other liquid form; and reserve requirements may be as high as 16.5 percent of net demand deposits. Of course, almost every state limits the interest rate that institutions can charge on various types of loans.

With the exception of loan interest rate ceilings, the major rationale for asset restrictions has been to keep institutions from making loans or from purchasing assets that are too risky or illiquid. For various reasons, however, asset restrictions may have contributed to greater inherent riskiness in banking operations than would otherwise exist. For example, because they cannot invest in all types of assets, banks, and especially thrift institutions, cannot fully diversify. The result may be to choose a portfolio with lower earnings and greater risk than in the absence of asset restrictions.

The dangers of insufficient diversification are obvious in the case of disintermediation suffered by thrift institutions in a period of rising interest rates. During these periods, when depositors withdraw their funds to invest directly in market security, portfolios with short-term assets would be more liquid than those with long-term mortgages. Studies have indicated that as little as 10 percent of the savings and loan portfolios allocated to consumer loans would provide sufficient liquidity.

The purpose of loan rate ceilings, such as state usury ceilings in the case of mortgage loans, is to protect consumers from paying unfairly high rates. However, when they are binding, such ceilings may restrict the supply of loans to consumers and adversely affect institutional soundness. Numerous studies have demonstrated that the quantity of consumer loans is substantially reduced as loan rate ceilings become increasingly binding. Thrift institutions, which usually must purchase mortgages as a chief asset, cannot afford to pay the higher deposit rates to keep deposit customers during high-rate periods, as long as usury ceilings keep them from earning high returns on new mortgages. In effect, the state usury ceiling and the deposit rate ceiling combine to cause the cyclical disintermediation problem for thrift institutions.

Supervision, Examination, and Deposit Insurance

Among the most important and least understood elements of financial regulation is the supervisory process. At the federal level alone, five agencies employ approximately 10,000 people and spend $280 million per year examining the financial condition of banks, savings and loans, and credit unions; supervising the institutions' efforts to expand or innovate; and making sure they adhere to the myriad federal and state laws and regulations. Commerical banks must be examined twice in every three-year period. Examination of a multibillion dollar bank might require a dozen person-years of effort and be conducted jointly by officials of two federal agencies and at least one state agency.

What is the point of this great expense? Presumably, it helps prevent unsound banking practices from leading to individual bank failures and possibly "runs" on the entire system. The supervision process is bolstered in this regard by deposit insurance (which acts to prevent runs by small depositors) and by the "lender of the last resort" posture of the Federal Reserve.

Apart from the question of whether supervision is generally effective in achieving its primary goal, there appear to be several philosophical questions concerning the supervisory process as it fits into the broad spectrum of regulation. First, why is it necessary or desirable to regulate financial institutions both by setting certain inviolable limits to their actions (rate ceilings or loan limits) *and* by monitoring their actions so as to determine when such behavior is not in the social interest? If the monitoring (supervisory) process is effective, at worst the operating limits reduce the flexibility and efficiency of firms that can and should operate outside the boundaries of the regulations. If, on the other hand, supervision is ineffective, then operating limits in one area (for example, liability price ceilings) will be offset by the firm's excesses in another area (for example, excessively risky lending practices). The regulator-imposed operating limits will not serve to reduce the probability of a financial institution's failure and, therefore, must be justified on other grounds. Since most such "limits" (usury ceilings, deposit rate ceilings, and so on) may result in operating or allocative inefficiencies, they become difficult to justify if the financial soundness rationale for their existence is missing.

A second aspect of the relationship between supervision and other regulations is that the social benefits of financial reform will depend on the efficacy and stringency of supervision. The possible benefits from repeal of Regulation Q, for example, depend on the willingness or ability of banks to raise deposit rates, bidding funds away from market instruments to the satisfaction of bank customers (depositors). However, effective and stringent bank soundness standards imply that banks will not be allowed to expand as rapidly as otherwise; that is, competition for deposit funds will be restrained. Hence, market-determined earnings on supply of loans (postrepeal of loan rate ceilings) would be lower under stringent soundness standards and the benefits accruing to depositors (borrowers) from the removal of deposit (loan) ceilings would be lessened.

Consumer Protection Regulations

Legislation and regulation aimed at consumer credit services have found widespread support for several reasons. First, such laws would tend to increase information to financial consumers, thus decreasing the "irrational" selection and use of debt. Second, consumer protection laws would serve to insulate consumers from the actions of unconscionable creditors. Finally, such laws may lead to a decrease in consumer spending and borrowing (and an increase in savings).

The Truth in Lending Law (TIL) is designed to improve consumer awareness of interest rates. It requires that lenders report the costs of credit in a common framework—the annual percentage rate. Batko, in "Consumer Financial Services: Compliance With the Truth in Lending Act," found that nearly 90 percent of the lending firms surveyed are currently in compliance with TIL regulations.[1]

While there was little difference in compliance among different types of firms, the evidence suggests that smaller lending institutions were somewhat less compliant (in responding to consumers' telephone inquiries) than were large firms. The overall record of compliance with TIL, as shown both in the Batko study and in earlier surveys, suggests that the law is working. However, the effectiveness of this type of information-expanding law will clearly depend on the existence and importance of rate ceilings, such as state usury ceilings. For example, the usefulness of the annual percentage rate (APR) concept is diminished if an effective state usury ceiling causes all firms to charge the APR ceiling. In the absence of a rate ceiling, however, it is more likely that an innovative firm (one with lower costs or one that is more aggressive) will find it profitable to advertise a lower rate. With very low ceilings, such a rate reduction may not be forthcoming unless precipitated by a substantial decline in costs.

Interest rate information laws are also likely to reduce reliance on nonprice forms of competition among financial institutions as consumers become more aware of interest rates. In Chapter Eight, "Public Regulation of Financial Services: The Truth in Lending Law," Shay and Brandt suggest that this may already be taking place. The authors find a strong link between APR awareness and consumer shopping behavior (that is, number of firms visited to obtain credit). Further, overall awareness is growing, suggesting greater pressure to foster rate competition rather than nonprice forms of competition. Unfortunately, awareness is not increasing as fast among minority groups or those with low income or low education. Thus, firms that deal with these customers may feel less competitive pressure.

Two major economic issues concern the antidiscrimination laws and regulations (for example, the Equal Credit Opportunity Act). First, under such legislation, creditors can no longer use certain information (race, sex, marital status) in their credit-scoring schemes when determining the credit rating of a potential borrower. Such categories of information, to the extent that they are low-cost proxies for the "true" financial characteristics of a customer, help minimize the cost of a credit search. Outlawing the use of these proxies, it is argued, would therefore lead to inceased costs for financial institutions and an attendant decline in the supply of consumer credit. Shay, Brandt, and Sexton investigated this possibility using two independent sets of credit application and loan account histories. In Chapter Nine, "Public Regulation of Financial Services: The Equal Credit Opportunity Act," they report that eliminating information on sex, marital status, and age did not decrease the accuracy of the credit-scoring system used by a national retail firm, because these categories had little or no usefulness as predictors of satisfactory performance. However, in the case of a large finance company, age and marital status were significantly correlated with credit performance. Their evidence suggests that the costs of ECOA in terms of reducing information to lenders so that their losses increase may not be substantial. However, such protected classes may be worse off in that they would have scored higher if this information had been supplied; now it must be ignored.

A second issue surrounding ECOA-type legislation is whether discrimination actually takes place in financial markets. In "Discrimination in Consumer Credit" (Chapter Ten) Marshall examines this issue by analyzing two samples of applications for credit. His results are mixed: the first lender appeared to discriminate against older people before enactment of ECOA but gave them preferential treatment afterward; a second lender appeared to discriminate against older people both before and after ECOA. The finding of discrimination in the Marshall study requires careful analysis. Specifically, although old age may not, in itself, imply greater credit worthiness, other high-scoring variables (such as time at present job) are easier to achieve with advancing age, thus giving older people, other things being equal, higher credit scores. For this reason, credit managers may soon learn from actual default experiences that they ought to require *higher* credit scores of older people to compensate for the credit-scoring model's tendency to overrate them.

What cannot be learned from the Marshall study and its predecessors is the extent to which true discrimination, in the economic sense, takes place. Such discrimination occurs when a lender refuses a loan to a member of a certain group even though such a refusal is not in the profit-maximizing interest of the firm. In such cases the discriminating manager is paying for his social prejudices by not taking advantage of a profitable situation (a loan) when it is presented to him.

It is in the area of true economic discrimination (as opposed to the use of social or racial characteristics as financial proxies) that an important relationship exists between ECOA legislation and legislation that affects market structure. Specifically, in highly competitive markets the possibility for actual discrimination is lessened; a bank manager could not *afford* to reject a profitable loan on racial or other grounds, because bank earnings would already be pushed to a bare minimum by competition. Moreover, with liberal entry and/or branching regulations, any racial or other social group that found itself credit-rationed on nonfinancial grounds ultimately would receive credit from new market entrants wishing to take advantage of profit potential. Hence, structural reform, such as increased thrift-bank competition for consumer loans or easing of branching restrictions, is likely to minimize the need for antidiscrimination legislation. Conversely, ECOA-type legislation is likely to have the greatest impact on credit flows in those states and local areas with the most concentrated, least competitive market structures.

The following two chapters by Haywood and Ebaugh describe the structure of the industry and the regulatory framework, respectively. They are followed by several chapters in which the costs and benefits of particular regulations are identified and analyzed. These regulations and the methodologies used to analyze them were chosen by agreement among the researchers, the advisory group, and the National Science Foundation. Regulations chosen for study are those for which the costs and benefits appear to diverge substantially— that is, particular groups have found the costs excessive. The studies themselves are diverse in their orientation. Some are empirical studies of regulation; others are primarily concerned with the development of methodologies that can be utilized when the appropriate data are available.

NOTES

1. Arnold A. Heggestad and John J. Mingo, eds., *The Costs and Benefits of Public Regulation of Consumer Financial Services,* Final Report to the National Science Foundation (Cambridge, Mass.: Abt Associates Inc., 1978).

TWO
Provision of Consumer Financial Services
Charles F. Haywood

Suppliers of Consumer Financial Services

Commercial banks, savings and loan associations, mutual savings banks, credit unions, finance companies, and retailers are the principal suppliers of the types of consumer financial services examined in this book. Over the past several decades, shifts have been made both in the number of institutions and in the percentage of services provided by each type of institution. This section outlines the growth of each type of financial institution, the factors affecting its growth, and the share of total consumer financial services it provided between 1950 and 1975.

There are approximately 14,650 commercial banks in the United States today—about the same number as there were in the late 1930s. The number of commercial banks increased rapidly starting in the 1870s and reached approximately 30,000 by 1920. From 1921 through 1929, failures, voluntary liquidations, and mergers outstripped the formation of new banks by an average of about 800 per year. From the beginning of 1930 to the end of 1933, the net decrease in the number of commercial banks was approximately 9,000. Thus, in the space of 13 years, the number of commercial banks in the United States was reduced by half.

At the end of 1975, there were 4,946 savings and loan associations in operation. The number has declined since about 1960, when there were 6,320 associations in operation. New savings and loan associations have been formed over the past fifteen years, but mergers have more than offset the number of new formations. The pace of mergers accelerated somewhat in the late 1960s. Between 1960 and 1965, 164 Federal Home Loan Bank System member associations were merged with other organizations. From 1966 through 1970 there were 374 mergers, and from 1971 through 1975 the total was 601.

Because of mergers and a few conversions to commercial bank form, the number of mutual savings banks has also declined, from 529 in 1950 to 476 in 1975. Sixteen of the seventeen states in which mutual savings banks are located permit either limited area or statewide branching. The number of mutual savings banks with branches increased from 195 in 1960 to 379 in 1975; the number of branch offices rose from 487 to 1,846. Further erosion of the number of mutual savings banks through merger and some additional expansion in number of branch offices can be expected. Regional concentration, however, limits the prospects for significant structural change. Federal chartering of mutual savings banks would, of course, open the door to expansion of the industry through conversion of savings and loan associations to mutual savings banks.

There are approximately 23,000 credit unions presently in existence. Credit unions have undergone considerable change since 1970, the year in which federal share insurance was established. From the late 1940s to 1970, expansion in the number of credit unions and growth in the size of individual credit unions could be explained by their appeal as relatively low-cost lenders. Credit unions were attractive to borrowers primarily because they offered installment credit at rates not in excess of 1 percent per month on the unpaid balance. Convenience, especially proximity to place of employment, was also a factor. Other favorable developments included growth in demand for consumer durable goods, particularly automobiles, and the increasing size and concentration of workers in industrial and commercial concerns and government entities. However, the growth of credit unions was constrained by the lack of federal insurance on share accounts and deposits. The advent of federal share insurance in 1970 opened new opportunities for growth through emphasis on the deposit function as well as the lending function. The powers of credit unions have since been greatly expanded. They are now able to offer mortgages, long-term consumer loans, and NOW accounts. Thus, their growth should continue.

Despite the large number of finance companies (3,376 in 1975), the consumer finance business is highly concentrated: 88 finance companies with loans of $100 million or more held 89.4 percent of the total assets of the industry in 1975. Looking only at consumer receivables, the companies with $100 million or more held 87.4 percent of the total. The Federal Reserve's 1975 survey of finance companies indicates little change in concentration since 1970 and an increase in the number of finance companies from 2,961 in 1970 to 3,376 in 1975. Formation of finance company subsidiaries by bank holding companies contributed to the pace of new entry between 1970 and 1975. A number of finance companies were also acquired by bank holding companies.

Retailers are also an important source of installment as well as noninstallment credit for consumers. However, since provision of credit is not the primary purpose of retailers, data on their numbers and growth will not be presented here, but the percentage of total consumer credit provided by retailers will be discussed later in this section.

Factors Affecting the Number of Suppliers

Prior to the mid-1930s, liberal chartering policies at the state and federal levels had resulted in a large number of uneconomic or marginally viable banks. Changes in the structure of the American economy during the 1920s (especially shifts of population from rural to urban areas), speculative excesses in the late 1920s, and the collapse of income and employment in the 1930s accentuated the weaknesses in the banking system and accelerated contraction in the number of banks. As a result of a wave of failures and liquidations caused by "overbanking," the earlier liberal chartering policies were replaced by more stringent standards, which required, among other things, proof of initial capital and management competence, evidence that income would probably be sufficient to assure economic viability within a reasonable period of time, demonstration of community need for a new bank, and documentation that there would be no apparent competitive damage to any existing bank. Bank charters became, in effect, certificates of public convenience and necessity.

The formation of new banks has reflected several patterns of economic change over the past thirty years or so. One is, of course, the increasing affluence of the U.S. economy. More influential forces have been regional shifts in population and economic activity. The demand for new banking services has stimulated expansion in the number of branch offices. Although new banks have been formed in such states, especially in those experiencing rapid economic growth, mergers have tended to offset new bank formations. This expansion in the *number* of commercial banks has been concentrated in states that prohibit or closely restrict branching.

States are usually grouped into three categories with respect to branching laws. At the present time, twenty states permit statewide branching, sixteen states permit branching within a limited area, and the remaining fourteen states essentially prohibit branching, although several of them now permit a limited number of branch offices or facilities to be established in close proximity to the home office or within the home office community. Furthermore, certain states usually listed under statewide branching prohibit de novo branching into communities with home offices or branch offices of other banks. Some limited branching states also have home office and branch office protection rules. Moreover, limited branching can mean branching in the home county and contiguous counties and/or branching within a geographic radius ranging from 25 to 100 miles of the home office.

Home office protection rules tend to have anticompetitive consequences. Entry through de novo branching by nonlocal banks is barred, and mergers are encouraged. In states permitting multibank holding companies, acquisition of a protected bank through the holding company may maintain home office protection, whereas acquisition by merger will terminate such protection if there is no other home office bank in the community. Home office protection rules are a neglected area of study in the field of banking structure.[1]

Much of the concentration in local banking markets reflects one or a combination of several factors: (1) state restrictions in de novo branching, (2) mergers that were consummated prior to the early 1960s, and (3) federal and state chartering policies since the mid-1930s. Expansion of bank holding companies since 1966 is also cited as a trend toward increased concentration in banking. However, a distinction should be made between the expansion of bank holding companies into closely related nonbanking activities and the expansion of multibank holding companies. Expansion of bank holding companies into closely related nonbanking activities may have procompetitive and/or anticompetitive effects, depending on the circumstances of the specific expansion. Expansion of multibank holding companies since 1966 has occurred in states that limit or prohibit branching. Acquisitions of banks by multibank holding companies have been mainly of the "market extension" variety—whereby the holding company acquires a bank in a market where it currently does not operate—and have not increased concentration in relevant market areas.

In addition to the impact of branching regulations on the concentration of banks in general, two types of banking institutions—savings and loan associations and credit unions—have been particularly affected by other economic and regulatory factors. For example, the merger movement in savings and loan associations appears to have been stimulated by several circumstances. Competition for savings balances and for mortgages has squeezed earnings margins.[2] Geographic expansion through merger has been attractive as a quicker and less expensive means of market penetration than de novo branching. Relatively significant economics of scale have been found in savings and loan associations, and these have apparently been given even greater dimension by electronic data processing and electronic funds transfer technology.

Federal branching policy has been favorable to savings and loan association mergers. Federally chartered savings and loan associations are not subject to the same statutory restriction as national banks, which must conform to state laws governing branching. The Federal Home Loan Bank Board has permitted associations to branch according to the prevailing mode of multioffice banking in an area; that is, it has permitted branching where multioffice banking is effected through holding companies and chain ownership, as well as through branching. In addition, branching in limited geographic areas, without regard to the prevailing mode or state law, has been permitted.

Antitrust standards with respect to product line and concentration have also favored savings and loan mergers. For the purpose of evaluating the competitive effects of bank mergers, the Supreme Court has defined commercial banking as the relevant line of commerce, or product line. However, acquisition of a savings and loan association has been considered to be in a line of commerce that includes the savings and residential mortgage business of commercial banks, as well as savings and loan associations. Concentration ratios pertinent to savings and loan mergers are thus defined on the basis of a broader product line than concentration ratios for mergers of commercial banks.

The structure of the savings and loan industry may be undergoing substantial change. Conditions seem to favor a continuation, perhaps even a further acceleration, of the merger movement. Also, conversions from a mutual form to a stock form of organization were suppressed, for a time, by a federal moratorium; only a limited number of conversions of federally chartered associations have been permitted. The conversion issue is affected by bitter opposition from sources that evidently believe there is political advantage (favorable legislative and regulatory treatment), as well as economic advantage, in maintaining the mutual character of the industry. Interest in conversions seems likely to increase, bringing greater pressure for some accommodation in federal policy. Two changes in federal policy could lead, in time, to a substantial decrease in the number of mutual savings and loan associations: liberalization of federal policy on conversions to stock form, or federal chartering of mutual savings banks.

With regard to credit unions, the introduction of federal insurance on share accounts and deposits encouraged credit union growth by emphasizing the deposit as well as the lending function of these institutions. In addition, credit unions recently entered the checking account business through issuance of share draft accounts. A share draft account is a savings account on which "payable through" drafts are drawn. Since December 31, 1980, they have been able to offer negotiable order of withdrawal (NOW) accounts.

With approximately 23,000 credit unions in existence, their entry into the checking account business could have a substantial effect on competition in the consumer financial services industry. Credit unions are not subject to Regulation Q ceilings or federal income taxes; moreover, they operate on an interstate basis, serving employees of the same company or government agency, wherever their actual places of employment are.

Although the requirement of a common bond as a basis for membership in credit unions has been an important factor contributing to economical and low-risk operation, it has also limited the expansion of individual credit unions. There has already been some erosion of the common bond requirement, and further relaxation seems likely. With share insurance, the common bond loses some of its significance as a factor making for safe and sound operations. Also, as credit unions get larger, economies of scale that might be realized from further expansion could offset the adverse consequences of an attenuated common bond requirement.

Continuing rapid growth of credit unions seems certain for some time to come. Further structural change also seems likely. Originally organized as "cooperatives," credit unions—at least the larger ones—should now be regarded as "mutual" organizations, in much the same fashion as mutual savings banks and mutual savings and loan associations. Professional management is becoming increasingly important in the credit union movement. Further growth of deposit services will accelerate the shift away from the traditional emphasis on credit unions as "self-help" cooperative lending institutions.

Percentage of Consumer Financial Services
Provided by Suppliers

As indicated in Table II-1, the savings and the time deposits of the household sector were estimated at $787.1 billion at the end of 1975. Commercial banks held $357.6 billion, or 46 percent, of the total. The balance was distributed as follows: savings and loan associations, $286 billion; mutual savings banks, $109.8 billion; credit unions, $32.2 billion; and consumer finance companies, $1.5 billion. Of the $195.4 billion of consumer credit shown in Table II-1, installment loans accounted for approximately $162.2 billion, and noninstallment credit, about $33.2 billion. Commercial banks held $78.7 billion of the installment debt, or 49 percent of the total. Finance companies had $36.2 billion, credit unions accounted for $25.4 billion, and retailers provided $17.9 billion. Other lenders, including mutual savings banks, savings and loan associations, and auto dealers, held $3.5 billion. The noninstallment debt fell into three categories of roughly equal size: single payment loans by commercial banks, charge accounts, and service credit.

Data on the growth of the major suppliers of consumer savings and time balances and consumer credit are shown in Table II-2. Commercial banks held approximately 48 percent of the savings and time balances of consumers at the end of 1950. Their share declined to 37 percent in 1960, increased to 45 percent in 1970, and edged up slightly to 46 percent by 1975. Since data on consumer ownership of commercial bank deposits are not reported as such and must therefore be estimated, small changes in relative position should not be taken too literally.

As demonstrated by the data in Table II-2, savings and loan

TABLE II-1 Assets and Liabilities of Households, Year-End 1975 (in billions of dollars)

Assets		
Money and "near moneys"		$ 969.4
Currency and demand deposits	$182.3	
Savings and time accounts	787.1	
Securities		945.4
Government securities	190.4	
Corporate and foreign bonds	62.1	
Corporate equities, at market	692.9	
Life insurance and pension fund reserves		512.9
Other financial assets (net)		28.6
Total financial assets		2,456.3
Nonfarm family loans		989.6
Durable goods		363.2
Total assets		3,809.5
Liabilities		
Consumer credit		195.4
Home mortgages		445.0
Other loans		53.7
Total liabilities		694.1
Net Worth		3,115.4
Total liabilities and net worth		3,809.5

Source: National Consumer Finance Association.

associations expanded rapidly in the 1950s, their relative share rising from 21 percent to 38 percent in the span of a decade. In the 1960s the growth of savings and loan associations slowed in comparison to the growth of consumer savings and time balances at commercial banks. From 1970 through 1975, the growth rate of savings and loan associations was about the same as that of commercial banks.

To some extent, the declining share of mutual savings banks reflects their concentration in the northeast region of the United States, which has lagged behind other regions in its rate of economic growth. In the states where they are concentrated, mutual savings banks have been experiencing a steady decline in market share, from about 45 percent in 1950 to 32 percent in 1975.[3] These market share reports, however, include corporate time deposits in the savings and

TABLE II-2 Growth of Major Suppliers of Selected Financial Services, 1950–1975 (in billions of dollars)

	1950		1955		1960		1965		1970		1975	
Savings and Time Deposits												
Commercial banks	$32.4	48%	$43.6	41%	$61.9	37%	$115.6	40%	$188.9	45%	$357.6	46%
Savings and loan associations	14.0	21	32.2	30	62.2	38	110.3	38	146.3	35	286.0	36
Mutual savings banks	20.0	30	28.1	26	36.3	22	52.4	18	71.6	17	109.8	14
Credit unions	0.9	1	2.4	2	4.9	3	9.2	3	15.5	4	32.2	4
Total	67.3		106.3		165.3		287.5		442.3		785.6	
Consumer Credit												
Commercial banks	5.8	40	10.6	37	16.7	39	29.0	42	45.4	44	78.7	48
Finance companies	5.3	36	11.8	41	15.4	36	23.8	34	27.7	27	36.7	23
Credit unions	0.6	4	1.7	6	3.9	9	7.3	10	13.0	13	25.4	16
Retailers	2.6	18	4.0	14	5.9	14	8.5	12	13.7	13	18.0	11
Others	0.4	3	0.8	3	1.0	2	1.3	2	2.3	2	3.5	2
Total	14.7		28.9		42.9		69.9		102.1		162.3	

Source: Board of Governors of the Federal Reserve System; U.S. Department of Commerce.

time balances of commercial banks, which grew rapidly during the 1960s and have been especially important in the deposit structures of commercial banks in the major metropolitan areas of such mutual savings bank states as New York, Massachusetts, Connecticut, and Pennsylvania. Although relevant estimates are not available, it seems reasonable to believe that exclusion of corporate time balances would show a less unfavorable trend in the relative position of mutual savings banks in the 1960s and might even reveal some improvement in market share in the 1970s.

Credit unions have experienced the fastest rate of growth of the several suppliers in the savings and time deposit market since 1950. Part of this growth was associated with expansion in the number of credit unions, which increased from 10,571 in 1950 to 22,806 in 1975.

In the consumer installment credit area, commercial banks experienced a decline in market share in the early 1950s but have shown strong expansion since the late 1950s. Finance companies have declined in relative position since the mid-1950s, with a substantial decrease since the mid-1960s. The strong growth of credit unions in installment lending, parelleling their growth in the savings account area, has gained them approximately 16 percent of the national total. Although installment lending by retailers did not expand as rapidly as total installment credit in the early 1950s, it grew at about the same pace from the mid-1950s to 1970. However, from 1970 to 1975, there was a significant slowing in the rate of expansion of installment loans by retailers.

Production of Consumer Financial Services

Consumer financial services fall into two broad categories: accumulation of financial assets for transaction purposes, short-term liquidity or precautionary needs, and long-term security; and assumption of liabilities, largely associated with the acquisition of homes and durable consumer goods. Banking institutions offer both categories of financial services, although the various types of banks differ in the particular services they offer. Finance companies and retailers do not provide deposit services but do offer both installment and noninstallment credit services. Because banks offer a full range of financial services, the production of services provided by these institutions will be treated first; the financial services provided by finance companies are discussed at the end of this section.

Banking origins can be traced to the safekeeping function—a function which in turn provides the funds that banks are able to lend and invest. A second function, clearing (the process of collecting funds deposited in a given bank), evolved in various ways in various societies according to the needs and technology of the time, and it is still evolving today. Although the functions of safekeeping and clearing are closely intertwined, it is convenient to describe them separately. Furthermore, since commercial banks provide the fullest array of both safekeeping and clearing services, they will be used to illustrate the way in which both functions are handled, while discussion of the way in which these two functions are handled by the other banking institutions will focus on differences peculiar to each type of bank.

Commercial Banks

Because of their role in the payments system, commercial banks have a more complicated production process than the other types of suppliers of consumer financial services. The relatively predominant position of commercial banks in the services selected for study suggests that the benefit-cost effects of regulation of commercial banks are especially important. Also, in certain instances benefit-cost effects on commercial banks can be generalized to other types of suppliers.

Commercial banks may obtain deposits, or lendable funds, from the public at lower cost than such funds would otherwise be available. By providing borrowers with funds at the time required, in appropriate amounts, and at convenient locations, commercial banks seek higher yields than can be obtained from investment in credit market securities. The net income of the banks is derived from the "spread" between costs and the yields on earning assets, in which payments for credit services are included.

According to data provided by the Federal Deposit Insurance Corporation, loans and securities make up more than 80 percent of the assets of commercial banks in 1975. Cash balances, including required reserves, account for about 13 percent. Fixed assets—land, buildings, furniture, and equipment—are less than 2 percent of total assets. The major categories of loans are commercial and industrial loans, real estate loans, and loans to individuals. Other types of lending that should be noted are loans to financial institutions, federal funds sold (overnight loans of excess reserves, mainly to other commercial banks), and farm production loans.

Commercial banks are highly leveraged enterprises, with equity funds making up only about 7 percent of total resources. Deposits contribute 84 percent of total resources, and nondeposit liabilities, including federal funds purchased, account for 9 percent. At the end of 1975 demand deposits (for example, checking accounts) were 40 percent of total deposits; time deposits, especially certificates of deposit, were almost 40 percent of the total; and savings accounts were about 20 percent.

Interest and fees on loans are, of course, the major source of income of commercial banks, contributing about 72 percent of total operating income in 1975. Income from investments contributed 17 percent. Tax-exempt interest on state and local government obligations is a relatively important source of net income after taxes. Income from sources other than loans and investments was 11 percent of total operating income in 1975.

On the expenses side, interest paid on savings and time accounts and on borrowed funds accounted for more than 50 percent of total expenses in 1975. Staff costs, including fringe benefits, were 23 percent of the total. Occupancy expenses, including furniture and equipment, were only about 5 percent. Other operating expenses, a relatively significant category, include items such as advertising, purchases of services (for example, data processing), and postage (a rapidly rising expense in recent years).

The first function of banks, the safekeeping function, can be divided into four components: (1) receipt and disbursement, (2) record keeping, (3) risk protection, and (4) maintenance of liquidity.

RECEIPT AND DISBURSEMENT. At first glance, receipt and disbursement procedures might seem relatively simple. The customer deposits currency and checks, listed on a deposit ticket, and obtains a receipt;[4] or the customer withdraws funds for which the bank obtains a receipt. These transactions, however, can take a variety of specific forms, and there is a good deal of technology involved.

In receiving a deposit, five steps are performed in addition to the issuance of a receipt. (1) The amount of currency and coin is verified. (2) Currency and coin are checked for counterfeits. (3) All items requiring endorsement are checked to see if proper endorsement has been made. (4) The items are checked to determine that all being accepted for deposit are "cash items." The distinction here is between cash items (usually checks), for which immediate credit can be given, and collection items (such as drafts, notes, and acceptances), for which credit is given only after actual collection. (5) The total amount of the deposit is verified. This last step—"proving deposits," or simply "proof "—has been an area of much technological and organizational innovation to reduce its labor intensiveness.[5]

At this point, discussion of the disbursement function will be limited to withdrawals from accounts; payment of checks will be discussed below under the deposit service of clearing. Withdrawals from bank accounts have traditionally required the use of written orders or receipts, although the recent advent of automatic teller machines and point of sale terminals eliminates this requirement. For checking accounts, the withdrawal instrument is usually a check drawn to "cash." For savings and time deposits, it is a bank form serving as a written receipt. For time certificates, withdrawal is effected by surrendering the certificate to the bank.

For these several types of withdrawals, disbursement is in the form of currency and coin, an officer's or cashier's check, or credit to another account, whatever the preference of the customer. Money orders and traveler's checks may also be requested, but issuance of these instruments should be regarded as a separate transaction, distinct from withdrawals as such.

RECORD KEEPING. A ledger record must be maintained for each deposit account; this is the record-keeping component of safekeeping. Deposits and withdrawals are posed to the account as soon as possible, normally not later than the following day. The difficulty of this task is in the accurate and rapid handling of a large volume of ledger entries at low cost. Until the late 1800s, posting and other record-keeping entries were made entirely by hand. From the late 1800s to the 1920s, the development of bookkeeping machines brought mechanization to the posting operations of many banks. Well-designed machines made their appearance after World War II, but in the late 1950s it became evident to some large banks, notably Bank of America NT&SA, that mechanization was not enough. It was projected that the personnel cost associated with manually operated machines would rise rapidly, and a paperwork breakdown seemed likely at some time in the future. By the late 1950s, the use of electronic equipment for record keeping was facilitated by the development of the technology of magnetic ink character recognition. It is estimated that more than 95 percent of the commercial banks in the United States now use electronic data processing to accomplish their deposit record keeping.

RISK PROTECTION. All banking firms must protect their assets from the risks of fraud, embezzlement, and other losses, for example, loans that are defaulted. The principal measures used to protect against risk can be described as follows:

1. *Dual control.* At least two persons perform certain tasks. In the receiving function, tellers must balance out their cash each day with the head teller or other supervisor; excess cash is turned over to the head teller or additional cash obtained as required. In some banks receipt of deposits and loan repayments by mail are handled by two persons. Dual control in the opening and closing of the vault is standard practice. Requirements that bank personnel take vacations in periods of at least one week are intended to assure that every task involving responsibility for or access to funds is placed under the scrutiny of a different person at least once a year.

2. *Security.* Technological improvements in vault design and alarm systems have reduced the incidence of bank burglaries, but robberies, or holdups, continue to be a serious problem. Techniques used to discourage holdups include cameras and telephonic alarms that can be activated from teller stations and packets of currency with recorded serial numbers and/or containing explosive devices that release a dye. Security standards for banks are specified by federal law and regulation.

3. *Audits and examinations.* Many banks have internal audit programs, as well as audits by public accounting firms. The directors of a bank have a legal responsibility to conduct an annual examination of the bank either through an outside audit or, in the case of small banks that regard the costs of an outside audit as high in relation to income, by a committee of the directors. Examination by federal and/or state supervisory agencies is not an audit. The purposes of supervisory examination are mainly to verify the value of the assets of a bank, to test for violations of laws and regulations governing the exercise of the bank's powers, and to assess the adequacy of bank management.

4. *"Blanket bond."* Banks typically purchase insurance protection for a broad range of possible losses, such as fire, robbery, burglary,

mysterious disappearance, embezzlement, and extortion.

5. *Diversification of loans and investments.* Federal and state laws limit the amount that can be loaned to one borrower or group of affiliated persons or companies. Further diversification depends upon the judgment of management and directors, the latter bearing the legal responsibility for loans and investments.

6. *Credit analysis and supervision.* Practice varies somewhat among banks in the evaluation of the credit worthiness of loan applicants. Adequate files, containing financial statements and other pertinent information on borrowers, are expected to be maintained in all banks. Large banks and many medium-size banks have credit departments, which are responsible for the maintenance of credit files, analysis of changes in the condition of borrowers, and analysis of loan applications. Supervision of certain types of loans after they are made is an essential aspect of credit administration. The scope of lending of some banks is therefore limited by their inability to supervise specific types of loans. Developing the knowledge or acquiring the personnel needed to supervise certain types of loans may be too costly in relation to prospective income.

7. *Federal deposit insurance.* The advent of federal deposit insurance in 1933 was one of the most important developments in the history of commercial banking in the United States. It contributed to the preservation of the highly proliferated, or decentralized, structure of commercial banking, brought almost all commercial banks under some degree of federal regulation and supervision, and provided the small depositor with full assurance of the safety of bank deposits. Although designed and established as an insurance scheme, deposit insurance is a federal guaranty for which the banks pay a franchise tax (denominated as an insurance premium), the proceeds of which are dedicated to payment of the costs of administration of the guaranty program and investment in U.S. government securities. Currently, deposit insurance coverage is $100,000 per individual interest in each bank and $100,000 for deposits of public agencies. Losses of depositors in failed banks since 1933 have been less than 2 percent of total deposits. In the case of a failed bank, the Federal Deposit Insurance Corporation (FDIC) may elect to pay off insured depositors, which may result in loss to depositors on amounts in excess of the insurance coverage, or provide financial assistance for all deposits to be assumed by a reorganized bank

or by another bank. Since the early 1940s, the policy of the
FDIC has been to choose the method that appears to be less
costly to the FDIC.

8. *Capital and "bad debt" reserves.* As observed above, commercial
   banking is a highly leveraged enterprise, and capital ratios—for
   example, the ratio of capital accounts to "risk assets"—have
   been declining over the past fifteen years or so. Capital and bad
   debt reserves provide a margin of protection for uninsured
   deposits, but the largest amounts of uninsured deposits are in
   the large banks, which tend to have the lowest capital ratios.
   Federal and state regulatory agencies use averages and capital
   positions. Increases in capital may be required by the regulatory
   agencies, especially as a condition for approval of additional
   branches. The capital adequacy problem has been debated for
   many years, and it continues to be an important and controversial issue.

MAINTENANCE OF ADEQUATE LIQUIDITY. The liquidity position of a
bank, which must be adequate for its operation, is a function of cash
assets, holdings of short-term marketable securities, and cash inflow
and outflow. The relevant cash assets include currency and coin in
the vault, excess reserves at Federal Reserve Banks, and deposits at
other commercial banks (over and above state reserve requirements
for banks that are not members of the Federal Reserve System).
U.S. Treasury bills and other government obligations within a year
or so of maturity are the principal types of securities held for liquidity purposes. Required reserve balances are a relatively minor
source of liquidity, and in the normal course of bank operation they
are regarded as a use rather than a source of funds. Consequently,
only excess balances at Federal Reserve Banks and correspondent
banks are usually counted among the assets held for liquidity purposes.

Normal sources of cash inflow to a bank include deposited funds,
loan repayments, maturing securities, and revenue. Normal cash
outflow includes deposit withdrawals, payment of checks drawn on
the bank, and expenses. Revenues and expenses are ordinarily
minor cash flow items. Certain revenue and expense transactions
may have only indirect effects on a bank's cash position, for example, crediting of interest on savings and time accounts or collection
of interest effected by debits to borrowers' deposit accounts. Loan
repayments and maturing securities are the major sources of cash in-

flow that can be planned with a reasonable degree of certainty.

The traditional emphasis of banks on short-term loans and investments has reflected liquidity requirements related to the demand and short-term nature of their deposit liabilities. Historically, the emphasis was upon short-term commercial and industrial loans, which were thought to be "self-liquidating" because they are associated with the production and distribution of goods. The fallacy of this view is well recognized today, but short-term loans continue to be preferred partly for their liquidity but also because it is less difficult to project risks of loss over short periods than over long periods. Repayment of loans in regular installments, or amortization of principal, did not become a widespread practice in commercial banking until the 1930s. With amortization of principal, banks found that home mortgage loans, consumer loans, and even intermediate-term loans to commerce and industry ("term loans") could be better sources of regular cash inflow than the traditional demand or short-term business loan. Today many banks regard repayments on consumer installment loans as an important part of their liquidity position.

Institutional arrangements to support the liquidity of commercial banks are extensive. A major reason for the formation of the Federal Reserve System in 1913 was to provide an "elastic currency," that is, to establish an ultimate source of liquidity for commercial banks through the rediscounting of "eligible paper" at Federal Reserve Banks. Such assistance today takes the form of short-term loans, or "discounts and advances," by Federal Reserve Banks. The federal funds market, involving purchases of excess reserve balances, is another important institutional arrangement. In addition, banks may obtain loans from other banks.

The second function of banks, the clearing function, concerns collection of funds deposited in individual accounts. Checks drawn on accounts held within the bank are collected by internal processing, that is, by debiting the accounts of the respective drawers within the bank. Checks drawn on other local banks are collected through a clearinghouse association if the number of banks and volume of activity are large enough to justify a formal arrangement.[6]

Checks on nonlocal banks, or transit items, may be collected by mailing them directly to the drawee banks, to one or more correspondent banks, and/or to the Federal Reserve Bank (or nearest branch) for the district in which the receiving bank is located. Since direct mailing to a number of drawee banks would be costly and time-consuming, it is used only when volume warrants or in special situations where depositors request direct collection of large checks. In using a correspondent bank or Federal Reserve Bank for collection of transit items, a bank is acting as a depositor; that is, the bank makes a deposit consisting of its transit items, and the correspondent bank or Federal Reserve Bank treats the deposit in much the same way as the bank treats the deposits of its customers.

Speed is of great importance in the collection of transit items. Ordinarily, the bank has credited the customer's account with the amount of the deposit but has not yet received "good funds" for placement in earning assets. Also, delay in transit increases the risk that items will be returned unpaid. The customer is thus exposed to the possibility of loss, and so is the bank, if return of unpaid items puts the customer's account in an overdrawn position.

Payment of checks is largely responsible for the high liquidity requirements of commercial banks. Settlement must be authorized when checks are presented, subject to return of any unpaid items. Banks maintain deposits at other banks and with Federal Reserve Banks to facilitate settlement. These deposits must be managed to assure their adequacy while avoiding loss of income from excessive balances. In small and medium-size banks management of the "money position" may take relatively little time each day, but the timing of decisions and actions is important. In large banks, especially those with accounts of large corporations, the task is somewhat more difficult and time-consuming.

Estimates of the costs of providing deposit services are shown in Table II-3. Due to variations in activity, each account in a bank has its own break-even point. Annual service costs per account in 1975 averaged $51.60 for small banks, $63.00 for medium-size banks, and $85.80 for large banks in the Federal Reserve's Functional Cost Analysis. Almost two-thirds of the checking accounts in banks have average balances of less than $500, and the income earned on most of these accounts falls below their service costs. Similarly, about two-thirds of the savings accounts in commercial banks have average balances below their break-even points. The dollar volume in demand and savings accounts above break-even points is sufficiently great to produce net earnings that more than offset the operating deficits on the large number of accounts below break-even points. The principal elements in the costs of demand deposits and savings and time deposits are operating costs and interest expenses. Personnel costs, both processing and overhead, make up about one-half of

TABLE II-3 Selected Costs of Commercial Bank Deposit Services, 1975

	BANK SIZE IN TOTAL DEPOSITS		
DEPOSIT SERVICE	*Under $50 million*	*$50 million to $200 million*	*Over $200 million*
Demand Deposits			
Account maintenance, per year	$22.20	$24.96	$32.40
Deposit, per ticket	.15	.16	.20
Check cashed, per check	.12	.13	.17
Home debit, per item	.08	.08	.11
Transit check	.04	.04	.05
Regular Savings Deposits			
Account maintenance, per year	8.13	8.65	9.16
Deposit, per ticket	.31	.34	.36
Withdrawal, per transaction	.60	.65	.69
Posting of interest, per transaction	1.18	1.28	1.44
Interest cost, per $100	4.72	4.77	4.57
Opening account	2.07	2.10	2.11
Closing account	1.10	1.15	1.16

Source: Board of Governors of the Federal Reserve System.

the total costs of demand deposit services. Interest expense dominates the cost picture for savings and time deposits.

Commercial banks make a variety of consumer loans for the purpose of expenditure—for example, real estate loans, automobile loans, and personal loans. Consumer installment loans by commercial banks also fall into two general categories: loans extended directly by the bank; and loans made indirectly through, or paper acquired from, "dealers," such as automobile dealers, mobile home dealers, and retailers of appliances and home furnishings. About 64 percent of the number of consumer installment loans outstanding at commercial banks in 1975 were direct loans, accounting for 58 percent of the dollar total of outstanding loans. Approximately two-thirds of the indirect loans were for purchases of automobiles, accounting for roughly one-half of the dollar total of indirect loans. Mobile homes made up the second largest category of indirect loans

TABLE II-4 Selected Costs of Direct Consumer Installment Loans
by Commercial Banks, 1975

	BANK SIZE IN TOTAL DEPOSITS		
TYPE OF COST	*Under* *$50 million*	*$50 million* *to $200 million*	*Over* *$200 million*
Acquisition, per loan	$37.33	$42.49	$55.48
Servicing and liquidation, per 12 payments	31.56	31.92	36.24
Annual loss rate, per $100	.51	.46	.59
Annual cost of money, per $100	4.84	4.78	4.57

Source: Board of Governors of the Federal Reserve System.

by dollar volume, with approximately 22 percent of the volume of
indirect loans outstanding.

Table II-4 presents cost data on direct loans by commercial
banks. At a medium-size bank, the costs of acquisition, servicing,
and liquidation—the administrative costs—are about $74 for a one-
year loan, $106 for a two-year loan, and $138 for a three-year loan,
regardless of the amount of the loan. Such administrative costs make
for what might be regarded as relatively high break-even points. At
an interest charge of $6.00 per $100, or an effective rate of 11 percent, the break-even points for the medium-size bank depicted in
Table II-5 would be $2,864 for a one-year loan, $1,933 for a two-
year loan, and $1,636 for a three-year loan, including cost of money
and loss rate, as well as administrative costs.

In Table II-5, the major cost elements in installment loan services offered by commercial banks are shown as proportions of total
costs. Processing costs and overhead—another way of looking at administrative costs—account for 38 percent of the costs of installment
loans in small and medium-size commercial banks and 41 percent in
large commercial banks. While all costs have risen on a per-unit
basis over the past fifteen years, the cost of money has increased as
a proportion of total costs.

Federal Reserve cost data indicate that the net yield on consumer
installment loans is above the average net yield on all loans for small
and medium-size banks but below such averages for large banks. In
1975 small banks had a net yield of 2.78 percent on installment

TABLE II-5 Commercial Bank Installment Loan Services, Analysis of 1975 Costs

	BANK SIZE IN TOTAL DEPOSITS		
COST ELEMENT	*Under* *$50 million*	*$50 million* *to $200 million*	*Over* *$200 million*
Processing	27.3%	27.3%	29.0%
Personnel	20.7	20.8	21.6
Overhead	10.9	10.6	12.1
Losses	6.9	5.4	6.8
Cost of money	55.9	56.8	52.1

loans, compared to an average net yield of 2.34 percent on all loans. The net yields on installment loans for large banks were 2.24 percent, compared with average loan yields of 2.57 percent. On consumer installment loans, large banks tend to have lower gross yields and higher operating costs than medium-size and small banks.

Savings and Loan Associations

Savings and loan associations originated as mutual building societies whose members pooled their funds through capital subscriptions to construct or purchase homes. The assets of savings and loan associations are concentrated in residential mortgages, and their liabilities are concentrated in savings and time accounts. Such specialization makes for a production process somewhat less complicated than that in commercial banking. Interest income and interest expense are the major forms of revenue and expense. Personnel costs are less important than in commercial banking, in terms of both proportion of total expenses and ratio to total assets.

Except in those states where NOW or checking accounts have been authorized, the deposit services of savings and loan associations are limited mainly to the safekeeping function. The introduction of NOW accounts in 1980 greatly increased the deposit safekeeping functions in savings and loans, as well as in other thrift institutions. With respect to the risk protection phase of the safekeeping function, the principal differences between commercial banks and savings and loans pertain to diversification of loans and investments, credit analysis and supervision, deposit insurance, and capital and "bad debt" reserves.

Diversification of loans and investments. The loan portfolios of savings
and loan associations are specialized and, in some significant
dimensions, lack diversification. Loans are concentrated in
residential mortgages and usually in the local market area of the
savings and loan association. A degree of diversification can be
achieved by locations and classes of residential properties within
the market area. Concentration tends, however, to prevail over
diversification, particularly where a savings and loan association
may be a major source of mortgage commitments in the development of a subdivision. The security of association loan portfolios
resides not in diversification, as this term is customarily used,
but in the values of the mortgaged properties, the owners'
equities in such properties, and the stability and variety of income sources of owners. Additionally, the existence of federal
and private firms that provide insurance against default on mortgage reduces their loss expenses.

Credit analysis and supervision. Evaluation of mortgage loan applications involves, of course, appraisal of the property to be mortgaged, as well as analysis of the income and employment status
and credit record of the applicant. Associations that make construction loans have the additional need to maintain close supervision of the financial condition of the builders to whom funds
have been loaned.

Federal deposit insurance. Insurance of accounts is provided by the Federal Savings and Loan Insurance Corporation (FSLIC),
established in 1934. Although holders of savings accounts in
mutual savings and loans are legally owners rather than
creditors, insurance on their deposits is identical to insurance on
bank deposits.

Capital and "bad debt" reserves. Most savings and loan associations are
mutual organizations. Stock savings and loan associations have
been a small segment of the industry nationally and are prominent in only a few states, notably California. The trend to convert to stock associations is increasing. The inability of mutual
savings and loan associations to increase capital through sale of
stock and their apparently limited ability to tap long-term debt
markets are regarded by some observers as signs of a structural
weakness that, in time, will inhibit growth and prompt conversions to stock ownership. Improvement of capital positions has
been aided by favorable tax treatment with respect to allocations
to "bad debt" reserves. However, such treatment is in the pro-

cess of being phased out according to a schedule that each year reduces the relative size of the tax-free allocation. Savings and loan associations operate on somewhat thinner net worth margins than commercial banks. The question of capital adequacy in savings and loan associations is as unresolved as it is in commercial banking.

Maintenance of liquidity has been a long-standing and sometimes serious problem in savings and loan associations. Although loan payments flow in on a monthly basis, the long maturities of the loans result in a loan repayment cash flow that is low relative to total liabilities payable on demand or short notice. Savings and loan associations operate with high loan-deposit ratios and relatively slim holdings of cash and short-term government securities. In periods of stable growth in the economy and with short-term interest rates significantly below long-term rates, savings and loan associations in general do not have a liquidity problem. Cash inflow is favored by a steady pace of growth in savings balances and by early repayment of loans associated with resale of homes. In periods of inflation and tight money, such as 1979, with short-term interest rates rising relative to long-term rates, savings may not only cease to grow but decline, and early loan repayments may diminish.

The Federal Home Loan Bank System, which was created in 1932 to help meet the liquidity needs of savings and loan associations, has been a major source of short-term funds for savings and loans. The sensitivity of savings and loan cash flows to swings in the economy and interest rates is one of the reasons that proposals have been made to extend consumer credit powers to savings and loan associations. Congress finally granted this authority in 1980. Analyses indicate that even modest holdings of consumer installment credit, for example, 10 percent of total assets, would significantly improve cash flow positions.

Savings and loan associations that belong to the Federal Home Loan Bank System are subject to minimum liquidity requirements. Holdings of cash and short-term marketable securities are expected to be at least 2.5 percent of total assets; "overall liquidity," in obligations defined by regulation, should be at least 6.5 percent.

Mutual Savings Banks

A mutual savings bank is a type of trust, or fiduciary, arrangement, under the direction of a self-perpetuating board of trustees. Depositors in a mutual savings bank have the legal standing of creditors and share a beneficial interest in the surplus, or capital accounts, of the bank.

A decade ago there was little or no expectation that mutual savings banks would play a leading role in changing the system of financial intermediaries. Little known outside the northeastern United States, mutual savings banks enjoyed a reputation of conservative management as savings institutions that had been established by business and community leaders to encourage thrift among working-class people. However, introduction of NOW accounts and successful efforts to gain checking account powers in Connecticut, Maine, and New York have placed mutual savings banks at the forefront of change in the financial structure.

Historically, mutual savings banks have been known as depository institutions. The trust investment concept of prudence has influenced asset portfolio management and regulation of the investment powers of mutual savings banks. Residential real estate mortgages have traditionally been prominent in the portfolios of mutual savings banks, because such lending was consistent with encouragement of thrift in working-class people, with the concept of savings as a source of funds for long-term investment, and with "prudent man" investment standards. In this regard, mutual savings banks have been major holders of federally underwritten residential mortgages. In 1965 mutual savings banks held 31 percent of the outstanding volume of FHA and VA mortgages, compared to their holdings of only 14 percent of total mortgages outstanding. Since the late 1960s, mutual savings banks have shifted their portfolios toward conventional mortgages, but they still hold about 18 percent of all federally underwritten mortgages, compared to 10 percent of total mortgages.

Table II-6 shows the assets and liabilities of mutual savings banks and their geographic distribution as of the end of 1975. Mortgage loans make up about 64 percent of total assets, and approximately four-fifths of these loans are on residential properties. Consumer installment loans are only about 5 percent of total assets; adding home improvement and guaranteed education loans would bring the total to 1.4 percent. Mutual savings banks hold corporate equities and bonds, as well as obligations of federal, state, and local governments. Categories of eligible securities are specified by law and regulation in the respective states.

Income and expense data for mutual savings banks in 1975 are set forth in Table II-7. Interest paid depositors equals about three-fourths of total operating income. Operating expenses, in relation to income or total assets, are somewhat less than in commercial banks and savings and loan associations. Specialization in the savings and mortgage business explains the difference with respect to commercial banks. Economies of scale apparently contribute to the difference with respect to savings and loan associations. The average size of mutual savings banks is about 3.7 times the average size of savings and loan associations.

The production of deposit services by mutual savings banks is similar to the production process in savings and loan associations and to the production of savings and consumer time deposit services in commercial banks. With respect to the safekeeping function, receipt and disbursement procedures and record keeping are much the same as in savings and loan associations and the savings departments of commercial banks. In the area of risk protection, mutual savings banks have more diversified asset portfolios than savings and loan associations. Deposit insurance for mutual savings banks is provided by the FDIC and, in the state of Massachusetts, by the Mutual Savings Central Fund, Inc. About 20 of the 166 mutual savings banks in Massachusetts have FDIC coverage, as well as membership in the Central Fund. Only 1 of the 476 mutual savings banks in 17 states is uninsured.

A small number of mutual savings banks in Delaware, Indiana, Maryland, New Jersey, Oregon, and Vermont have had checking account powers either by statute or specific charter authority since the early 1930s, but little or no use was made of these powers until the late 1960s and early 1970s. Even as recently as the second quarter of 1976, thirty mutual savings banks in the six states noted above had only $156 million in checking accounts. A significant change came in 1972 with the introduction of NOW accounts in Massachusetts and New Hampshire, which can be regarded as chequable savings accounts or as interest-bearing checking accounts. Federal legislation subsequently limited NOW accounts to these two states until February 1976, when NOW account authority was extended to depository institutions in Connecticut, Maine, Rhode Island, and Vermont. State legislation provided checking account authority for mutual savings banks in Maine in October 1975, in Connecticut in December 1975, and in New York in May 1976. In

TABLE II-6 Assets and Liabilities of Mutual Savings Banks, by State, December 31, 1975 (in millions of dollars)*

	Total	New York	Mass.	Conn.	Penn.	N.J.	Wash.	N.H.	Me.	R.I.	Md.	All Other States
Assets												
Cash and due from banks	$ 2,330	$ 1,329	$ 215	$ 192	$ 144	$ 155	$ 88	$ 40	$ 35	$ 17	$ 26	$ 90
U.S. government obligations	4,740	2,391	902	314	252	297	77	88	102	49	110	158
Federal agency obligations	2,767	1,057	753	176	227	215	76	60	50	65	26	62
State and local obligations	1,545	1,053	123	100	138	51	12	9	16	2	6	35
Mortgage-backed securities	3,367	2,135	232	79	332	386	82	21	21	32	21	27
Corporate and other bonds	17,536	10,301	2,242	723	2,321	917	232	96	149	65	97	393
Corporate stock	4,322	2,074	854	641	205	109	68	110	97	57	21	88
Mortgage loans	77,221	42,974	11,751	6,715	4,435	3,584	1,841	1,239	1,141	918	742	1,879
Other loans	4,023	1,648	827	572	165	141	122	140	100	77	141	89
Guaranteed education loans	557	332	54	60	39	28	15	4	6	10	3	5
Consumer installment loans	608	—	214	182	—	4	18	49	34	19	73	15
Home improvement loans	444	207	85	63	3	13	6	16	6	11	21	12
Federal funds	1,110	544	255	132	22	65	25	18	22	12	3	13
Passbook loans	615	267	146	76	21	24	9	18	15	13	5	22
All other loans	690	298	74	59	80	7	48	35	18	12	36	22
Bank premises owned	1,075	550	163	102	48	63	34	24	25	23	8	34
Other real estate	426	213	58	82	8	6	39	6	2	3	—	8
Other assets	1,703	1,065	159	127	131	65	29	14	12	28	38	35
Total assets	121,056	66,791	18,277	9,823	8,407	5,989	2,699	1,849	1,751	1,336	1,237	2,898

	Total	New York	Mass.	Conn.	Penn.	N.J.	Wash.	N.H.	Me.	R.I.	Md.	All Other States
Liabilities												
Regular deposits	109,291	60,442	16,477	8,790	7,692	5,351	2,471	1,641	1,584	1,188	1,066	2,599
Ordinary savings	69,653	38,850	10,429	5,720	4,683	3,308	1,521	1,091	1,138	639	875	1,399
Time and other	39,639	21,592	6,048	3,071	3,009	2,043	950	550	446	549	191	1,190
School and club	199	94	17	13	45	13	3	2	2	2	2	7
Other deposits	383	168	5	9	5	127	6	2	4	••	30	27
Total deposits	109,873	60,704	16,500	8,810	7,743	5,492	2,480	1,645	1,589	1,190	1,098	2,623
Borrowings and mortgage warehousing	555	294	16	77	15	45	29	8	4	15	—	52
Other liabilities	2,200	1,311	319	153	141	95	24	32	17	29	41	39
Total liabilities	112,628	62,308	16,835	9,040	7,898	5,631	2,533	1,685	1,611	1,234	1,139	2,713
Capital notes and debentures	185	55	4	37	50	17	6	3	1	—		11
Other general reserves	8,243	4,427	1,438	746	458	341	160	160	140	101	98	174
Total general reserve accounts	8,428	4,483	1,442	783	508	358	166	164	140	101	98	185
Total liabilities and general reserve accounts	121,056	66,791	18,277	9,823	8,407	5,989	2,699	1,849	1,751	1,336	1,237	2,898
Memoranda												
Cash and investments												
Maturing within one year	6,154	2,981	1,188	562	309	393	161	114	109	72	97	169
Maturing within five years	11,816	5,634	2,359	928	720	731	314	230	220	151	188	340
Total mortgage loans	77,221	42,974	11,751	6,715	4,435	3,584	1,841	1,239	1,141	918	742	1,879
Residential	63,095	34,633	9,695	5,604	3,514	3,299	1,404	1,033	963	759	700	1,490
FHA	14,525	9,913	1,365	435	1,195	745	178	113	111	84	123	262
VA	12,602	7,767	1,614	393	1,271	703	113	146	209	84	156	147
Conventional	35,967	16,953	6,716	4,777	1,048	1,850	1,114	774	643	591	421	1,081
Nonresidential	14,075	8,331	2,042	1,107	921	285	437	204	176	159	43	370
Farm	51	10	13	4	••	••	1	3	1	—	••	19
Number of banks	476	118	166	67	8	20	8	28	32	6	3	20

*Data for cash and investments maturing within one year and five years, including cash, federal funds, securities, and open market paper.
**Less than $500,000.

Source: National Association of Mutual Savings Banks.

TABLE II-7 Income and Expenses of Mutual Savings Banks, by State, 1975 (in millions of dollars)

	TOTAL	NEW YORK	MASS.	CONN.	PENN.	N.J.	WASH.	N.H.	ME.	R.I.	MD.	ALL OTHER STATES
Total operating income	8,117	4,419	1,242	682	551	399	193	131	123	91	84	202
Interest and dividends on securities	2,159	1,206	323	122	222	122	35	23	28	16	16	47
U.S government and agency obligations	626*	334	n.a.	32	53	52	14	10	11	9	10	14
Other securities	1,533*	872	n.a.	90	169	70	21	13	17	8	6	33
Net interest and discount on loans	5,781	3,113	901	546	321	268	150	106	93	72	63	148
Mortgage loans	5,460*	2,978	n.a.	495	307	257	139	93	84	65	51	139
Other loans	321*	135	n.a.	51	14	11	11	12	9	7	11	9
Other operating income	177	101	18	14	8	10	9	2	2	2	5	6
Operating expenses and taxes	1,422	744	223	131	82	72	41	26	24	21	19	40
Net operating income after expenses and taxes	6,695	3,675	1,019	552	469	328	153	105	99	70	65	161
Interest paid depositors	6,165	3,450	895	492	438	297	142	94	87	63	57	150
Net operating income after expenses, taxes, and interest	530	224	124	59	31	30	11	12	12	7	8	11

Net realized gains or losses											
on assets	-89	-43	-33	-5	-4	-2	-2	-1	-1	-1	**	**
Securities	-32*	-10	n.a.	-4	-1	-2	1	-1	-1	-1	**	**
Real estate mortgage											
loans	-33*	-19	n.a.	-1	-1	**	1	**	**	**	**	**
Real estate	-11*	-7	n.a.	1	**	**	**	**	**	**	**	**
Other	-12*	-6	n.a.	**	-2	**	**	**	**	**	**	**
Retained earnings	441	182	91	55	27	28	13	10	11	11	7	11

*Partly estimated; separate data for Massachusetts are not available.
**Less than $500,000
Source: National Association of Mutual Savings Banks.

the second quarter of 1976, 231 mutual savings banks in Connecticut, Maine, Massachusetts, and New Hampshire had 493,334 NOW accounts with a combined total balance of $456.5 million. In Connecticut, Maine, and New York mutual savings banks had 397,245 checking accounts, with a combined total balance of $137.9 million.

In the production process NOW accounts are handled in the same manner as checking accounts, except that interest payments are periodically posted to NOW accounts. Institutions could invoke the withdrawal notice requirements of savings accounts on negotiable orders of withdrawal, but notice requirements on savings accounts were abandoned in practice long ago.

Partly because of their orientation to depository institutions, mutual savings banks have traditionally maintained somewhat stronger liquidity positions than savings and loan associations. The attractiveness of federally underwritten mortgages to mutual savings banks can be explained not only by their safety but also by their liquidity. In addition, mutual savings banks are eligible for membership in the Federal Reserve System and in the Federal Home Loan Bank System; sixty-eight were members of the latter system at the end of 1975. Another source of external liquidity is the Savings Bank Trust Company in New York City.

Mutual savings banks operate on relatively slim earnings margins. Total operating income in 1975 was 7.02 percent of total assets, interest paid was 5.33 percent, and operating expenses and taxes were 1.23 percent. The spread between income received and interest paid was thus only 1.69 percent of total assets, or 24 percent of operating income. Net earnings after operating expenses and taxes were .46 percent of total assets, or 6.6 percent of total operating income.

The ratio of operating expenses to total assets or total income has been rising since the late 1960s and especially since 1972. This trend can be explained in part by the pace of inflation, but some of the upward drift in operating expenses is undoubtedly associated with the entry of mutual savings banks into the checking account business. Mutual savings banks have been rather successful in gaining cost benefits from the use of electronic data-processing equipment. Favorable experience in this regard, as well as the capacity potential offered by the use of electronic data-processing, probably played some role in stimulating expansion into NOW and checking account services.

Credit Unions

As noted earlier, credit unions have been the fastest-growing sector of the consumer financial services industry during the past twenty-five years. Organized under federal and state laws as "cooperatives," credit unions limit membership to persons with a "common bond." Three types of common bond provide the basis for membership: occupational, for example, employees of the same company, government agency, or political subdivision; associational, for example, members of the same fraternal or religious organization or consumer cooperative; and residential, for example, residents of a well-defined and usually small local area. The predominant type of membership is occupational.

Until recent years credit unions have been highly specialized in their functions, receiving members' savings in the form of share accounts or deposits and making installment loans to members. About 86 percent of total credit union resources are in the form of paid-in capital in share accounts. Savings deposits are approximately 3 percent of total resources. Reserves and undivided earnings come to approximately 10 percent of the total. Loans are about three-fourths of total assets and about 90 percent of members' savings. Loans are mainly consumer installment loans and a relatively small volume of short- to intermediate-term residential real estate loans. The extent to which credit unions will exercise their new mortgage and credit card powers remains to be seen.

The average size of credit unions is approximately $1.4 million. Based on 1973 and 1974 data reported in the *National Credit Union Administration Quarterly,* average annual income can be estimated at about $125,000, of which roughly half is paid out as dividends and interest. Annual operating expenses are approximately $50,000. However, these estimates are skewed by the inclusion of some relatively large credit unions; the income and expenses of the typical credit union would fall below these averages.

The safekeeping function of credit unions is comparable to that of the other financial intermediaries. Risk protection in credit unions is affected by several factors related to their form of organization. The common bond basis of membership tends to limit risk exposure on individual loans and is conducive to good collection experience. However, the common bond also makes for concentration of risks, especially where the basis of membership is occupational. Reliance upon elected officers and other volunteers, including committees for review of loan applications, is generally successful, but maintenance of interest and commitment is sometimes difficult. The treasurer is the key position in a credit union, and the success or failure of the union often turns on the capabilities and integrity of the person filling that position.

A program of federal credit union share insurance, comparable to FDIC and FSLIC coverage, was established in 1970. The program is directed by the National Credit Union Administration (NCUA). Sixteen states have also offered share insurance programs—nongovernmental insurance under state supervision.

The liquidity requirements of credit unions have been closely related to the stability of membership. A reduction in force at place of employment or a sudden increase in the turnover rate, as in state governments or political subdivisions after an election, can quickly reduce a credit union's ability to redeem shares. This ability is a function of the credit union's holdings of cash and marketable securities (which have averaged about 22 percent of total assets in recent years); installment loan repayments; and external sources of borrowing, including commercial banks. In the normal course of business, credit unions seldom have a liquidity problem. When one does develop, though, it is often rather serious, because it is linked to instability in membership.

A basic precept in the credit union movement has been that the maximum rate of interest on loans should be 1 percent per month on the unpaid balance. (Six states permit higher rates.) As the return paid on share capital is in the form of dividends, declarations of dividends can be tailored to actually realized net income. Flexibility in this regard, however, is limited by the fact that the viability of credit unions depends upon payment of competitive rates of return on savings balances. In small credit unions reliance on volunteer and part-time workers and in-kind assistance reduces operating expenses. The amount of this cost savings decreases as credit unions increase in size. Growth is also conducive to rates on certain types of loans being set below the maximum of 1 percent per month. Local competitive conditions, especially in regard to automobile loans, and general economic and financial trends also affect rate patterns.

According to National Credit Union Association data for 1973–74, the estimated average yield on credit union loans and investments was 9.6 percent in 1974. Operating expenses equaled 3.6 percent, and dividends and interest were 4.9 percent of total loans and investments. The net yield on loans and investments was thus 1.1 percent. Comparison with average net yields on loans and investments of commercial banks is difficult because credit unions are exempt from federal taxation of income.

Finance Companies

Finance companies in the consumer installment lending field include sales finance companies, consumer finance (or small loan) companies, industrial loan companies, and industrial banks (also known in some areas as "Morris Plan" banks or "thrifts"). Included are corporations, partnerships, and single proprietorships ranging in size from one office to nationwide systems. The essential common characteristic is that they are privately owned businesses engaged in direct consumer installment lending and/or indirect lending to consumers through the purchase of installment sales paper. A further distinguishing feature is that these businesses are not depository institutions, except for some of the industrial banks and industrial loan companies; that is, they rely on borrowed money and equity as sources of loan funds.

Data on the assets and liabilities of finance companies are presented in Table II-8. Income and expense data, on a percentage basis, are shown in Table II-9 for 233 companies, accounting for approximately 47 percent of the total assets shown in Table II-8. Information on the assets of these 233 companies is presented in Table II-10; information on liabilities, capital, and surplus is presented in Table II-11.

Sales finance companies account for the bulk of the business receivables shown in Table II-8. The data in Table II-10 are indicative of the share attributable to these companies, which are primarily involved in the purchase of consumer installment paper, or indirect lending, rather than in direct lending to consumers. Important in this regard, of course, are the finance companies that are subsidiaries of automobile manufacturers. Independent sales finance companies have shifted somewhat into the direct lending field. However, the data for sales finance companies are strongly influenced by the larger companies engaged in business installment lending or in the purchase of consumer installment paper. The data

TABLE II-8 Assets and Liabilities Outstanding at Finance Companies, by Size of Receivables, June 30, 1975 (in millions of dollars)

		SIZE OF COMPANY (IN THOUSANDS OF DOLLARS OF SHORT- AND INTERMEDIATE-TERM LOANS OUTSTANDING)								
	TOTAL	$100,000 & over	$25,000– 99,999	$5,000– 24,999	$2,500– 4,999	$1,000– 2,499	$500– 999	$250– 499	$100– 249	Under $100
ASSETS										
Consumer receivables	$42,760	$37,378	$2,712	$1,253	$419	$416	$268	$181	93	40
Retail passenger car paper	9,938	9,351	290	91	53	70	49	19	9	5
Mobile homes	3,461	3,247	170	30	2	8	2	1	1	
Revolving consumer installment credit	5,752	5,304	395	36		14		1	1	
Personal cash loans	16,715	13,122	1,661	895	312	279	188	147	78	33
Loans secured by second mortgages	1,946	1,064	449	264	62	58	25	18	5	1
Other	14,769	12,058	1,213	631	250	221	164	129	72	31
All other consumer installment loans	6,895	6,354	196	200	52	45	28	13	5	2
Business receivables	39,286	35,930	2,148	904	147	99	25	20	9	4
Wholesale paper	10,945	10,297	532	60	24	19	8	4	1	1
Automobiles	7,713	7,632	58	13	4	2	3	1		
Other consumer goods	1,273	1,031	193	26	10	6	3	2	1	
All other	1,960	1,634	280	21	11	10	1	2	1	

Retail paper	11,067	340	122	17	19	4	3	3	1
Commercial vehicles	5,012	5	22	6	7	3	1	1	
Business, industrial, and farm equipment	6,055	335	100	11	11	1	2	2	1
Lease paper	8,065	293	151	31	7	5	1	2	
Auto paper	2,343	23	18		3	1			
Business, industrial, and farm equipment	3,950	243	106	30	4	2	1	1	
All other	1,772	26	28			2			
Other business credit	9,208	983	572	75	55	9	11	2	3
Loans on commercial accounts receivable	3,388	309	303	34	34	4	3	3	
Factored accounts receivable	1,400	326	30	15	12	3	1		
Advances to factored clients	203	47		17			1	1	
All other receivables	4,218	301	239	9	9	2	6	1	2
Other receivables	3,948	127	37	9	15	4	4	3	1
Total receivables—gross	85,994	4,986	2,195	575	530	298	205	105	45
Less: reserves for unearned income	7,684	448	230	60	53	31	21	8	2
Less: reserves for losses	1,623	100	58	18	17	8	7	3	1
Total receivables—net	76,687	4,438	1,906	496	460	259	177	94	42
Cash and noninterest-bearing deposits	2,667	267	98	25	23	12	9	5	5
Time deposits	202	37	11	6	18	10	4	2	2

TABLE II-8 (cont.)

SIZE OF COMPANY (IN THOUSANDS OF DOLLARS OF SHORT- AND INTERMEDIATE-TERM LOANS OUTSTANDING)

	TOTAL	$100,000 & over	$25,000- 99,999	$5,000- 24,999	$2,500- 4,999	$1,000- 2,499	$500- 999	$250- 499	$100- 249	Under $100
ASSETS										
Other loans and investments	6,745	6,220	296	81	26	78	14	13	9	7
U.S. government securities	63	36	21	2		2	1			
Other marketable securities	683	611	36	4	4	18	4	2	3	1
All other loans and investments	5,998	5,573	239	75	22	58	9	11	6	6
All other assets	2,416	1,929	272	97	20	41	22	15	12	8
Total assets—net	88,716	79,299	5,310	2,193	573	620	317	219	122	64
LIABILITIES AND CAPITAL										
Loans and notes payable to banks	8,617	5,829	1,485	783	207	175	73	35	22	7
Short term	7,900	5,518	1,351	654	161	123	51	24	14	4
Long term	718	312	134	130	46	52	22	11	7	3
Commercial paper	25,905	25,167	632	85	19	1				
Directly placed	23,686	23,360	247	59	19	1				
Dealer placed	2,218	1,807	385	26						

Other short-term debt	2,815	1,842	446	351	57	51	30	22	9	7
Deposit liabilities and thrift certificates	1,480	834	413	119	45	44	16	6	2	2
Other current liabilities	3,113	2,497	463	67	19	25	24	11	4	3
Other long-term senior debt	23,404	22,614	530	119	30	59	21	19	8	3
Long-term subordinated debt	5,609	4,875	410	173	56	53	22	17	2	1
All other liabilities	3,823	3,600	60	71	30	29	13	9	9	3
Capital, surplus, and undivided profits	13,951	12,039	872	423	111	182	119	100	67	39
Total liabilities, capital, and surplus	88,716	79,299	5,310	2,193	573	620	317	219	122	64
Memoranda:										
Short-term debt	36,620	32,527	2,428	1,090	238	176	81	47	23	11
Long-term debt	29,730	27,801	1,074	422	131	165	64	47	18	8
Total debt	66,350	60,328	3,503	1,512	369	340	146	94	41	19
Number of companies	3,376	88	102	204	162	338	415	563	641	863

Source: Board of Governors of the Federal Reserve System.

TABLE II-9 Gross Income of Finance Companies, 1975 (percent distritution)*

	Consumer Finance Companies	Sales Finance Companies	All Reporting Companies
Gross income from receivables	81.0%	89.3%	85.2%
Gross income from insurance	10.9	2.7	6.7
Other income	8.1	8.0	8.1
Total gross income	100.0	100.0	100.0
Expenses, excluding cost of borrowed funds and federal income taxes	59.3	36.0	47.4
Salaries and wages	21.7	16.0	18.8
Advertising and publicity	1.2	0.5	0.8
Losses and loss reserves (net after recoveries)	13.9	8.7	11.3
Other operating expenses	22.5	10.8	16.5
Cost of borrowed funds	26.5	49.0	38.0
Federal income taxes	3.9	6.7	5.3
Net income	10.3	8.3	9.3
Total gross income reported (in thousands of dollars)	$2,658,630	$2,785,254	$5,443,884
Number of companies reporting	192	41	233
Number of offices covered	11,402	3,665	15,067

*Parts may not add to totals due to rounding.
Source: National Consumer Finance Association.

TABLE II-10 Reported Assets of Finance Companies, 1975
(in thousands of dollars)

Accounts and Notes Receivable	Consumer Finance Companies	Sales Finance Companies	All Reporting Companies
Retail automobile paper	$212,937	$8,465,531	$8,678,468
Mobile homes	67,523	2,665,856	2,733,379
Revolving consumer install- ment credit	29,150	113,221	142,371
Personal loans	10,933,822	2,634,445	13,568,267
Home improvement loans	5,611	152,620	158,231
All other retail consumer goods credit	949,762	1,421,246	2,371,008
Subtotal—consumer goods	12,198,805	15,452,919	27,651,724
Wholesale paper	67,997	4,674,164	4,742,161
Retail paper on business, in- dustrial, and farm equipment	67,417	1,153,942	1,221,359
Lease paper	107,767	2,365,089	2,472,856
All other accounts and notes receivable and business credit	216,146	1,392,708	1,608,854
Total receivables	12,658,132	25,038,822	37,696,954
Deduct reserves for unearned income	1,901,921	2,323,922	4,225,843
Subtotal	10,756,211	22,714,900	33,471,111
Deduct reserves for losses	397,079	373,055	770,134
Subtotal	10,359,132	23,341,845	32,700,977
Cash and bank balances	607,966	580,105	1,188,071
Other loans and investments	3,654,791	3,427,345	7,082,136
Other assets	597,515	339,979	937,494
Total assets	15,219,404	26,689;274	41,908,678
Number of companies reporting	192	41	233
Number of offices covered	11,402	3,665	15,067

Source: National Consumer Finance Association.

TABLE II-11 Reported Liabilities, Capital, and Surplus of Finance
Companies, 1975* (in thousands of dollars)

Liabilities, Capital, and Surplus	Consumer Finance Companies	Sales Finance Companies	All Reporting Companies
Bank loans	$1,754,336	$2,356,709	$ 4,111,045
Commercial paper	1,844,662	7,594,046	9,438,708
Other short-term debt	361,587	1,682,595	2,044,182
Deposit liabilities and thrift certificates	696,657	173,146	869,803
Long-term indebtedness (excluding subordinated debentures)	5,040,653	6,143,175	11,183,828
Subordinated debentures	1,144,438	1,602,786	2,747,224
All other liabilities	1,114,807	4,632,362	5,747,169
Capital, surplus, and undivided profits	3,262,264	2,504,455	5,766,719
Total	15,219,404	26,689,274	41,908,678
Number of companies reporting	192	41	233
Number of offices covered	11,402	3,665	15,067

*Parts may not add to totals due to rounding.

Source: National Consumer Finance Association.

on consumer finance companies shown in Tables II-9 and II-10 may
therefore be more useful for analysis of the production of consumer
installment loan services.

As indicated in Table II-9, operating expenses, including losses
and net allocations to loss reserves, were equal to 59.3 percent of the
income of consumer finance companies in 1975. Operating expenses
accounted for 12.4 percent and the cost of borrowed funds for 5.6
percent of year-end receivables. The relatively substantial operating
expenses reflect several factors. The average size of loans outstanding at the end of 1975 was about $1,000 (excluding unearned
charges) for the consumer finance companies reported on in Tables
II-9 and II-10. The personal loan receivables at year-end included
about 10 million separate loans, and most of these loans were made
during the preceding year. With such a large number of loan transactions relative to total dollar volume, personnel and other processing costs are necessarily high in relation to income. It should be
noted, too, that receivables averaged only $943,000 per loan office.

The net earnings of consumer finance companies are especially sensitive to changes in the costs of their sources of funds. Net income per loan before cost of funds and profits tends to be rather constant, reflecting legal loan rate ceilings on the one hand and relatively fixed operating expenses on the other. The cost of borrowed funds, federal income taxes, and net income add up to 40.7 percent of total income, with the cost of borrowed funds amounting to 26.5 percent (see Table II-9). An increase in the cost of borrowed funds to 29.1 percent of total income (interest rates rising by one-tenth) would decrease before-tax net income from 14.2 percent to 11.6 percent of total income (a relative decline of 18 percent). It is estimated that between 1972 and 1974, increases in the costs of borrowed funds cut before-tax net income from 20.7 percent of total income to 13.3 percent.

Retailers

The credit function of retailers is perfomed by a broad range of firms. At one end of the spectrum are small, local retail establishments; at the other end are the nation's leading retail organizations with stores throughout the country and/or extensive mail-order businesses. Intermediate types of organizations include local and regional multistore operations and specialty mail-order businesses. In the smallest organizations the credit function may be performed on a part-time or full-time basis by one or two persons, one being designated, perhaps, as the credit manager. In larger organizations the credit function is performed by a department organized separately from the sales side of the business, and the large regional and national companies have extensive credit divisions.

The credit function of retailers is affected by several trade-offs. A stringent credit policy may adversely affect sales, but a lax credit policy, while favoring sales, may result in undue credit losses and/or collection expenses. Resolution of this conflict can be pursued through more thorough investigation of credit applicants, but this in turn increases the costs of administration. Low-cost investigation, billing, and collection procedures have traditionally been emphasized in the retail credit field.

Many retailers now use a technique of credit evaluation known as "credit scoring." Credit-scoring formulas are based on empirical analysis of the characteristics of good and bad credit risks. Predictors of credit performance are identified through multivariate analysis of past experience with customers. Such predictors may include years at present address, years at present place of employment, age of automobile, possession of credit cards or charge accounts, home phone, and credit bureau rating. Weights or points are assigned for characteristics falling within the range of variation of each predictor. Loss ratios are predicted for various total point levels. The minimum point level for approval of credit is determined by the retailer according to the loss ratio regarded as acceptable.

Inclusion of such predictors as race, age, sex, and marital status in credit-scoring formulas has come in conflict with equal credit opportunity regulations. However, some observers argue that credit scoring is less discriminatory than other techniques of credit evaluation, because it is empirically based and is therefore more objective than other approaches. Also, applicants can qualify on the basis of total points, whereas with other approaches to credit evaluation a particular characteristic may by itself result in denial of credit. It seems likely that credit-scoring techniques will be adjusted to comply with equal credit opportunity requirements and that wider use will be made of such formulas in the future.

Interaction Among Suppliers of Consumer Financial Services

In addition to offering financial services to consumers, commercial banks provide deposit and loan services to the other suppliers of consumer financial services. The processing of credit union share drafts by commercial banks is currently a subject of some controversy, but the deposit services provided the other types of consumer financial institutions are a normal part of the general deposit business of commercial banks. On the lending side, commercial bank loans to mutual savings banks, savings and loan associations, and credit unions are relatively small in relation to the total resources of these institutions and are mainly made to meet liquidity needs. However, commercial bank loans to finance companies (including commercial paper) and to retailers are a major source of funds for these types of consumer lenders.

Commercial bank lending to organizations that compete with commercial banks in the consumer loan area does not pose a conflict and is not especially remarkable. Although there is some overlap in the consumer loan markets between commercial banks on the one hand and finance companies (mainly in the area of automobile financing) and retailers on the other, finance companies and retailers are largely oriented to types and sizes of installment loans that would be unprofitable or less profitable for commercial banks than other types of lending. It should also be recognized that the major proportion of commercial bank loans is made to large finance companies and large retailers by money center and large regional banks. Competition in local markets for consumer loans occurs between local banks and finance companies or large retailers financed mainly from sources outside the local area.

Common ownership of commercial banks and finance companies has increased somewhat since 1970. From the beginning of 1971 to the end of 1975, bank holding companies acquired 104 finance companies. The major incentive for acquisition of finance companies has been geographic expansion, especially on an interstate basis. Since 1956, bank holding companies have been prohibited from acquiring banks outside the state in which their principal subsidiary bank is located.[7] Commercial banks have long been prohibited from branching across state lines, and in various states branching is prohibited or limited to local areas. Bank holding companies are permitted, however, to own and operate certain types of closely related nonbank financial institutions on an interstate basis. Finance companies have become a significant vehicle for interstate expansion of bank holding companies.

About twenty stock savings and loan associations are owned by bank holding companies on a ''grandfathered'' basis; that is, they were acquired by one-bank (unregistered) holding companies prior to 1970. Since one-bank holding companies were brought under federal regulation in 1970, the Federal Reserve has declined to permit them to acquire stock savings and loan associations. Acquisition of savings and loan associations in the same market areas as the subsidiary banks of the holding company would obviously have antitrust implications, but that is not the issue in dispute. It is clear, too, that the savings and loan business is closely related to banking, as the Federal Reserve has acknowledged. Opposition to bank holding company authority to acquire stock savings and loan associations has come from the Federal Home Loan Bank and the mutual segment of the savings and loan industry. Underlying this opposition is the apparent belief that conversions from mutual form to stock form would be stimulated by bank holding company acquisitions. The concern seems to be that such conversions would change not only the structure but also the character of the industry and would ultimately bring less favorable legislative and regulatory treatment.

Director interlocks between commercial banks and savings and loan associations have been extensive. Bankers and/or bank shareholders were active in the organization of a number of mutual as well as stock savings and loan associations some years ago, and traditional relationships have been maintained in many instances. In general, these relationships are less significant than they were fifteen to twenty years ago, when commercial banks began to come into closer competition with savings and loan associations. However, in some local market areas commercial banks continue to be less competitive with respect to residential mortgage loans than would be the case in the absence of traditional ties with local savings and loan associations. The problem is not so much in director interlocks as such, many of which might be innocuous with respect to competitive performance, as it is in the structure and history of specific markets.

Commercial banks and consumer finance companies are sometimes linked in local market areas through common personal ownership. An individual or closely related group of individuals may own controlling interest in one or more banks and one or more small loan or industrial loan companies. Since 1970, a number of "chains" of this type have been reorganized as holding companies. Such chain arrangements today tend to be relatively small and located in states that restrict branching and do not permit multibank holding companies.

NOTES

1. *United States v. Marine Bancorporation et al.* illustrates the anticompetitive implications of home office protection. The government was unable to establish that the instant merger was in violation of the Clayton Act, due mainly to the fact that state law barred the acquiring bank from entering the market by any means other than merger.

2. An increase in Regulation Q ceilings tends to have a two-fold effect on net earnings of financial intermediaries. The cost of funds rises, and generation of a larger volume of savings flows through intermediaries tends to increase competition for the types of earning assets held by intermediaries, thereby decreasing or dampening any rising trend in interest rates on new loans.

3. National Association of Mutual Savings Banks, *1976 National Fact Book of Mutual Savings Banks* (Washington, D.C., 1976), pp. 47–48.

4. A receipt for a deposit can take several forms: a duplicate deposit

ticket, a stub of the deposit ticket or separate form imprinted at the time of receipt with the depositor's account number and the amount of the deposit, or an entry initialed by the receiving teller in the customer's passbook.

5. If the deposit includes only currency and coin, proof is a simple procedure: the teller must verify the amount of currency and coin before a receipt is issued. If the deposit includes checks, as well as currency and coin, the amount of currency and coin must be verified before issuing a receipt, but verification of the total of the checks may be deferred. A bank acts as the depositor's agent in accepting checks, and the total is subject to adjustment for errors, as well as to adjustment for checks returned unpaid by the bank on which drawn. Verifying the total of checks and other items that may be included in a deposit is usually too time-consuming to be done routinely by a teller prior to issuance of a receipt. Also, the circumstances are not conducive to minimization of errors.

6. A clearinghouse works essentially as follows. Each bank batches the checks to be presented to each of the other banks. At stated times during the day, the batches are brought to a central location and swapped through a "round robin" process. Each bank comes out of the exercise with a net deficit or net surplus. A memorandum is prepared indicating the net amounts to be paid and to be received by the respective banks. This memorandum is transmitted to the local bank, correspondent bank, or Federal Reserve Bank holding the clearing accounts for the association, and the appropriate credits and debits are made. Transmittal of the memorandum is by messenger or wire, depending on the location of the clearing bank.

   Specific arrangements and practices vary. Some clearinghouses have paid staff and their own facilities; others are managed by the participating banks on a rotating basis; and some arrangements continue to have the informality of their coffeehouse origin. Development of automated clearinghouses is currently in progress but is limited by the fact that checks must be physically presented for collection; that is, the role of automated clearinghouses is limited to types of transactions not involving checks, such as payrolls on magnetic tape.

7. Exception is found in Iowa; under state law conforming to the federal requirement in this regard, an out-of-state holding company which had been active in Iowa prior to 1954 has been permitted to make several acquisitions in recent years.

THREE
The Users and Providers of Consumer Financial Services: A Legal Framework
Dwight D. Ebaugh

Introduction

Law imposes many limits on the development of consumer financial services. A mixture of statutes, regulations, interpretations, and judicial decisions, the law comes from the federal government and from the fifty state governments; it comes from legislatures, administrative agencies, and courts; and it affects all aspects of consumer financial services. The law differentiates the powers and characteristics of our financial institutions. It regulates the number of providers that enter the financial services business and the growth of these providers after their entry. The law affects the prices and other characteristics of consumer financial services, as well as the operations of financial institutions. The law imposes standards for the provision of consumer credit information, for the collection of consumer debts, and for discrimination by creditors among credit seekers.

This chapter outlines the framework of laws surrounding consumer financial services, examines the private and social goals of these laws, and identifies the competing interests that are served or hindered by changes in them. Every significant change in the legal framework triggers complex disruptions in the existing pattern of consumer financial services, and no single change can satisfy all of the interests and goals at stake.

Users and Providers

Consumer financial services are deposit services (checking and savings accounts); credit services (loans for the purchase of cars, homes, and other consumer goods and services); and miscellaneous items, such as traveler's checks, safe deposit boxes, money orders, Christmas clubs, and credit card accounts. The users of consumer financial services are individuals and households; excluded are business organizations, government units, and users of commercial financial services.

Consumers can obtain financial services from commercial banks, thrift institutions (savings and loan associations, credit unions, mutual savings banks, and industrial banks), finance companies, and a variety of other sources (for example, retail stores, insurance premium financers, pawn shops, savings bond programs, and retirement plans).

Commercial banks offer the widest range of consumer financial services and, until recently, they were the only financial institutions offering checking accounts.[1] In addition to checking accounts, commercial banks offer savings accounts and lend money to consumers for almost any consumer purpose. They also provide safe deposit boxes, U.S. savings bonds, traveler's checks, credit card accounts (for example, VISA and Mastercharge), currency exchange, money orders, certified checks, Christmas clubs, individual retirement accounts (IRAs), automobile leasing, receipt of utility payments, notarization services, and the like.

In the past, thrift institutions offered a limited mixture of financial services. By way of generalization, thrifts differed from commercial banks because their deposit services did not include demand deposits, their consumer lending capabilities were restricted to varying degrees, and their miscellaneous services were less extensive. Today, largely as a result of federal laws such as the Depository Institutions Deregulation and Monetary Control Act (DIDMCA) of 1980, the differences between thrifts and commercial banks are diminishing.[2]

With regard to deposit services, all depository institutions were authorized to offer negotiable order of withdrawal (NOW) accounts, effective December 31, 1980.[3] The NOW account permits consumers to write checks (negotiable orders of withdrawal) against interest-bearing savings accounts.[4]

With regard to consumer loan services, savings and loan associations are authorized to make personal loans, to carry on credit card operations, and to exercise trust powers, as well as to operate in their traditional area of residential mortgage loans.[5] Credit unions, once restricted to making personal loans, are now authorized to make certain residential mortgage loans as well.[6]

Mutual savings banks are authorized in only nineteen jurisdictions (mainly states in the Northeast). They may offer checking and savings accounts, and they provide consumer loan services similar to those offered by commercial banks.[7]

Twenty-three states authorize some form of industrial banks, known variously as thrift and loans, industrial savings banks, loan and investment companies, or Morris Plan companies. These industrial banks generally accept savings deposits and make consumer installment loans. In some states industrial banks have the same powers as commercial banks.[8]

In addition to the services provided by banks, limited consumer financial services are provided by two other types of institutions—finance companies and retail stores. Finance companies are nondepository lending institutions that specialize in a single consumer financial service—personal loans.[9] That is, finance companies typically lend money to individuals and households on an installment loan basis for consumer purposes.

In terms of the volume of credit they extend to consumers, retail stores are the most significant of the "other" providers of consumer financial services. The revolving credit accounts and installment purchase plans offered by retailers (for example, Sears) are similar in many respects to the consumer loans extended by banks, thrifts, and finance companies. Other providers of consumer financial services include providers of consumer credit services, such as insurance premium finance companies and pawn shops, and providers of consumer savings services, such as the U.S. government (savings bonds) and private employers (retirement-deferred compensation plans).

The Law

The providers of consumer financial services are specialists by law as well as by choice. The law from which they derive their authority consists of statutes, regulations, interpretations, and judicial decisions. In the United States, it must be remembered, laws are enacted both at the federal level by the Congress of the United States and at the state level by fifty separate and distinct state legislatures. Thus, the laws that shape consumer financial services consist of federal statutes, regulations, interpretations, and judicial decisions side by side with state statutes, regulations, interpretations, and judicial decisions. The so-called ''dual banking system'' reflects the fact that some of our financial institutions were created under federal law, others are creatures of state law, and most are affected at both levels.

Consider this example, which highlights consumer financial services law within the dual banking system. Fred Fisher, an Iowa resident, occasionally used a BankAmericard credit card issued by the First National Bank of Omaha in Omaha, Nebraska.[10] Fisher used this card to make small credit purchases from Iowa merchants, and on one occasion Fisher's wife used the card to obtain a $250 cash advance from an Iowa bank. The First National Bank of Omaha charged interest under its BankAmericard plan at a rate of 1.5 percent per month (18 percent per year) on the previous month's unpaid balance up to $499.99, and 1 percent per month (12 percent per year) on previous balances of $500 or more. Fred Fisher sued the First National Bank of Omaha, alleging that the bank's interest charges were usurious and in violation of the National Bank Act.

The relevant provision of the National Bank Act does not spell out a particular interest rate that is usurious; rather it allows a national bank to charge the rate of interest allowed by the state where the national bank is located.[11] In this case, Nebraska statutes prescribed a range of maximum interest rates, with particular rates depending on the nature of the loan and the lender (from 9 percent for ''ordinary loans'' to 30 percent on certain small personal installment loans made by small loan companies licensed under Nebraska statutes).

In deciding the case against Mr. Fisher, the Federal Court of Appeals, 8th Circuit, made a number of instructive observations. First, if a national bank in one state makes a loan in another state and if there is a differential between the maximum rates allowable on the loan by the two states, the national bank may charge the higher of the two rates.[12] Second, a *national* bank is not limited to the interest rate that a *state* bank may charge with respect to a particular type of loan if another lender in the state is permitted to charge a higher rate of interest on the same type of loan.[13] Thus, regardless of the limitations imposed on state banks by Nebraska law, a national bank may legally charge for credit card transactions the rates allowed to small loan companies under Nebraska statutes.

The Fred Fisher case illustrates the dual banking system and the components of the law—statutes, regulations, interpretations, and judicial decisions—that shape consumer financial services. Numerous statutes were involved in the Fisher case, including the National Bank Act (a federal statute) and Nebraska state statutes limiting the interest rates chargeable on various loan transactions.

Statutes are the basic laws enacted by senators and representatives in the U.S. Congress and the legislatures of the fifty states. Frequently, the fixed words and phrases of a statute are not enough to resolve a dispute that is governed by the statute. For example, in the Fisher case it was clear that the First National Bank of Omaha was bound under the National Bank Act to charge interest at the rate allowed by the laws of Nebraska.[14] It was not clear, however, whether the bank's credit card rates were limited by the laws of Nebraska governing ordinary loans, the laws of Nebraska governing personal installment loans by Nebraska state banks, or the laws of Nebraska governing licensed small loan lenders. The court held that the national bank could charge the highest of these state rates for the same type of loan. Thus, the court's decision is a component of the law governing interest rates chargeable by national banks.

Judicial decisions are not made in a vacuum. The courts draw upon other judicial decisions, indications of legislative intent, established legal principles, and the like. In the Fisher case the court gave weight to a regulation of the Comptroller of the Currency: "A national bank may charge interest at the maximum rate permitted by State law to any competing State-chartered or licensed lending institution."[15] A regulation, such as the one just cited, is neither a statute nor a judicial decision, but it is another component of the law. Congress often enacts a statute and delegates authority to the administering agency (in this case the Comptroller of the Currency) to publish regulations that implement the statute.

A final component of the law is administrative interpretation. Frequently, questions arise in the consumer financial services community that cannot be answered with certainty by reference to statutes and regulations. Rather than proceeding at the risk of a lawsuit and an adverse judicial decision, the concerned party asks the appropriate agency, "If I do this, will I be in violation of the law?"

The agency's response or interpretation becomes part of the consumer financial services law.[16] Here is an example of a Federal Reserve Board interpretation of its own truth in lending regulation (Regulation Z):

> Lay-away plans as extension of credit—many vendors offer lay-away plans under which they retain the merchandise for a customer until the cash price is paid in full and the customer has no contractual obligation to make payments and may, at his option, revoke a purchase made under the plan and request and receive prompt refund of any amounts paid toward the cash price of the merchandise.
>
> A purchase under such a lay-away plan shall not be considered an extension of credit subject to the provisions of Regulation Z.[17]

Virtually every action taken by a provider of consumer financial services is governed by some combination of statutes, regulations, interpretations, and judicial decisions. It is the responsibility of each provider to be aware of, and comply with, this network of law. Since it takes some time and effort for the providers to maintain their legal awareness and compliance, this is an important cost of operation.

Regulatory Agencies

The major federal agencies that regulate consumer financial services are the Federal Reserve Board; the Comptroller of the Currency; the Federal Deposit Insurance Corporation (FDIC); the National Credit Union Administration (NCUA); the Federal Trade Commission; and the Federal Home Loan Bank Board and its subsidiary, the Federal Savings and Loan Insurance Corporation (FSLIC). The primary consumer financial regulatory agencies at the federal level and the consumer financial institutions that they affect are shown in Table III-1.

The Federal Reserve Board (that is, the Board of Governors of the Federal Reserve System) was created in 1913, along with the Federal Reserve System, by the Federal Reserve Act.[18] The board probably is known best for its role in influencing the nation's money supply and economic policy, but it also has wide-ranging regulatory authority. Examiners from the Federal Reserve System examine certain commercial and mutual savings banks.[19] The Federal Reserve Board regulates certain interest rates, certain bank mergers, and cer-

TABLE III-1 Primary Consumer Financial Regulatory Agencies

Consumer Finance Services Institutions	PRIMARY FEDERAL AGENCIES*					
	FRB	C of C	FDIC	FHLBB/FSLIC	NCUA	FTC
National banks	x	x	x			
State member (FRB) banks	x		x			
State-insured nonmember banks			x			
State-uninsured nonmember banks						x
Federal S&Ls				x		
State-affiliated (FHLBB-FSLIC) S&Ls				x		
State-unaffiliated S&Ls						x
Federal credit unions					x	
State-insured (NCUA) credit unions					x	
State-uninsured credit unions						x
Mutual savings banks (FRB members)	x					
Consumer finance companies						x
Retail creditors						x

* FRB = Federal Reserve Board
C of C = Comptroller of the Currency
FDIC = Federal Deposit Insurance Corporation
FHLBB/FSLIC = Federal Home Loan Bank Board and Federal Savings and Loan
                   Insurance Corporation
NCUA = National Credit Union Association
FTC = Federal Trade Commission

tain bank holding company activities; it also implements various federal statutes, such as the Bank Holding Company Act, the Federal Reserve Act, the Equal Credit Opportunity Act, the Truth in Lending Act, the Fair Credit Billing and Reporting Acts, the Consumer Leasing Act, and the Home Mortgage Disclosure Act.[20] In addition, the Federal Reserve Board is responsible for enforcing certain legislation with respect to certain banks.[21]

Similarly, the other agencies are responsible for examining certain institutions, regulating certain activities, and implementing and enforcing various acts of Congress. It is easier to describe the responsibilities of these agencies by looking at the institutions they regulate and the statutes they enforce than by looking at the agencies themselves. For example, all national banks (that is, banks chartered by federal as opposed to state government) are examined and regulated primarily by the Comptroller of the Currency. This is true despite Section 2 of the Federal Reserve Act, which requires that all national banks be members of the Federal Reserve System and be insured by the Federal Deposit Insurance Corporation. State banks that are members of the Federal Reserve System are examined and regulated primarily by the Federal Reserve Board. The Federal Deposit Insurance Corporation is the primary examiner and regulator of insured nonmembers, that is, state banks that are insured by the FDIC but are not members of the Federal Reserve System.

The only commercial banks that escape direct supervision by the federal banking agencies are state banks that have no federal deposit insurance and no Federal Reserve membership. Of the approximately 15,000 commercial banks in the country, only about 250 fall into this category.[22]

The regulatory jurisdictions depicted in Table III-1 have been incorporated into the enforcement provisions of many of the federal consumer financial services statutes discussed in this chapter. As an illustration, the Bank Merger Act requires merging banks to receive prior approval from one of the banking agencies: the Comptroller if the surviving bank is a national bank, the Federal Reserve Board if the survivor is a state member, and the FDIC if the survivor is an insured nonmember.[23] All acquisitions by bank holding companies, regardless of the affiliations of the banks involved, are reviewed by the Federal Reserve Board.

If we shift our view from commercial banks to savings and loan associations, the federal regulatory scheme is not so confusing (see

Table III-1). All federally chartered savings and loans are members of the Federal Savings and Loan Insurance Corporation, a subsidiary of the Federal Home Loan Bank Board.[24] State-chartered savings and loans are subjected to federal supervision only if they insure with FSLIC or affiliate with the Home Loan Bank System.

The National Credit Union Administration insures all federal and state credit unions that apply and meet the NCUA standards.[25] NCUA is authorized to supervise and examine all federal credit unions.[26]

Generally, if a financial institution (as opposed to a nonfinancial institution, such as a retail store) does not fit within the federal regulatory scheme, it is supervised at the state level. There are, of course, fifty different approaches to state regulation. In Michigan, for example, the authority to enforce state laws that deal with state-chartered financial institutions is divided between the state's Financial Institutions Bureau and the Attorney General's office.[27] The state's Banking Code, Savings and Loan Code, Credit Union Code, Small Loan Act, and Motor Vehicle Finance Act all specify the Financial Institutions Bureau as the agency responsible for enforcement. The Deceptive Advertising Act, Retail Installment Sales Act, and Home Improvement Finance Act all specify the Attorney General's office as the agency responsible for their enforcement.

All providers of consumer financial services fall within the jurisdiction of several government (state and/or federal) agencies with regard to some combination of supervision, regulation, examination, enforcement, and implementation of consumer financial services law.[28] State-chartered banks, for instance, are typically supervised and examined by an agency of state government, and most are also supervised and examined by federal banking agencies in connection with Federal Reserve System membership or federal deposit insurance. National banks, on the other hand, may avoid direct supervision at the state level, but they are subject to some direction from each of the three federal banking agencies.

Laws Governing Entry and Expansion

The supply of consumer financial services and access to them depend on the number of businesses providing these services—a number that is regulated by law. If a group decides to open a bank (or a thrift institution or a small loan company), it first must obtain a charter or a license from the appropriate state or federal agency. Thus, the number of sources of consumer financial services—the number of banks, thrifts, loan companies, and so forth—depends on the number of charters and licenses that are· granted by the agencies in accordance with the law. Banks, savings and loans, and credit unions may apply for charters at either the state or the federal level. Mutual savings banks, industrial banks, and finance companies apply for charters or licenses at the state level.[29]

The primary rationale for regulating entry into the financial services business is to minimize business failures that result from "overbanking," "excessive competition," and the entry of organizations with insufficient financial and managerial resources. Bank and thrift failures are socially undesirable because they cause depositors to lose savings and may have destabilizing ripple effects throughout the economy of the community.

On the other hand, lawmakers recognize the advantages of chartering a sufficient number of financial institutions to serve the needs of the community adequately. Thus, the chartering and licensing statutes generally require the administrative agency to find a need for an additional institution and assure that the soundness of other financial institutions will not be impaired by the additional competitor. In addition, the new institution must demonstrate that it has sufficient financial and managerial resources to operate safely and profitably.

The law regulates not only the number of providers that enter the financial services business, but also the expansion of ongoing concerns. A chartered financial institution must obtain approval from the appropriate regulator before it may open a branch office, merge with another financial institution, or affiliate with a bank holding company.

Consider a bank that wants to open a branch office.[30] Regardless of the bank's charter source, state law determines the geographic limits on such a branch, because national banks are permitted by federal law to branch only to the same extent as state banks within the state in question. Some states allow branches throughout the state, some states restrict branches within counties or regions of the state, and some states flatly prohibit branches. If a bank is permitted to branch, there must first be a regulatory determination similar to the determination made for chartering. Would the convenience and needs of the community be served by the proposed branch? Is the proposed branch consistent with the financial capabilities of the branching organization? Will the proposed branch create a risk of overbanking and bank failure?[31]

Next, consider a bank that wants to merge with another bank. The merger must be compatible with state branching limitations, because after the merger, the merged bank will be a branch of the survivor, and it may proceed only with the prior approval of the appropriate state and federal banking agencies. Under the Bank Merger Act, the appropriate federal agency may approve the merger only if its anticompetitive effects are outweighed by the probable effect of the transaction in meeting the convenience and needs of the community.[32]

Now consider a bank holding company (that is, a company owning one or more banks) that wants to purchase another bank. The result of such a transaction seems similar to that of a merger. In the latter case banks A and B merge to become a larger bank A; in the former case banks A and B are both purchased by C, a bank holding company. In the bank holding company case, however, the offices of bank B are not legally branches of bank A, and the offices of bank A are not legally branches of bank B. Therefore, in a state such as Michigan, where branching is restricted, it is illegal for a Detroit bank to merge with a Lansing bank, but it is permissible for a holding company to own banks in both Detroit and Lansing. The holding company laws vary from state to state, with some states prohibiting them and some states limiting their activities. All bank holding company acquisitions are governed by the Bank Holding Company Act, which directs the Federal Reserve Board to deny anticompetitive acquisitions unless the anticompetitive effects are clearly outweighed in the public interest by the probable effect of the transaction in meeting the convenience and needs of the community.[33] The board also is required to consider the financial and managerial resources and future prospects of the banks concerned. Again, the law demonstrates a concern for maintaining competition, meeting community needs, and assuring bank soundness. In addition, once a bank merger or a bank holding company acquisition has been approved by the appropriate state and federal regulatory bodies, it is subject to scrutiny by the Antitrust Division of the U.S. Department of Justice under the federal antitrust laws.[34]

Finally, consider a bank that wishes to establish an electronic funds transfer (EFT) service, such as an automated teller machine (ATM), so that bank customers can deposit or withdraw cash at any time of the day or night by using an unattended machine, or so that shoppers can pay for goods at retail stores by debiting their accounts electronically, using a terminal at the point of sale.[35] EFT systems and ATMs are recent innovations among consumer financial services, and they have run into many legal difficulties. In 1974 the Comptroller of the Currency issued an interpretation of the National Bank Act that allowed national banks to establish ATMs without regard to state branching restrictions. The interpretation was hotly debated in Congress, court challenges were brought, and the interpretation was withdrawn in October 1975. At this time, no federal statute regulating ATMs (or EFT systems in general) has been enacted, and only about half the states have enacted EFT legislation. The EFT laws in New York, for example, apply to banks, savings banks, and savings and loans. An EFT facility is considered a branch, automated teller machines and point-of-sale terminals are permitted, numerical restrictions on new branches for savings banks and savings and loans do not apply, and unmanned facilities are treated the same as manned facilities.[36]

Although these few examples involve commercial banks, almost all financial institutions must obtain regulatory approval before expanding to new locations.[37] Federally chartered savings and loan associations seek this approval from the Federal Home Loan Bank Board. State-chartered savings and loans and credit unions typically apply to a state agency. However, federally chartered credit unions are not required to obtain regulatory approval before branching. Consumer finance companies must follow the same procedures before expanding as they do before beginning to do business in a state: they must obtain a license from the state. Similarly, in states where they are allowed to exist, mutual savings banks and industrial banks obtain their charters (or licenses) and their permission to branch from state authorities.

Laws Governing Deposits, Loans, and Other Services

The law not only distinguishes among financial institutions and determines their location, it also shapes many of the consumer financial services offered. Many of these legal constraints are so commonplace that we take them for granted.

For example, prior to DIDMCA, when consumers selected a bank to open a checking account, they inquired about the service charges on the account, not about the amount of interest they would be paid on their deposit balances. The reason was not that banks were unable to produce earnings with checking account deposits, but that the law prohibited the payment of interest on checking accounts.[38]

Consumers also may notice that, with regard to savings deposits, competing banks tend to pay the same rate of interest. Competing thrifts also tend to pay the same rate of interest; however, the thrift rate may be .25 percent above the commercial bank rate. The reason for this is that various federal agencies are directed by law to set the maximum rates that may be paid by different financial institutions.[39] DIDMCA will lift these restrictions in the future.

The legislative rationale for banning interest on checking deposits and limiting interest on savings deposits was to assure stability in the financial community. Fixed interest rates were believed to inhibit banks and thrifts from engaging in vigorous price competition. This, in turn, reduced the likelihood that an institution would take risks, suffer unacceptable losses, and collapse. The reason for allowing thrift institutions to pay slightly higher interest rates was to offset their disadvantages with respect to commercial banks and to coax money into deposits which would be used for the housing industry. Under DIDMCA, limitations on deposit interest rates will be phased out because the lawmakers are now concerned that limitations discourage persons from saving money, impede competition among depository institutions, and fail to provide an even flow of funds for home mortgage lending.

The interest charged on consumer loans also is limited by law to protect borrowers from unreasonably high rates.[40] Legal interest rate limitations on loans are a matter of state law, since federally chartered lenders are directed by federal law to observe the rate ceilings prescribed by the state in which they are located.[41] Most states impose interest rate ceilings on mortgage loans, installment loans, revolving charge accounts, auto loans, and so forth. The limits may be associated with particular types of loans, regardless of the lender (for example, auto financing) or with particular types of lenders (for example, pawnbrokers). Under DIDMCA, state mortgage usury ceilings are eliminated by federal preemption unless the state overrides the preemption by adopting a new statutory mortgage interest ceiling by April 1, 1983. Interest rate limitations on other consumer loans are not affected by DIDMCA. To charge an interest rate higher than allowed by statute constitutes usury. Depending on the state, penalties for usury range from forfeiture of the interest in excess of the allowed rate to voiding of the entire contract.

Most financial institutions that accept deposits advertise that accounts up to $100,000 are insured by either the FDIC, FSLIC, or NCUA. This insurance coverage is the result of federal legislation designed to protect depositors from being wiped out by the collapse of a bank or thrift.[42]

A host of other laws and regulations are aimed at maintaining the soundness of financial institutions by regulating their exposure to risk. Banks and thrifts are required to maintain levels of capital sufficient, it is hoped, to absorb the losses that occur from time to time. They are also required to make loans and investments in such a way that their overall risk exposure is acceptable. For example, loan losses are analyzed, and various collateral requirements are observed. With regard to deposits, all the institutions must maintain a portion of their deposits in the form of reserves so that they can supply their customers' daily needs for cash.[43]

All of these regulations aimed at minimizing risk and maintaining financial soundness have an effect on consumer financial services. Banks, for example, may be limited in the volume of home mortgage loans that they can extend. Similarly, in response to regulations, credit unions may restrict their volume of unsecured loans; savings and loan institutions may reduce the percentage of home purchase values they are willing to finance; and, as they did until recently, banks may emphasize their commercial business and downplay consumer services.

Consumer financial services have also been affected by the historical split between banking and commerce. The laws that define and limit consumer financial services are based on the premise that any mixture of banking and commerce is bad because (1) a financial institution financing its own commercial endeavors as well as its competitors' would constitute a conflict of interest, and (2) commerce is too risky for the financial community. As a result, the law generally prohibits financial institutions from investing in real estate, stock, or other "nonbanking" assets.

In 1970 certain national banks proposed to offer their customers (consumer as well as commercial) an investment service whereby the banks would operate collective investment funds in competition with mutual funds and open-end investment companies. The Comptroller of the Currency approved this financial service, but a lawsuit was brought by the Investment Company Institute. In 1971 the Supreme Court held that the practice would involve banks in the underwriting, issuing, selling, and distributing of securities, which would violate the Glass-Steagall Act.[44] Thus, strict adherence to the separation between banking and commerce and the overriding concern for bank soundness have, at times, meant that consumer financial services are not provided.

A significant amendment to the Bank Holding Company Act was enacted in 1970.[45] It directed the Federal Reserve Board to determine whether certain nonbanking activities were ". . . so closely related to banking or managing or controlling banks as to be a proper incident thereto." The amendment also specified:

> In determining whether a particular activity is a proper incident to banking or managing or controlling banks the Board shall consider whether its performance by an affiliate of a holding company can reasonably be expected to produce benefits to the public, such as greater convenience, increased competition, or gains inefficiency, that outweigh possible adverse effects, such as undue concentration of resources, decreased or unfair competition, conflicts of interests, or unsound banking practices.[46]

Thus, the legislature expressed some of the objectives (greater convenience, increased competition, and gains in efficiency) of allowing banks to venture into nonbanking activities. As a result of this change in the law, bank holding company affiliates are now providing more consumer financial services: consumer finance loans, mortgage loans, credit card services, industrial banking, trust services, automobile leasing, and certain insurance services.

Creditor Remedies and Debtor Protections

The total cost of making loans includes the cost of recovering principal and interest from borrowers who do not repay their loans as agreed. In a society in which debtors had no defenses against legal actions by their creditors, loans would be extended more readily because losses would be an insignificant problem. At the opposite extreme, if creditors had no legal remedies in the event of loan defaults, consumer financial services would become scarcer and more expensive. The real situation is, of course, somewhere in the middle.

Creditors can use certain statutes and other laws in collecting money that has been loaned.[47] Other laws limit the reach and effectiveness of creditor remedies in favor of other principles, such as encouragement of business entrepreneurship, maintenance of legal due process, and no punishment for mere indebtedness. The effect of these laws on consumer financial services is not as obvious and direct as, say, an 18 percent per year finance charge usury ceiling, but they nevertheless have an impact.

For instance, it is often noted that a primary purpose of the Federal Bankruptcy Act[48] is to relieve the honest debtor from the weight of oppressive indebtedness and permit him or her to start afresh.[49] The debtor's fresh start, however, is at the expense of providers of consumer financial services, whose claims may become uncollectible following the debtor's discharge in bankruptcy. The Bankruptcy Act undoubtedly affects the cost and availability of unsecured consumer loans, although the magnitude of the effect may defy measurement, and it may be impossible to make an objective comparison between the social benefits of fresh starts and the social costs of discharged debts.

The same kind of analysis can be made of creditor remedies, such as garnishment. Technically, in a situation between creditor X and debtor Y, garnishment refers to a claim by X against any property belonging to Y in the hands of some third party. The term is generally used interchangeably with wage garnishment, in which a creditor collects a debt by tapping the debtor's wages while they are still in the hands of the debtor's employer. Garnishment aids in the debt collection process, it probably results in lower overall loan losses, and it may be a legal factor that contributes favorably to the availability of credit. On the other hand, the potency of the garnishment remedy has been diluted over the years in favor of other social objectives. Prejudgment wage garnishment (that is, garnishment prior to a judicial hearing and determination as to the debtor's liability) has been restricted by law to preserve legal due process.[50] The size of wage garnishments has been limited by federal law to a fraction of each paycheck (25 percent of after-tax, take-home pay, as a rule of thumb), and most states allow a judgment debtor to obtain a court order for the payment of a debt in installments without threat of garnishment.[51] These limitations on the amount of wage garnishments arguably give debtors an incentive to continue working since they can salvage a portion of each paycheck without resorting to bankruptcy.

There are, of course, numerous other laws in this area.[52] For example, as a result of Michigan's Married Women's Property Act, a married woman is liable if she cosigns a promisory note with her husband, but judgment entered on the note may be satisfied only out of property held jointly with her husband; the wife's separate property is not liable unless the borrowed money directly benefitted her separate property.[53] Another example is the law regarding self-help repossession (that is, repossession of loan collateral by a creditor in accordance with a written security agreement but without prior notice or court procedures). Many debtors have challenged this creditor remedy as unconstitutional deprivation of property without due process of law, but most courts have upheld self-help repossession as a lawful creditor remedy.[54] As a final example, many debtor and creditor litigants are shocked to learn that each party must bear their own litigation expense regardless of who wins. There are some specific statutory exceptions to this rule, but frequently a potential litigant must weigh his or her attorney's fees against the potential award of damages before proceeding to court.

Without specifying the details and mechanics of other laws, the point is that credit remedies and debtor protections constitute another body of law that affects consumer financial services. Any changes in these remedies and protections will affect both the users and providers of consumer financial services.

Discrimination Among Credit Seekers

In order to operate profitably and succeed as private enterprises, all financial institutions must discriminate among loan applicants on the basis of credit worthiness (that is, the risk of default or probability of repayment). Lenders must constantly strive to lend money only to borrowers who are likely to repay. Discrimination based solely on credit worthiness is consistent with the goals of private business, as well as with the generally accepted social and legal principle that borrowed money should be repaid.

Several laws are designed to insure that credit discrimination is, in fact, credit discrimination and not discrimination based on race, sex, marital status, national origin, location of collateral (redlining), or the like.[55] Regulations implementing equal credit opportunity, like those implementing truth-in-lending disclosures, are issued by the Federal Reserve Board and enforced by various federal agencies. The regulations appear as Regulation B of the board.[56]

The Equal Credit Opportunity Act (ECOA), Title VII of the federal Consumer Credit Protection Act, prohibits discrimination on the basis of sex, marital status, race, color, religion, national origin, age, the fact that a borrower's income derives from public assistance, or the fact that a borrower has exercised any right granted under the Consumer Credit Protection Act.[57] The types of discrimination prohibited by the ECOA are applicable to all creditors, including those who offer thirty-day accounts with no finance charge imposed. Thus, they are applicable to doctors, lawyers, plumbers, electricians, and retailers who bill consumers for work performed or merchandise sold. However, certain types of "incidental credit" are exempted from various disclosure requirements, though the basic prohibition against discrimination is applicable. To be eligible for the incidental credit exemption, the following criteria must all be met: (1) no credit card is involved; (2) no finance charge, late payment, or other fee is or may be imposed; and (3) there is no agreement by which the credit may be paid in more than four installments. Except where an application is made by telephone or an existing credit limit is to be increased, all creditors—other than those qualifying for the incidental credit exemption—are required to supply each applicant with an ECOA notice.

Certain ECOA rules concern the handling of credit applications. A retailer may not refuse, on the basis of sex or marital status, to open a separate account to a credit-worthy applicant. Furthermore, a creditor may not prohibit an applicant from opening an account in a birth-given first name and surname, even though the applicant may in fact be married. Thus, a married woman is permitted to use her maiden name for credit purposes. If an applicant applies for a separate account (for example, a woman asking for an account in her own name), a creditor may not ask the applicant's marital status, except in a community property state or as required to comply with state law governing permissible finance charges. If the applicant applies for a joint account or if the above conditions are met, the creditor may ask about marital status only in terms of "married," "unmarried," or "separated."

For every account established after November 1, 1976, the creditor must determine whether it is a joint account (that is, the applicant's spouse will be permitted to use it), designate it accordingly, and furnish information to a credit-reporting agency in a manner that will enable the agency to have access to both names. In practical terms, therefore, this will require accounts to be designated in the first names of both parties, rather than as Mr. and Mrs.

Under the ECOA, a creditor may request and consider information concerning an applicant's spouse (or former spouse) only under the following conditions: (1) if the spouse will be permitted to use the account (as in a joint account); (2) if the spouse is contractually liable on the account; (3) if the applicant is relying on the spouse's income in seeking the credit; or (4) if the applicant is relying on alimony, child support, or maintenance payments. A creditor may also request the name in which another account is carried if the applicant discloses the account in applying for credit. Where alimony, child support, and maintenance payments are disclosed, the creditor must consider them as income to the extent that such payments are likely to be made regularly.

A creditor may not arbitrarily discount income on the basis of sex or marital status, nor may the creditor discount income solely because it is derived from part-time employment. However, the creditor may consider the probable continuity of such income in evaluating credit worthiness.

A creditor *may* ask about an applicant's liability to pay alimony, child support, or maintenance. Furthermore, if the creditor first discloses to the applicant that income from these sources need not be revealed, a creditor may also inquire as to whether any of the applicant's income comes from alimony, child support, or maintenance payments. In addition, amendments to the ECOA permit the creditor to inquire about an applicant's age or whether income derives from public assistance programs, if the inquiry is for the purpose of determining credit or the amount of income derived from public assistance.

Also under the ECOA, a creditor must notify a consumer of action taken on a credit application within thirty days of receipt of the application. Each rejected applicant is entitled to a statement of reasons for such action. This may be done in one of two ways: (1) routinely providing a statement of reasons in writing, or (2) giving written notification of the adverse action and disclosing the applicant's right to receive specific reasons and the name of the person or office from whom the reasons should be solicited. In addition, the Fair Credit Reporting Act requires that the creditor notify the applicant of the name and address of the credit bureau supplying information, if the rejection is based in whole or in part on that information.

The most controversial aspect of the ECOA is the so-called "effects test," a judicial doctrine that originated in *Griggs vs. Duke Power Company*, a decision by the U.S Supreme Court dealing with employment discrimination.[58] The *Griggs* decision prohibits not only discrimination based upon discriminatory intent, but also practices that have the effect of discriminating against protected classes, regardless of the motive or intent of the employer. According to a footnote to Regulation B, the legislative history of the ECOA indicates that Congress intended that an "effects test," such as that developed in equal employment opportunity laws (for example, *Griggs*), be applicable in determining whether a creditor's judgment of credit worthiness is discriminatory. Regulation B did not define an effects test, however, because so far the courts have applied the effects test only to areas closely related to employment discrimination.

Application of the effects test to credit-granting policies raises some fundamental questions about procedures now in use by the providers of consumer financial services. During the past two decades, the larger creditors have turned away from judgmental systems of evaluating credit applicants to empirically derived systems of predicting the probability that an applicant will default on a credit application. These systems allocate points according to a weighting scheme based upon the creditor's recent experience with credit applicants, using generally accepted statistical techniques for sampling and validation. Although such systems, on their face, would appear to be lacking in any discriminatory intent, they may often result in effects that would present a prima facie case of illegal discrimination. To deal with such a contingency, Regulation B contains an absolute prohibition against considering a person's sex, race, religion, or other attributes, except age, in the credit-granting decision. Thus, credit-scoring systems cannot use these attributes even if past experience indicates that they are the best predictors of credit worthiness. If a credit-scoring system has met the regulation's test of being demonstrably sound and empirically derived, the amended act permits age to be considered but forbids the assignment of a negative point value for age if the applicant is sixty-two years or older.

Another federal antidiscrimination statute is the Home Loan Mortgage Disclosure Act, which was prompted by the congressional finding that "some depository institutions have sometimes contributed to the decline of certain geographic areas by their failure pursuant to their chartering responsibilities to provide adequate home financing to qualified applicants on reasonable terms and conditions. . . ."[59] The practice of refusing to lend in certain geographic areas is usually called "redlining" because of allegations that mortgage lenders draw red lines on their lending maps to indicate blighted sectors of the community where no loans will be made.

The purpose of the Disclosure Act is not to outlaw redlining but instead to reveal institutional mortgage-lending patterns to the public so that an assessment of these patterns can be made. Also, the purpose of the act is not to compel lenders to make riskier or less profitable loans: "Nothing in this chapter is intended to, nor shall it be construed to, encourage unsound lending practices or the allocation of credit. . . ."[60] Many have argued that it will have this effect, however.

As with creditor remedy and debtor protection laws, anti-discrimination laws affect the availability and cost of consumer financial services. Under the ECOA, for instance, people who were formerly denied financial services may now be entitled to them as a matter of law. A statute such as the ECOA may also increase the cost of credit. At least in the short run, when lenders are required to revise their practices, there are added costs associated with more careful credit screening, use of new forms and notices, additional postage, and increased litigation. Thus, the antidiscrimination laws have a variety of effects on consumer financial services.

Credit Information

Provision of comprehensive market information to consumers theoretically enables them to purchase better services at the same price or to purchase the same services at a lower price. According to the same theory, the most efficient providers of services experience relative success, and inefficient providers have an incentive to shift their resources to other enterprises. For example, consider consumers shopping for car loans. In order to get the best loan, it is necessary for them to have comparable information from all lenders regarding such things as amount financed, interest rate, monthly payments, and length of loan. If consumers have ready access to such information, then we would expect the lenders with the best deals to be the most successful. In theory, then, full information enables the market to function and leads to a desirable allocation of resources. However, as we have seen with debtor protection legislation and antidiscrimination laws, these benefits are obtained at some cost. In the case of financial information laws, the costs are those of compiling and disseminating the information.

The most important credit information law is the Consumer

Credit Protection Act, which includes Truth in Lending, Fair Credit Reporting, Fair Credit Billing, and the Consumer Leasing Act.[61] These statutes were designed to guarantee (1) strengthened competition among institutions engaged in the extension of consumer credit, (2) meaningful disclosure of credit terms to avoid the uninformed use of credit, (3) protection of consumers from inaccurate and unfair credit billing, (4) assurance that "credit agencies" adopt reasonable procedures for meeting the needs of commerce in a manner that is fair and equitable to the consumer, and (5) meaningful disclosure of the terms of consumer leases.[62] The heart of the disclosure requirement under the Consumer Credit Protection Act is a determination of the finance charge to be levied on a credit transaction and its conversion into an annual percentage rate calculated to the nearest .25 percent.[63] The finance charge, as defined in the law, is the total cost of credit and includes almost all direct and indirect charges that a consumer would not have to pay if a cash purchase were made.

In addition, certain specific disclosures are required in open-end credit transactions (sometimes called revolving credit or department store credit), and these must be made both before the first transaction occurs and with each periodic billing statement. These disclosures include the conditions under which a finance charge may be imposed, the method of determining the amount of the finance charge, the minimum periodic payment required, and the customer's right to question billing errors. The law also spells out a procedure that creditors must follow in resolving billing disputes. Disclosure requirements for closed-end (installment) credit are similar.

Various titles of the Consumer Credit Protection Act (for example, Truth in Lending, Fair Credit Billing, and Consumer Leasing) are implemented by Regulation Z. Written by the Federal Reserve Board, Regulation Z spells out a procedure for determining whether state-required disclosures are inconsistent with federal requirements and thus pre-empted. Where state and federal requirements do not conflict, creditors must meet both. Some states have specifically provided that compliance with the federal law will be considered compliance with the disclosure requirements of state law.

An Example

A hypothetical example that covers much of the material in this chapter involves Ms. Consumer, who wishes to bor-

row $1,000 without security for a thirty-six-month period to buy
household furniture. She seeks a lender near her home in Stefan
County, Michigan. The lenders in Stefan County include a commercial bank, a savings and loan association, several credit unions, a
small loan company, and (for furniture purchases) the local furniture
store. Michigan does not allow mutual savings banks or industrial
banks (Michigan industrial banks are the same as commercial
banks), and there are no pawn shops in Stefan County. In a typical
Michigan county, Ms. Consumer would be able to select from approximately four banks, twelve credit unions, one savings and loan,
and one consumer finance company.[64]

Ms. Consumer must rule out the credit unions, because she is not
associated with any group that has formed one. She must also rule
out the furniture store, because it only extends credit that is secured
by the furniture purchased.

Ms. Consumer inquires first at the commercial bank, the First
National Bank of Stefan County. Under Michigan law, the bank
could offer Ms. Consumer a credit card loan, an installment loan,
or a term loan. The First National Bank of Stefan County is a national bank, as its name indicates. Although some of the powers of
national banks are specifically authorized by federal law, the power
to extend a loan to Ms. Consumer is implied from the federal law
that authorizes national banks "to exercise all such incidental
powers as shall be necessary to carry on the business of banking."[65]

As we learned in the *Fisher* case, a national bank located in a particular state may charge interest rates equal to that state's statutory
rates for comparable loans. Under Michigan law, the interest rate
on a bank credit card loan may not exceed 1.5 percent of the unpaid
balance per month, or 18 percent annual percentage rate (APR).[66]
On installment loans, the maximum rate is specified as "interest
added in advance at the rate of seven percent per annum or less on
the entire amount of the loan from date of disbursement to date of
maturity."[67] In order to convert this 7 percent add-on rate to an
APR, some calculations must be made or a table must be consulted.
The calculations depend on the amount financed, the finance
charge, and the number of monthly payments. If Ms. Consumer applied for $1,000 at 7 percent add-on with thirty-six equal monthly
payments, the annual percentage rate would equal 12.75 percent.[68]

On other loans, state-chartered Michigan banks "may charge,
collect, and receive interest and other charges in the same manner
and at up to the maximum rate or amount permitted by law for the

same type of loans made by national banking associations authorized to do business in this state."[69] This Michigan provision is an example of a "trailer statute," which is enacted by the state legislature in an effort to preserve competitive equality between state and national banks.[70] Such legislation is enacted if a state legislature is not able to respond sufficiently quickly to a ruling, for example, by the Comptroller of the Currency, giving national banks a significant competitive advantage over state banks in the form of a new or increased authority.

The result of all of this is that when Ms. Consumer goes to the First National Bank of Stefan County with her loan request, the bank offers two options: revolving credit at 18 percent APR and installment credit at 7 percent add-on. Other banks may have offered a third option in the form of a term loan with no principal payment due until the end of the loan period. However, First National Bank of Stefan County does not offer term loans to consumers with whom it has had no prior banking contracts.

Another provider of consumer financial services in Stefan County is the local savings and loan association, a state-chartered institution. In Michigan state savings and loan associations may make small "any purpose" loans, which include all small loans up to $5,000 that are not specifically authorized under the state's statutes.[71] The maximum interest rate on such a loan is 8 percent add-on, the rate specified by Michigan's law governing savings and loan associations.[72] Under Ms. Consumer's terms ($1,000 with thirty-six equal monthly payments), 8 percent add-on is equivalent to an annual percentage rate of 14.5 percent.[73]

A final Stefan County source for Ms. Consumer's loan is the state-licensed consumer finance company, which makes loans up to $1,500 at rates "not exceeding 2.5 percent per month on that part of the unpaid principal balance of any loan not in excess of $400, and 1.25 percent per month on any remainder of such unpaid principal balance."[74] Under Ms. Consumer's terms, the annual percentage rate is 24.2 percent.

Ms. Consumer fills out loan applications at the bank, the savings and loan association, and the consumer finance company. As a result of discrimination laws (for example, the Equal Credit Opportunity Act) and information laws (for example, Truth in Lending and other provisions of the Consumer Credit Protection Act), each of the potential lenders will make certain disclosures and refrain from certain practices. For example, under the Equal Credit Opportunity Act and Regulation B implementing the act, they may not make statements discouraging Ms. Consumer's application on the basis of her sex or marital status, and they may not refuse, on the basis of her sex or marital status, to grant a separate account to Ms. Consumer if she is married and credit worthy. They must provide Ms. Consumer with a written notice identifying the federal agency that administers compliance with the act: the Comptroller of the Currency in the case of the national bank, the Federal Home Loan Bank Board in the case of the savings and loan (with FSLIC insurance), and the Federal Trade Commission in the case of the consumer finance company. The three lenders will also furnish information to Ms. Consumer under Truth in Lending and Regulation Z. The information and the manner in which it is disclosed will vary depending on whether open-end credit (the bank's revolving credit plan with a credit card) or other than open-end credit (the various installment loan arrangements) is being offered.

Within thirty days after the lenders receive a completed application from Ms. Consumer, they must notify her of the action taken.[75] If her application is denied, Ms. Consumer is entitled to a statement of the lender's reasons for denial. If one or more applications are approved, Ms. Consumer may select the loan with the most satisfactory rate and terms. Later, if Ms. Consumer defaults, the creditor may take action against her, but such action is limited by state and federal law, and of course if a debtor lacks the ability to pay, there is nothing a creditor can do.

NOTES

1. Throughout this chapter, references will be made to a compilation prepared by the law firm of Weil, Gotshal & Manges, New York City, in connection with a research project funded by the National Science Foundation and performed at Purdue University. This source, hereafter referred to as *Purdue Compilation,* is available from the Credit Research Center, College of Business, Purdue University, West Lafayette, Indiana. With regard to commercial banks in general, see *Purdue Compilation,* pp. 641–674, 861–863, 872–878, 908–910, and 916–917.
2. The Depository Institutions Deregulation and Monetary Control Act of 1980, 94 Stat. 132, 12 USC 226.
3. Consumer Checking Account Equity Act of 1980—Title III of the Depository Institutions Deregulation and Monetary Control Act of 1980.

4 . The NOW account was introduced by mutual savings banks in
Massachusetts and New Hampshire in 1972 and, because of its controversial nature, it quickly became a subject of federal legislation,
which prohibited NOW accounts in federally insured financial institutions in all states except Connecticut, Maine, Massachusetts, New
Hampshire, Rhode Island, and Vermont. In three additional
states—Illinois, Maryland, and Minnesota—NOW accounts (or
noninterest-bearing NOW accounts) were authorized for state-chartered
financial institutions. In August of 1974, two years after the NOW
account experiment began, federal credit unions were given authority
via a temporary regulation of the National Credit Union Administration to offer third-party payment services (checking accounts)
to their members. A six-month pilot program involving five
credit unions was then instituted. After the pilot period, the program
was expanded and, as of September 1976, 333 credit unions were
offering share drafts. (Information regarding credit union share
drafts is from *Final Report of the Governor's Advisory Commission on the
Regulation of Financial Institutions,* State of Michigan, August 1977,
p. 30; hereinafter *Michigan Governor's Report.* In the meantime, the
American Bankers' Association sued to bar the credit union share draft
practice. In March 1978 the U.S. District Court for the District of
Columbia declared that federal credit unions could offer the check-like
services to their members under the "incidental powers" clause of the
Federal Credit Union Act.

5. Title IV of the Depository Institutions Deregulation and Monetary
Control Act of 1980.

6. 91 Stat. 49.

7. *Purdue Compilation,* pp. 736–791, 867, 879–882, 911, and 922.

8. *Purdue Compilation,* pp. 792–813, 868, 869, 884–886, 913, and 923.

9. Although consumer finance companies and small loan companies do
not accept deposits, as do commercial banks and thrifts, some finance
companies are free under state law to sell "certificates of indebtedness"
or the like, and the sale of such notes is similar to a deposit service. On
consumer finance companies generally, see *Purdue Compilation,* pp.
155–166.

10. The facts concerning Fred Fisher and the First National Bank of
Omaha appear in *Fisher v. First National Bank of Omaha,* 548 F.2d 225
(1977), hereinafter *Fisher.*

11. The provision in question is 12 U.S.C. 85. See *Fisher,* p. 257.

12. *Fisher,* pp. 257–258.

13. *Fisher,* p. 259.

14. Actually, there was an issue as to whether the laws of Nebraska or the
laws of Iowa applied to a credit card transaction where the account was
in Nebraska and the customer-merchant transaction occurred in Iowa.

The court held that ". . . it really makes no difference. . ." (p. 257), relying on a decision in *Fisher vs. First National Bank of Chicago*, 538 F.2d 1284 (7th Cir. 1976).

15. 12 C.F.R. 7.7310, which appears in *Fisher,* p. 260.

16. The degree to which an inquirer may safely rely on an administrative interpretation depends on the authority granted to the agency by statute and the conditions placed on the interpretation by the agency.

17. 1969 *Bulletin* 443; 12 C.F.R. 226.201

18. 38 Stat. 251. Much of the Federal Reserve Act, as amended, appears at 12. U.S.C. 221, et seq. Also, see footnote 22 below.

19. The Federal Reserve System includes the Board of Governors in Washington, D.C. and 12 Federal Reserve Banks located in Boston, New York, Philadelphia, Richmond, Atlanta, Minneapolis, Chicago, Cleveland, Kansas City, Dallas, St. Louis, and San Francisco. Each Reserve Bank performs the examination functions and has contact with the member banks in its defined district. See footnote 21 below.

20. The Bank Holding Company Act of 1956 (70 Stat. 133) is implemented by the Board's Regulation Y (12 C.F.R. 225). The Federal Reserve Act (38 Stat. 251) is implemented by several of the board's "alphabet regulations"; for example, Regulation A (12 C.F.R. 201) implements Section 13 of the act, and Regulation Q (12 C.F.R. 217), which deals with the payment of interest on deposits, implements Section 19 of the act. The Equal Credit Opportunity Act, Consumer Credit Protection Act, Truth in Lending Act, Fair Credit Billing Act, Fair Credit Reporting Act, and Consumer Leasing Act are all contained within the Consumer Credit Protection Act (82 Stat. 158), as amended, which is implemented by Regulations B (12 C.F.R. 202) and Z (12 C.F.R. 226). The Home Mortgage Disclosure Act of 1975 (89 Stat. 1125, 12 U.S.C. 2801, et seq.) is implemented by Regulation C (12 C.F.R. 203).

21. For example, the Federal Reserve Board has primary jurisdiction under the Bank Merger Act (74 Stat. 129, as amended) over bank mergers in which the surviving bank is a state-chartered member of the Federal Reserve System. With regard to the same set of banks, the board is the supervisory agency under such acts as the Bank Protection Act of 1968 (82 Stat. 294), which deals with physical security, robberies, and the like.

22. *Michigan Governor's Report,* Exhibit F-2.

23. This provision of the Bank Merger Act appears as Section 18 of the Federal Deposit Insurance Act, 12 U.S.C. 1828(s) (2).

24. The Federal Home Loan Bank Board was made an independent agency in the executive branch of the federal government under the Housing Amendments of 1955 (69 Stat. 640; 12 U.S.C. 1437). The board supervises the Federal Home Loan Bank System, the Federal

Savings and Loan System, and the insurance of accounts of savings and loan associations. The Federal Home Loan Bank System was created under the authority of the Federal Home Loan Bank Act (47 Stat. 725; 12 U.S.C. 1421, et seq.). See 3 CCH Federal Banking Law Rep. 40,001 et seq.

25. National Credit Union Administration, *Your Insured Funds* (Washington, D.C.: January 1975). The applicable federal law is the Federal Credit Union Act (48 Stat. 1216; 12 U.S.C. 1751, et. seq.).

26. In Michigan NCUA relies entirely on the examination report made by the state's Financial Institutions Bureau. *Michigan Governor's Report*, p. 71.

27. *Michigan Governor's Report*, p. 73.

28. For an excellent chart of the division of responsibilities between the federal and state regulators of financial institutions, see Exhibit F-1, *Michigan Governor's Report*.

29. On chartering and licensing laws generally, see *Purdue Compilation* under the headings of the various financial institutions.

30. On branching laws generally, see *Purdue Compilation*.

31. Some states have laws that, in certain cases, eliminate all regulatory discretion and impose so-called home office protection. For example, in Michigan: "a branch shall not be established in a city or village in which a state or national bank or branch thereof is then in operation." MCLA 487.471(1).

32. 12 U.S.C. 1828(c)(5).

33. Section 3(c) of the Bank Holding Company Act of 1956 (70 Stat. 133), as amended, 12 U.S.C. 1842.

34. The Sherman Act (26 Stat. 209; 15 U.S.C.A. 1-7, as amended) and the Clayton Act (38 Stat. 730; 15 U.S.C. 12-27, as amended).

35. The information in this paragraph regarding ATMs and EFT systems is from *Purdue Compilation*, pp. 924–941.

36. *Purdue Compilation*, p. 936.

37. For a comparison across financial institutions of federal and state chartering and branching laws and standards, see Exhibits D-1 through D-4 in *Michigan Governor's Report*.

38. Section 19 of the Federal Reserve Act provides in part: "No member bank shall, directly or indirectly, by any device whatsoever, pay any interest on any deposit which is payable on demand. . . ." 12 U.S.C. 371a.

39. Under the authority of Section 19 of the Federal Reserve Act (12 U.S.C. 371a), the Federal Reserve Board regulates the maximum rates payable by member banks on time and savings deposits (see Regulation Q, 12 C.F.R. 217). See, generally, *Purdue Compilation*, pp. 887–889.

40. See footnote 11, above.

41. On loan rate ceilings generally, see *Purdue Compilation*, pp. 115–282, and *Michigan Governor's Report,* pp. 10–12.

42. On deposit insurance at the various financial institutions, see appropriate volumes of CCH Federal Banking Law Rep. at pp. 26,131 and 19,033.

43. Legally imposed reserve requirements differ for Federal Reserve System members and nonmembers. Members are required to keep reserves in noninterest-bearing form: vault cash or reserves held by the system. Depending on state law, however, some nonmembers may keep reserves in the form of income-producing government securities or correspondent balances.

44. *Investment Company Institute v. Camp,* 401 U.S. 617, 91 S.Ct. 1091 (1971).

45. 84 Stat. 1760.

46. 84 Stat. 1763; 12 U.S.C. 1843.

47. On creditor remedies and debtor protections generally, see *Purdue Compilation,* chapters V–VII.

48. Bankruptcy Reform Act of 1978, 11 U.S.C. 101 et seq.

49. *Local Loan vs. Hunt,* 292 U.S. 234, 244 (1934).

50. See, for example, the line of cases beginning with *Sniadach v. Family Finance Corp.,* 395 U.S. 337, 89 S.Ct. 1820 and *Fuentes v. Shevin,* 407 U.S. 67, S.Ct. 1983 (1972).

51. Federal restrictions upon the garnishment of wages are found in the Consumer Credit Protection Act, 301–307; 82 Stat. 163–164; 15 U.S.C. 1671–1677. With regard to state installment provisions, see, for example, Chapter 62 of Michigan's Revised Judicature Act, MCLA 600.6201, et seq.

52. A partial list of topics in this area includes the holder in due course doctrine, cognitive judgments, wage assignments, bankruptcy, security interests, repossession, deficiency judgments, attorneys' fees, acceleration clauses, garnishment, debt collection practices, laws. In addition to *Purdue Compilation,* for a general treatment see David G. Epstein, *Debtor-Creditor Law in a Nutshell* (St. Paul, Minn.: West Publishing Co., 1973).

53. See MCLA 557.52–54 and *City Finance Company v. Kloostra,* 47 Mich. App. 276 (1973).

54. See, for example, *Hill v. Michigan National Bank,* 58 Mich. App. 430 (1975) and *Turner v. Impala Motors,* 503 F.2d 607 (6th Circ., 1974).

55. On antidiscrimination statutes, see *Purdue Compilation,* pp. 20–69.

56. The following summary of ECOA provisions is from James Goldberg, *Retailer's Handbook of Federal Credit Regulations* (Washington, D.C.: London & Goldberg, 1976, pp. 7–9).

57. See footnote 20.

58. This discussion of the effects test is from Robert Shay, "Anti-

Discrimination Laws in Consumer Credit Markets,'' in *Public Regulation of Financial Services: Costs and Benefits to Consumers,* eds. A. Heggestad and J. Mingo, Phase I Interim Report to the National Science Foundation (Cambridge, Mass: Abt Associates Inc., 1977) pp. 320–322. The Griggs case is at 401 U.S. 424 (1971).

59. 12 U.S.C. 2801.

60. Ibid.

61. See footnote 20

62. See the ''Congressional findings and declaration of purpose'' sections under the various titles of the Consumer Credit Protection Act (82 Stat. 158, as amended). Note that Title VI of DIDMCA, the Truth in Lending Simplification and Reform Act, is designed to provide consumers with simpler, more understandable information, make compliance easier for creditors, limit creditors' civil liability to significant violations, and strengthen administrative restitution enforcement.

63. This material on credit information law is from *Purdue Compilation,* pp. 81–114; and Goldberg, *Retailer's Handbook of Federal Credit Regulations.*

64. Derived from the totals in Exhibit F-2 of *Michigan Governor's Report.* Based on 83 Michigan counties.

65. 12 U.S.C. 21.

66. MCLA 487.491(a).

67. MCLA 487.491(c).

68. This conversion was made by consulting *Truth in Lending—Regulation Z—Annual Percentage Rate Tables* (Washington, D.C.: Board of Governors of the Federal Reserve System, no date).

69. MCLA 487.491(d).

70. On trailer statutes, see *Purdue Compilation,* pp. 672–674.

71. MCLA 489.755.

72. MCLA 489.755 and 770e(3).

73. MCLA 489.755.

74. MCLA 483.13.

75. Section 701(d) of the Equal Credit Opportunity Act, as amended. See footnote 18, above.

FOUR
Proposals for Regulatory Reform in the Consumer Financial Services Sector
William Batko

Introduction

Several proposals for regulatory reform of the consumer financial industry have been made in the past few years. These proposals have had extensive exposure through legislative hearings, commission reports, economic studies, and interest group activities. The public record is full of charges and countercharges about the various reform packages. In this chapter empirical studies are used to shed some light on the worth of the proposed reforms and the validity of the public argument.

Three things should be kept in mind when discussing these proposals for regulatory reform. First, they must be viewed primarily as coherent packages, rather than as collections of individual reforms. The Hunt Commission stated the case strongly: "The recommendations are interrelated, and the Commission believes that piecemeal adoption of the recommendations raises the danger of creating new and greater imbalances."[1]

Second, the reform packages were designed to be implemented, and thus they take into account the political as well as the social and economic world. As such, they reflect the relative powers of concerned interest groups and contain implicit trade-offs among sections of industry and consumers. The packages should be considered not necessarily the best of the various reform ideas, but rather the survivors of the political process.

Third, current consumer credit protection laws and the structure of consumer credit markets must be considered. Any changes that occur will be the result of interaction between proposed reforms and current reality.

This chapter focuses on proposals for structural reform and proposals for consumer protection reform, which are treated separately. The reform packages analyzed here were chosen because they have generated the most discussion and are closest to implementation. In addition, these proposals, along with critiques of them, reflect a broad range of opinion within the political arena. The approach taken with regard to each package of reforms is to describe briefly the proposed reforms and then to analyze the implications of the package for the major issues concerning either structural or consumer credit reforms. In each instance the analysis will attempt to answer the following questions:

1. *Who will receive the benefits? Who will incur the costs?* In the debate over alternative packages, mention is often made of increasing competition in the various credit markets, with resulting aggregate benefits accruing to society. The proposals, however, affect groups of consumers and types of institutions in different ways. These expected effects, some of which are known empirically, must be considered.

2. *What will be the long-term consequences of a regime?* The proposals discussed here represent general overhauls of the present system. As such, they are expected to remain in place, if implemented, for some time. The long-term consequences of a reform package may well have an opposite effect from both the intended and the short-term effects. While difficult to measure and ascertain, these long-term consequences are very important to consider.

3. *What will be the relationship between federal and state law?* Both federal and state legislatures have jurisdiction over structural code and consumer credit law. Some of the packages contain proposals for new federal and state laws to coexist with current law. Others mandate the supercession of state law by the federal code. The current situation is an evolving one and is delicately balanced. The implementation of major reforms will have a profound effect on this balance.

This analysis is especially important in light of the Depository In stitutions Deregulation and Monetary Control Act (DIDMCA), passed in 1980. Many of the issues raised in previous reform packages are addressed by this act; however, many others have been evaded—victims of the same political forces expended in earlier reform attempts.

Proposals for Structural Reform

During the past decade and a half, there has been a growing concensus among regulators, economists, consumer groups, and the financial industry that financial institutions need major structural reform. The last such reform was introduced in the 1930s (Banking Act of 1933, Glass-Steagall Bill of 1935). This legislation, evolving during the Depression, was especially concerned with the safety and stability of the institutions, and with assuring adequate funding for specific economic sectors through tailored institutions (for example, funding for commercial enterprise by the commercial banks, for housing by the savings and loan associations, and for consumer credit by the credit unions and finance companies).

Recent empirical studies have argued against the unduly restrictive nature of some of these safety considerations. The institutions themselves have evolved in ways that stretch the legislative and regulatory limits imposed on them. Furthermore, legislation and regulation have narrowed institutional parameters of action in some instances, but have broadened them in others. What remains is a hodgepodge of laws and regulations, with inconsistent policies and inconsistent enforcement.

The Commission on Money and Credit

One of the first attempts at structural reform was made by the Commission on Money and Credit, initiated in 1958 by the Ford Foundation.[2] In 1961 the commission recommended equalization of reserve requirements on demand deposits for Federal Reserve commercial banks, repeal of reserve requirements on time and savings deposits, repeal of FHA and VA mortgage rate ceilings, federal chartering of mutual savings banks, and liberalized branching laws for federal depositories operating under restrictive state law. Although its major proposals were not implemented, the commission fueled the debate over structural reform, which was carried on through economic studies and position papers by industry groups. Another report, issued in 1961 by the Kennedy-appointed Committee on Financial Institutions, struck a similar note of easing anticompetitive regulations and suffered the same fate as the report of the Commission on Money and Credit. The movement for structural reform did not coalesce again until 1969, with the appointment of the Hunt Commission.

The Hunt Commission

The President's Commission on Financial Structure and Regulation (popularly known as the Hunt Commission after its chairman, Reed Hunt) was initiated by President Nixon in 1969. It commissioned numerous studies and took testimony and related materials from economists and industry lobbyists. The pressure for some type of reform was strong, and the Hunt Commission's recommendations relating to federal action were contained in the Financial Institutions Act (FIA) of 1973. A lengthy hearing record was developed, but the legislation was not passed; neither was a somewhat modified version issued two years later—FIA 75. The Hunt Commission's recommendations were finally passed in the Depository Institutions Deregulation and Monetary Control Act (DIDMCA) of 1980.

The recommendations covered a broad range of reforms. Interest rate ceilings would be phased out on time and savings deposits after ten years, but payment of interest on demand deposits would still be prohibited. Thrift institutions could make consumer loans and offer checking accounts. Credit union assests could include longer term consumer and mortgage loans than is presently possible. Credit unions could offer lines of credit, though not checking accounts, to their members. Reserve requirements on demand deposits would be equalized across institutions, and reserve requirements on time and savings deposits would be eliminated. Commercial banks and thrift institutions would be permitted to branch throughout their home state. Institutions holding mortgages would receive a tax credit based on the percentage of their assets contained in mortgages. States would be encouraged to remove mortgage rate ceilings, "unreasonable" restrictions on loan-to-value ratios, and legal impediments to the use of variable rate mortgages, and to permit life insurance companies to offer flexible interest rates on policy loans.

The FINE Report

Viewing the FIA 73 and FIA 75 as Republican bills, the Democratic Congress presented its own proposals for structural reform. The most ambitious attempt was made by the House Committee on Banking, Currency and Housing. Spurred by Representatives Reuss (chairman of the committee) and St. Germaine (chairman of the Subcommittee on Financial Institutions) in 1975, this committee issued the Financial Institutions in the Nation's Economy (FINE) "Discussion Principles," a committee staff report outlining major themes to be included in a reform package. Again, a lengthy hearing record and supporting economic studies were produced. Most of the principles were contained in the Financial Reform Act of 1976. This act, like the preceding FIAs, was not passed.

The FINE report proposed major structural reform. Deposit interest rate ceilings (including the prohibition on interest paid on demand deposits) would be repealed after five years. Thrifts and credit unions could issue third-party payments and could initiate or expand consumer lending (through loans, credit cards, and lines of credit). All institutions would become members of the Federal Reserve System, and reserves would be equalized for institutions of similar size. Institutions would collect a mortgage tax credit only for their mortgage holdings on low- to moderate-income housing. Intrastate branching would be allowed if not in conflict with state law, and branching into metropolitan areas larger than 2 million in population would be permitted despite conflicting state law.

National Commission on Consumer Finance

Under the legislative mandate of the Consumer Credit Protection Act of 1968, the National Commission on Consumer Finance (NCCF) started work in 1969 and completed it in 1972. Because most of the NCCF recommendations focused on consumer protection rather than structural reform, only those concerned with institutional entry into consumer credit markets will be discussed in this section.

The NCCF proposals that affect structure relate to the provision of consumer loans. The only criterion for finance company entry into a local market would be the "good character" of the proprietors. Depository institutions would be encouraged to branch into areas only if the resulting market concentration would be reduced. Finance companies would be federally chartered, and federal laws on finance company entry would supercede state laws within four years, if the states did not liberalize their own entry provisions. Thrift institutions would be permitted to make consumer loans up to 10 percent of their assets.

The DIDMCA, passed in May 1980, accomplishes most of the goals formulated by the reform movement for the thrift institutions. It permits negotiable order of withdrawal (NOW) accounts and establishes common reserve requirements on transaction balances for all depository institutions. It widens the asset powers of thrift institutions by permitting them to offer consumer loans to a maximum of 20 percent of their assets. In addition, savings and loans may offer credit cards and trust services. The act lifts consumer loan usury ceilings unless the states vote to reinstate the ceilings. Finally, it allows for the phased removal of Regulation Q over the next five years.

Major Issues of Structural Reform

The thrust of all of the proposed reforms is to ease the entry of depository institutions and nondepository consumer loan institutions into markets for consumer deposits and loans. This would be done in three ways: (1) liberalizing branching provisions for thrift institutions and commercial banks, membership provisions for credit unions, and market entry provisions for consumer loan companies; (2) removing interest rate ceilings (and differentials between rates paid by different institutions) on deposits; and (3) permitting an expanded portfolio choice for the thrift institutions and credit unions.

Any of the proposed regimes, if implemented, would have a strong influence on the structure of credit and deposit markets. The effects of an oligopolistic market structure—where market activities are concentrated in a few institutions—are known both to economic theorists and to empirical observers. A highly concentrated credit market is associated with low supplies of consumer credit,[3] high interest rates on consumer loans,[4] credit rationing in the case of commercial loan customers with access only to local markets,[5] high rates on commercial loans to small businesses,[6] and conservative bank management.[7] A high level of concentration will have the strongest effect on those consumers with the greatest need to obtain credit from the local market, either because they are marginal risk applicants (generally, lower income) or because they have been credit-rationed.[8] Nader also predicts a reduced incentive for institutional efficiency in a highly concentrated market because of the increased probability of federal assistance if a large institution encounters operating difficulty.[9]

At issue here, however, is not the effects of market concentration, but rather the effects of the alternative reform packages upon concentration. The NCCF recommendations dealt with this question explicitly by permitting institutions to branch only when it would not cause a domination of the market structure. De novo branching was preferred to branching through merger or acquisition. Some critics of Hunt and FINE, however, have remarked on the unreliability of insuring competition through their proposals. For example, in reviewing the Hunt recommendations, Robertson observed that ". . . the ultimate outcome of competition is large units. . . ."[10] Herman was more explicit:

> There is a curious tendency observable in the Hunt Commission report, in [Federal Reserve] Board decisions, and elsewhere, to assume that diversification by entry into closely related fields, even via merger, is procompetitive, or at worst neutral in effect. One deficiency in this view is that it rests on an unduly narrow time horizon. If General Motors enters the fields of bus or locomotive engine manufacture, the long-run effect of the presence of such a powerful force in a market is, at a minimum, much more obscure.[11]

If these arguments are correct, the net long-term effects of the alternative regimes (with the possible exception of the NCCF recommendations) will be at odds with their stated intention of increasing competition.

All three reform packages propose a stronger federal role in institutional structure. The NCCF expressed the rationale: state legislation especially has tended to constrain competition and unnecessarily segment the consumer credit market.[12] In some cases this view is expressed explicitly, for example, in the recommended federal chartering of mutual savings banks in the thirty-three states that do not charter those institutions. In other cases it is implicit, for example, in setting deposit interest rate ceilings for federal depositories. These actions would serve to undermine the role of state regulators and diminish the leverage states have in dealing with their own particular problems.

The remainder of this section considers the possible effects of each of the three reform packages—Hunt, FINE, and NCCF—if changes are made in liability rate ceilings, branching regulations, other provisions governing market entry, reserve requirements, and asset restrictions.

Liability Rate Ceilings

Interest rate ceilings exist on all deposits in national and state depositories, with the exception of certificates of deposit over $100,000 in national commercial banks and deposits in credit unions in some states. In reviewing the history of interest rate ceilings, Albert Cox concludes that

> . . . the regulations pertaining to interest rates on bank deposits do not represent the ultimate in economic wisdom. The historical foundation of these regulations—destructive rate competition for bank deposits in the twenties—lack solidity. It is doubtful whether the banking climate has changed enough since the twenties to now validate the destructive rate competition argument. Meanwhile, both logic and available data indicate that the regulations have had a number of adverse effects on the banking system and on the economy.[13]

All of the proposals include provision for time and savings accounts in federally regulated depositories. The NCCF goes one step further in recommending that the removal of ceilings supercede state law, so that all depositories come under the same rate provisions. FINE and NCCF, though not Hunt, would also remove ceilings on demand deposit interest rates. The Financial Reform Act (FRA) of 1976 would keep ceilings, but permit them to be set at higher then zero percent after two years. Both Financial Institutions Acts and FRA legislated a five and a half year period of transition, during which time and savings rate ceilings would still be imposed. After the transition period, the ceilings would be dropped.

The rationale for these proposals consists of two parts. Small savers, it is argued, are being discriminated against by rate ceilings. Corporate treasurers and large savers can obtain larger interest rates through money market instruments (Treasury bills, certificates of deposit in commercial banks of $100,000 or over, and so forth), while small savers are tied to their accounts because they do not have enough savings to gain higher rates. Kane estimates that

Regulation Q has cost small savers $30 billion since its inception.[14] It is also argued that rate ceilings restrict efficient allocation of funds. Classical economic theory indicates that competition through price mechanisms provides the greatest aggregate benefits to society. With rate ceilings, depositories are forced to rely on nonprice competition (for example, services, gifts, advertising, less than full-cost pricing on checking accounts) to attract funds. The economic inefficiencies arising through advertising and gifts would be reduced if rate ceilings were removed and institutions were allowed to compete through interest rates offered on deposits.

Critics of these proposals argue that the rate ceilings and rate differential between institutions serve to channel funds into the housing market by making savings accounts at thrift institutions more attractive. Less money might be available to these institutions—and hence to the social priority area of housing—if the ceilings were abolished. Tom Scott of the U.S. League of Savings Associations argued, "... extension of rate control is absolutely imperative for the health of thrift institutions and the housing industry. Also, it is imperative that the savings and loan business receive an adequate rate advantage as necessary protection to attract funds for the housing market."[15]

Supporters of these proposals cite several recent econometric models[16] to buttress their claim that housing credit would not be reduced under the alternative proposals. Hendershott's study, for instance, found that interest rates on mortgage loans would decline and effective demand would increase through reforms. Other parts of the reform package (savings and loan associations could offer checking accounts and make consumer loans) guarantee that the decreased percentage of mortgage assets held by the savings and loans would be more than made up for by their increase in total assets and by increased mortgage holdings by commercial banks and life insurance companies. Critics of these studies, however, argue that the models predicting a net increase in housing credit are improperly estimated, using data gathered under existing regulations to predict events under new regulations.[17] Thygerson also claims that Hendershott erred in specifying commercial bank savings and demand deposit rate-setting behavior without rate ceilings, which would have a major effect on the results of the model. If these critics are correct, the net impact upon housing credit from removing deposit interest rate ceilings is unclear.

Another argument against removing liability rate ceilings points to the differing effects of rate reform on different sizes and types of institutions. Easterly, speaking for the Independent Bankers' Association of America, claimed that under conditions of tight money, the elimination of rate controls will divert credit to metropolitan banks.[18] Using computations of profitability, Thygerson forecast that savings and loan associations would not be able to compete with commercial banks for deposits. For example, large commercial banks might be able, under these proposals, to reduce competition through predatory price arrangements, which are used successfully in other industries (such as retail food). Banks have had the opportunity to use predatory nonpricing mechanisms (advertising, credit allocation) in the past, but there is no evidence that they have used them to drive out competitors. Furthermore, interest rates on commercial bank certificates of deposit of $100,000 or more do not currently have a ceiling. It is with these deposits that the prime effects of tight money conditions are felt, and they will not be changed by the alternative regime proposals. In addition, savings and loan profitability should be enhanced by the provisions that allow expansion of their assets and liabilities. It seems unlikely, then, that fears of large banks driving out the competition—through predatory or competitive price arrangements—would be realized. Without protection from law (for example, deposit rate ceilings) or regulations, however, this issue is by no means settled.

A third argument concerning liability rate ceilings emphasizes the small debtor, rather than the small saver. Leary computed an average 2 percent increase in the cost of consumer loans, or a reduced availability of these loans, resulting from an average 5 percent rate paid on demand deposits.[19] Small savers would benefit; small debtors would not. This implies, however, that commercial banks occupy a monopoly position within consumer credit markets, an analysis not supported by empirical studies. Smith, for example, wrote, ''The competitive influence of consumer finance companies was observed to have a significant effect on bank rates and portfolio composition.''[20] If banks charged higher loan rates, consumers would shift to other sources for financing. In addition, Mingo argues that removal of liability rate ceilings would improve the positions of *both* small savers and small debtors, due to increased efficiencies gained through reduction of nonprice competition.

In summary, allocative efficiency and benefits to small savers will undoubtedly be gained through elimination of liability rate ceilings, but the major question of the effect upon mortgage credit remains unanswered. As with other reforms, both the amount and nature of benefits will depend largely upon the interaction of the reform with the local market structure.

Branching

The major reform scenarios have favored liberalized branching regulations for federally regulated commercial banks and thrift institutions. Combined with the provisions in the packages for federal chartering of mutual savings banks and an easy transition between state and federal charters for depositories, the reform regulations would have a direct impact on all states and virtually all depositories, and an indirect impact on the remaining nonfederal institutions.

Hunt, FINE, and NCCF all propose statewide branching for federally regulated institutions. FINE goes one step further in proposing that interstate branching be permitted where it is not prohibited by state law and that intrastate branching within metropolitan areas of greater than 2 million in population be permitted without respect to state law.[21]

Previous studies have documented the consumer benefits that can be gained by liberalizing branching laws. Schweiger and McGee found that branch banks have higher loan-to-asset ratios than unit banks in similar communities (especially for banks with less than $100 million in deposits), have more diversified portfolios (including a larger percentage of consumer and mortgage loans), and charge lower interest rates on consumer loans.[22] Eisenbeis found that banks in unit-banking states export a larger percentage of their assets to local markets than do branch banks (for business loans).[23] Banks in branch-banking states tend to have more offices per capita, provide more convenient services, and possibly offer greater competition than do banks in unit-banking states.

Some observers fear the long-term effects of branching on the competitiveness of the market structure. While more offices exist per capita in branch-banking states, there are fewer banks per capita. States with highly concentrated markets all permit branch banking, while low-concentration states have either unit banking or limited branching.[24] Beighley and McCall, studying consumer installment loans in local markets, found that ". . . bank market power is greater in branch banking markets, other things being equal."[25] Although economies of scale for certain banking processes (such as demand deposits) could result in higher prices paid to consumers in competitive markets, these economies exist for the bank as a whole and not for the branch.[26]

The above arguments refer to uniform (across all states) statewide branching proposals, not to branching within any specific market. The existing market structure will largely determine the effects on competition and concentration of any entry reform. The NCCF recommendations attempt to deal with this issue by encouraging branching that decreases concentration ratios within a market and discouraging mergers and acquisitions that increase concentration.

A third argument against liberalized branching is that state law would be preempted by federal law in those states that do not permit statewide branching and in all states if metropolitan branching were permitted. While this is an important issue, it is becoming less so. As Jacobs and Beighley point out, such developments as electronic funds transfer systems, multibank holding companies, and sales finance companies within banking markets will considerably lessen the importance of state law in regulating banking structure in the future. State control over banking structure will depend on how the states treat these developments, as well as branching reforms.[27]

Other Entry Provisions

The regulatory reform packages propose other means, in addition to branching, to ease institutional entry into the markets for consumer loans and deposits. Federal chartering of mutual savings banks, proposed by all three regimes, would allow these institutions to operate in the thirty-three states where they are currently prohibited. NCCF would permit the federal chartering of finance companies and would permit their entry into states simply upon demonstration of "good character." The Credit Union Amendments to the FIAs would eliminate the common bond requirement for credit unions, permitting these institutions to expand membership—and thus potential consumers of credit union consumer loans—beyond locational, fraternal, or job-related requirements. Finally, and perhaps most important, all three reform packages would permit thrifts and credit unions to offer third-party payment services, notably checking accounts.

The purpose of these proposals again is to encourage competition in the marketplace. The prime beneficiaries would be consumers in the aggregate. Permitting mutual savings banks in a few New

England states to offer NOW accounts caused a net inflow of deposits from commercial banks to mutual savings banks, with resulting revenue benefits for consumers. In order to meet the competition, the local commercial banks received permission to offer their own NOW accounts, paying interest on deposits and leaving consumers of both types of institutions in better positions. Increasing finance company access to the local consumer credit market has been shown to result in greater supplies of available consumer credit[28] and reduced interest rates on bank consumer loans.[29] In addition, the granting of third-party payment powers to thrift institutions is seen as an economic necessity if the institutions (and, by implication, the housing industry) are to remain competitive when the interest rate differentials favoring the thrifts are lifted.

It should be noted, however, that free entry into a market does not necessarily mean easy entry.[30] Other barriers to entry, besides regulation, are scale economies for demand accounts, primarily through electronic computers.[31] Banks in branch-banking states may already occupy the preferred sites, especially for gathering deposits, leaving only marginal locations for competitors in some markets. Thus, in most states removal of entry restrictions would probably not mean wholesale changes in the depository market structure.

Free entry into consumer credit markets does not necessarily imply consumer acceptance of that policy, even though supplies of credit may increase and interest rates drop upon entry. In a study done in Maine after that state effectively restricted the operations of finance companies, Benston found that 55 percent of the respondents who had been customers of finance companies before they closed operations felt better about the new situation, and only 22 percent felt worse. One-half of those surveyed had obtained financing elsewhere (credit unions, other finance companies, commercial banks).[32]

Reserve Requirements

Both Hunt and FINE advocate an equalization of reserve requirements across institutional and geographic lines. Hunt requires equal reserves for different size categories of institutions, but FINE does not make that requirement explicit. Hunt would also drop all reserve requirements on savings and time deposits.

Reserve requirements are a critical aspect of the Federal Reserve

Board's monetary policy. Without such requirements on proposed demand deposits at savings and loan associations and mutual savings banks, as well as at state-chartered, nonmember commercial banks, the Federal Reserve Board has both less information and less control over the supply of money in the country. Equalizing reserve requirements across institutional and geographic lines would adversely affect neither savings and loan associations nor mutual savings banks (which presently cannot accept demand deposits and so would not be losing anything by giving up a portion of their new powers to nonearning assets), but the reform would have an impact on state banks that are not members of the Federal Reserve System. Requirements for these banks are currently set by the states and vary widely. The reform proposals would raise the percentage of nonearning assets in states such as Kentucky and Iowa and would transfer earning reserves into the nonearning category in states such as Georgia and Florida. In addition, advocates of changes in the reserve requirements stress a need to equalize the competitive ground rules. Currently, thrifts and credit unions have far more liberal requirements than commercial banks, for which required reserves differ, depending on the size and location of the bank and whether it is a member of the Federal Reserve System. In some states interest is paid on reserves deposited by certain types of banks. National banks and banks in other states, however, cannot earn interest.

Guttentag has argued that the primary beneficiaries of changes in reserve requirements will be nondepository lending institutions (finance companies, mortgage bankers, and the like), not necessarily consumers. Costs and benefits will be felt by different institutions, and the degree of price competition and regulator preferences will determine where these cost and benefits will be passed along to consumers.[33] The local market structure will be important in determining which institutions pass the costs and benefits to consumers.

Removal of Asset Restrictions

Hunt, FINE, and NCCF all advocate giving thrift institutions a limited right to make consumer loans—to 10 percent of assets in FINE and NCCF, to 10 percent of assets plus any amount up to 3 percent of assets from "contigency funds" in Hunt. Both FINE and Hunt would give credit unions increased asset power by lengthening terms permitted on consumer and mortgage loans and increasing consumer loan amounts. Hunt would also encourage states to allow life insurance companies to provide policy loans at flexible rates. All of these powers have now been granted.

Advocates of these proposals have stressed the procompetitive benefits to the consumer flowing from increased competition. They point out that since consumer loans generally have a higher interest rate and are shorter term than mortgage loans, they will increase the liquidity and profitability and, by implication, the safety of thrift institutions. The savings and loan industry, in fact, argues that these reforms do not go far enough. They advocate that thrifts be mandated to maintain 30 percent of their assets ". . . in any type of investment approved by the Federal Home Loan Bank Board that is related to the needs of individuals or families or to real or personal property. . ." or that is a nonfederal public security.[34] While the cycles of consumer credit fluctuate somewhat more widely than normal business cycles,[35] they fluctuate less than mortgage credit and reach their peaks and troughs at different times in the business cycle. Thus, a portfolio containing both would be more balanced.

Critics of these proposals argue that housing loan availability would be reduced if thrifts could expand their asset powers. Mann and Friedman state both sides: "A possible serious disadvantage of portfolio regulation is that, by reducing the portfolio flexibility of S&Ls, it leads to a lower level of profitability. . . . On the other hand, a shift from portfolio regulation to expenditure or tax inducements for lending institutions in socially desirable sectors carries a serious risk of reducing the overall availability of funds to these sectors. . . ."[36] Liberalization of asset restrictions would be part of an entire package, however. Thus, if reforms on deposit holdings and rates can direct additional funds into savings and loan associations and mutual savings banks, then the decreased percentage of thrift institution mortgage holdings would not necessarily mean a decreased amount of mortgages. Furthermore, mortgage loans are often used as a form of consumer loan, especially second mortgages and refinancings. This form of credit is probably used most by those low-income borrowers with few assets besides their homes.[37] If the supply of consumer credit were expanded, especially to customers currently "rationed" by commercial banks, credit for housing ownership transfers and construction might not be affected, even if the total value of mortgage credit declined. Little is known, however, about the use of mortgage credit for nonhousing expenditures. The effects of increasing asset powers on housing credit thus remain unclear.

Proposals for Consumer Credit Reform

In the past few decades there has been a vast increase in the use of consumer credit. From 1950 to 1971, consumer credit rose in absolute terms ($21.5 billion to $137.2 billion) and as a percentage of total public and private debt in the United States (4.4 percent to 6.9 percent). Consumer credit is also playing a greater role in the purchase of consumer goods. Corresponding to this trend is the proliferation of instruments available to consumers who obtain credit. Credit cards and "instant" lines of credit through overdraft checking accounts now complement the traditional sales and loan credit instruments.

As the use and importance of consumer credit have increased, so has the push for consumer protection reform. Over the past decade, numerous states have implemented strong consumer protection proposals. Similarly, antidiscrimination laws have recently been expanded to cover consumer credit. The protective scope of these laws has been increased. Although, traditionally, consumer protection legislation and regulation have remained at the state level, the federal government has recently passed strong laws and regulations guaranteeing consumer rights in credit practices.

While agreeing that some reforms are necessary, many critics of recent consumer credit laws (especially among economists and industry spokespeople) argue that too strict regulation of the credit industry will prove counterproductive to consumers and to the economy. They argue that creditors must be able to discriminate between consumers in their ability to repay loans and that effective remedies must be available to prevent or minimize the loss from loan default. Without these measures, creditors will be forced to offer less credit to marginal-risk consumers (generally low- to moderate-income classes) and/or raise the prices of credit to cover the costs of loan losses.

Even if the industry arguments are true, it is unclear that consumer credit protection reform is unnecessary. Four distinct reasons for protection can be cited: decreasing consumer spending (and increasing savings), decreasing the irrational use of debt and rationalizing the process, increasing consumer information, and increasing consumer protection from unconscionable creditors. These reasons are often conflicting and are rarely stated explicitly.

Portions of the reform packages to be discussed herein are currently in use in some states. The focus of this section, however, is a more general application of the proposals, up to and including uniform state laws and federal laws that would supercede state regulation.

The Uniform Consumer Credit Code

The Uniform Consumer Credit Code (UCCC) is the major reform package proposed through the National Conference of Commissioners on Uniform State Laws. The final draft of the UCCC was prepared in 1967; since then, over a dozen states have adopted the code in total or in part. The UCCC has attracted both strong support (for instance, from the National Business Council for Consumer Affairs)[38] and strong criticism (for example, from the Consumer Federation of America).[39]

Disclosure provisions in the code are almost identical to those in the federal Truth in Lending regulations and in the Consumer Credit Protection Act. Loan rate ceilings on closed-end credit are 36 percent on the first $300, 21 percent on the next $700, and 15 percent on anything over $1,000, or (alternatively) a flat annual percentage rate of 18 percent. The ceilings for revolving charges are 2 percent per month on the first $500 and 1.5 percent per month on anything above that. Other fees can be collected by the creditor for delinquency, deferral, refinancing, closing, filing, insurance, consolidation, and creditor legal fees, if judgment goes against the debtor. Prepayment of the loan amount is permitted without penalty and includes a rebate on prepaid interest. The use of negotiable notes in consumer sales or lease transactions is prohibited, as are confessions of judgment, wage assignments, and garnishments before judgment. A limitation is placed on the amount to be garnished (as a percentage of the consumer's income), and limitations are placed on security interests other than for goods sold on credit. Balloons (higher monthly payments at the final stages of the payment schedule) are permitted, but they can be refinanced by the consumer without penalty and at terms equal to or better than the original loan to equalize monthly payments. Acceleration of debt upon the delinquency of any payment is permitted the creditor, as is acceptance of cross-collateral.

The Model Consumer Credit Act

The Model Consumer Credit Act (MCCA) was written by the National Consumer Law Center as a direct response to the UCCC. Proponents of the MCCA see the UCCC as an industry code with too much reliance on creditor remedies and not enough protection given the consumer. The authors of the MCCA were guided by three major principles:

> First, consumer credit is a commodity clothed with the public interest and, as such, should be closely regulated by an active administrative body similar to that which the public expects for insurance and utilities. . . .
>
> Second, adequate private remedies must exist so that consumers affected by illegal practices can obtain effective judicial redress. . . .
>
> Finally, practices and remedies undertaken to collect consumer debt must be confined to those which respect the realities of modern economic life. There is no question but that everyone should be expected to pay their legitimate debts. But no remedy or practice should be available which deprives an individual of resources necessary to meet the essential needs of the family.[40]

The MCCA is substantively based on previously enacted Wisconsin statutes. It prohibits discrimination in the granting of consumer credit by source of income and political affiliation, and also maintains the federal equal credit opportunity provisions. It does not define loan ceilings uniformly, leaving the matter to the states. However, it sets a twenty-five-month limit on the tenure for high-interest loans and a thirty-seven-month maximum tenure for low-interest loans. As in the UCCC, the refinancing rate must be equal to or less than the original rate, prepayment can occur at any time without penalty, and wage assignments are prohibited. Balloon payments are directly prohibited by the MCCA (unless payments are tied to the cyclical nature of the consumer's income), as is the doctrine that the holder in due course has no liability. Property necessary for a moderate standard of living is exempt from the satisfaction of judgment. Fees can be levied against creditors for contract default. The MCCA places limitations on default charges, executory transactions, and security interests. No creditor may receive fees or other benefits from offering credit life insurance, and there is no fee for credit insurance if the amount financed is $500 or less.

Additional disclosure terms and forms supplement the federal Truth in Lending legislation.

The National Commission on Consumer Finance

The National Commission on Consumer Finance (1969–1972) was criticized because of the issues it chose to study.[41] Its proposed reforms include permission for the creditor to accelerate debt collection and deficiency judgments only if the amount financed is $1,765 or more. Confessions of judgment are prohibited, as are cross-collateral and the holder-in-due-course doctrine. Wage assignment is permitted but limited in amount and conditions. Similarly, garnishment is permitted only after judgement and with limitations on amount. Balloons are permitted but can be refinanced without penalty. As in the other reform packages, unfair collection practices are prohibited. Prepayment is permitted without penalty. Disclosure requirements are increased, including terms related to the time-price doctrine. Federal Truth in Lending law supercedes state law, and the legislation applies to oral as well as written disclosure. As in the MCCA, legal fees are borne by the loser in case of judgment.

Major Issues in Consumer Credit Reform

The four major issues that concern the proponents of the various consumer credit reform packages are (1) the effects of creditor restrictions on the availability and pricing of credit, (2) the equality of creditor/debtor remedies and rights, (3) uniformity, and (4) enforceability. These issues are central to the discussion of specific proposals that follows.

In regard to the effects of creditor restrictions on the availability and pricing of credit, both the UCCC and the NCCF recommend rate ceilings that would be higher than those currently existing in many states. All fifty states have laws regulating creditor remedies to achieve full payment of debt packages. These laws permit certain creditor actions and prohibit others upon delinquency of payment. Proponents of the reform packages that are less restrictive to creditors (such as UCCC) argue that an unduly low rate ceiling and the lack of an effective remedy package limit the availability of credit in a state. They cite numerous studies showing that marginal-credit applicants (in many cases, lower income people) are denied credit when creditors are too restricted.[42] Lifting the restrictions would thus work to the benefit of marginal-credit applicants by making credit more available.

Opponents of these reforms argue that in many specific instances the rate on available credit rises to the legal maximum without reflecting true industry costs and that remedies are used more harshly than the situation warrants. They cite ghetto merchants and loan companies, which serve a clientele through a cartel imposed by social and political, as well as economic, forces. Critics argue that creditor restrictions should be lifted only when, on a state-by-state basis, it can be demonstrated that the current restrictions are, in fact, reducing the availability of credit to marginal groups. This argument has been somewhat confused by data limitations and by market aggregation in empirical studies (for instance, the use of statewide data to represent local markets).

In terms of the issue of equality of creditor/debtor remedies, the MCCA takes a consumer position (leaning toward removal of creditor remedies), while the NCCF strikes a middle ground between the UCCC and the MCCA. UCCC proponents believe their package reflects an adequate and fair balance between the rights of creditors and those of debtors. Consumer representatives view the UCCC as an industry bill, which is better than consumer credit laws in some states but worse than credit laws in other states. They point out that the bill favors creditors; for example, creditors who win a suit are entitled to up to 15 percent of their legal fees from the debtor, while the debtor, if successful, cannot obtain fees from the creditor; also, loan limits are indexed to rise with the cost of living rate, but not to drop if the rate drops.[43]

Disclosure

All three regimes support the federal Truth in Lending statute but differ in two respects: whether state or federal agencies should administer the law's provisions and whether additional truth in lending disclosure is needed.

UCCC advocates state administration, while NCCF and MCCA advocate federal administration. Proponents of the latter argue that a strong law is on the books and could be severely watered down if every state proposed different, and possibly weaker, regulations. Backers of the UCCC argue that many federal agencies are currently involved in Truth in Lending regulation, which is as confusing as state administration. The NCCF considers *both* federal and state enforcement procedures of disclosure laws inadequate to the task, calling them a "mixed bag."

NCCF would add time-price doctrine information and oral disclosure to the federal law. MCCA would use state statutes to subject additional items and forms to disclosure. Both claim these additional disclosures would provide a marginal increase in consumer knowledge and hence would lead to more informed choices and an increase in competitive activity. As with most information laws, these would have a greater impact on the educated middle class than on low-income, less educated, and minority consumers, who have been generally less aware of the annual percentage rate on consumer loans.[44] Day and Brandt found that rate knowledge also depends on previous credit experience.[45] Deutscher found, however, that the awareness of rates plays no part in the consumer's decision to purchase on credit as opposed to using cash.[46] Deutscher also found that rate awareness plays a role in the consumer search for financing *within* a specific lending group (banks, finance companies, credit unions, and so forth). As the NCCF points out, only consumers sensitive to marginal differences in interest rates are able to perform a policing function on the industry.

FINE and others promote a "truth-in-savings" provision, whereby interest rates paid on deposits within any given market area would be made public by each depository institution. As with the additional truth in lending proposals, benefits would initially accrue to the extent that (1) the regulations were enforced; (2) consumers were aware of and understood the disclosure; and (3) consumers were sensitive to interest rates in their savings behavior. The benefits would be a higher median rate on savings and a rise in institutional competition. Consumers would probably be more sensitive to savings rates than loan rates, as there is little psychological trauma associated with a savings account. The effects of a truth-in-savings provision, much as for truth in lending, depend largely upon the level of competition within the market and upon the level (and existence) of rate ceilings. The more stringent the rate ceilings, and the more concentrated the market, the smaller the effect of rate disclosure upon consumer or institutional behavior.

A different form of disclosure is exemplified by the Federal Home Mortgage Disclosure Act of 1975. This legislation mandates that commercial banks and thrift institutions disclose the number and amount of mortgage and rehabilitation loans given by geographic area. Alternative proposals have appeared in many states, for example, loan term disclosure in California and expansion of the type of institution covered by this disclosure in Pennsylvania. One purpose of these proposals is to attract deposits into those institutions that lend most heavily to the locality. An analysis of benefits and costs similar to that done for the other disclosure proposals would apply here with three additions: (1) consumers would need to be sensitive to the effects of local lending, a more complex effort than the simple comparison of savings or loan interest rates; (2) the prime beneficiaries would become those banks or thrifts investing most heavily locally and (presumably) the locality, which would have additional amounts of housing financing available; and (3) institutions that invested less heavily locally would bear the initial costs through decreased deposits.

Loan Rate Ceilings

The NCCF staff recommended higher ceiling rates than those that exist in most states, though the commission itself did not specify rates; the UCCC recommended somewhat lower ceilings; and the MCCA left this section blank, expecting the states to establish their own ceilings. Three issues are involved in this decision: should ceilings be uniform across states, what should the level of these ceilings be, and should there be automatic increases in the ceilings at periodic times?

Proponents of uniform ceilings argue that consumer credit is a national market. Without uniform ceilings, credit could not flow freely within its market, and its allocation would thus be disrupted. Opponents say that conditions in the different states and cities mandate different ceilings. What is good for Wyoming, argues Berlin, is not necessarily good for Watts.[47] The consumer credit reform bill for the District of Columbia (introduced in 1968) originally defined loan limits, but pressure from local politicians and citizens caused the limitations on rates to be left undefined.[48]

The ceiling level is the second issue. Consumer groups argue that, in many instances, actual loan rates rise to the ceilings, independent of the specific costs associated with lending. They cite market concentration and the limited access of many consumers to nonlocal credit markets as reasons for this. Speaking for the Consumer Federation of America, Angevine said, ". . . existing maximum rates shall not be increased without convincing evidence that existing rate ceilings are so low consumers are not being reasonably served.

Whenever feasible, rate ceilings should be lowered."[49] Proponents argue that availability of credit is reduced in the presence of ceilings—and this reduction has the greatest effect on low-income consumers—and that too low ceilings can lead to the inefficiencies of nonprice competition. As Senator Paul Douglas stated: "Higher or lower rate ceilings do not raise or lower finance company profits but, rather, determine credit availability. The higher the ceilings, the more marginal risk borrowers can be accommodated. This is confirmed by data showing a high positive correlation between the rate ceilings and bad debt charge-offs."[50] Studies by Shay, Greer, and others support this conclusion.[51] Johnson agrees with this appraisal of cash credit and cites the importance of interest rates on sales credit for low-income consumers. The important price differences between the low-income and the general market lie with the markup on goods or services sold, compared to which, finance charges amount to little.[52] Senator William Proxmire, in criticizing the work of the NCCF, sharply disagreed with their analysis of the effects of rate ceilings.[53] In addition, a study by Fand and Forbes shows that bank participation (which, at least for commercial loans, is a function of market concentration)[54] and per capita income are stronger determinants of the supply of credit than interest rate ceilings.[55] Studies by Shay support this finding, but he cautions ". . . it does not necessarily follow that the enactment of high rate ceilings in small loan laws could not be counted upon to expand the amount of installment credit."[56]

The third issue concerns automatic periodic increases in the ceilings. The UCCC would accomplish this by indexing the maximum amounts for a specific rate percentage (for example, $300 for 36 percent) to the cost of living or a similar measure. As written in the UCCC, the maximum amounts would rise with the cost of living but would not drop if the index fell. Consumer advocates argue that rates should be increased only upon demonstration of supply limitations caused by the rate ceilings and that it is inequitable to the consumer that rate ceilings be indexed to increases in the cost of living but not to decreases.

Creditor/Debtor Remedies and Rights

Large sections of all three reform packages address the issue of creditors' rights and remedies upon avoidance of payment, including deficiency judgments, wage assignments, garnishments, cross-collateral, confessions of judgment, acceleration of debt, and "unconscionable" methods of inducing payment. Similarly, all three regimes specify debtors' rights and remedies upon action by the creditor contrary to the contract terms: refinancing balloons, prepayment without penalty, fees levied against creditors for contract violation, and payment of legal fees.

The basic issue here is to balance the level of "unconscionability" in the remedies available to creditors, on the one hand, and the economic need of the creditors to avoid a deluge of loan default, on the other hand. The UCCC excludes numerous possible creditor remedies and includes some consumer remedies, and the MCCA includes many creditor remedies and excludes some consumer rights. However, proponents of the UCCC argue that the package is essentially a tool by which the creditor can insure payment. While many of these creditor remedies are not used often (banks, for example, seldom use garnishment as a remedy), they have an in terrorem effect on the consumer. Without these remedies, delinquencies and defaults on consumer credit would be more numerous. To remain viable, grantors of consumer credit would be forced either to adopt stricter standards in giving credit or to increase interest rates. Either measure would impact primarily on low-income consumers.

Greer found that acceleration, consumer payment of attorney's fees, and repossession were used often and valued highly by creditors, as were garnishment and deficiency judgments. Confession of judgment, holder in due course, wage assignment, and waiver of defense were neither valued nor used often. He also found a positive relation to interest rates and a negative relation to credit supply upon restriction of garnishment, attorney's fees, waiver of defense, and holder in due course.[57]

Bailey quoted the Prefatory Note to Working Draft No. 6: "too low ceiling rates, too substantial restrictions on creditors' rights and remedies, or too great enhancements of debtors' rights or remedies, might deprive the less creditworthy of lawful sources of credit and drive them to 'loan sharks' and other illegal credit grantors in whose hands they will enjoy no legal protections."[58] Kripke goes even further: "In the writer's opinion an effort to strike down the abuse of overextension of credit by restricting the remedies of the creditor is wrong. The [UCCC] is mild and restrained compared to the proposals of some consumer advocates, but it still goes too far."[59]

Opponents of these remedies argue that they are not necessary, that consumer payment records in those instances when in terrorem devices were legislated out of existence were not worse than before. In Canada, for example, strong remedy packages are sharply limited (four provinces deny deficiency claims and have restrictions on repossessions; one province restricts a sales creditor to repossession and the realization of security interests), without a clearly adverse effect on consumers or on institutions. Furthermore, in the few cases studied in Canada, the severity of remedy packages had no effect whatsoever on the per capita volume (and hence availability) of consumer debt in different provinces.[60] Both Benston, for the NCCF, and Barth, for the Federal Trade Commission, found small effects on credit supply and rates from restriction of creditors' remedies.[61] Barth argues that Greer has misspecified his model and thus makes erroneous conclusions. Jordan and Warren support the UCCC remedy package: ". . . it is becoming increasingly doubtful whether many of the traditional creditor remedies are needed by legitimate creditors. . . . The consumer today is very dependent upon credit, and if his ability to get credit depends upon paying his bills, he will pay them without the coercion of the State."[62] As Greer points out, "very few people incur debts with no intention of repaying them which suggests that debtors are generally motivated by integrity and the desirability of maintaining a good credit record," rather than by the fear of creditor remedies upon default.[63] Opponents argue that basic human rights are violated when the creditor is given use of a whole range of these devices, without corresponding strong debtor remedies, such as those found in the MCCA.

Holder in Due Course

The NCCF, the UCCC, and the MCCA would abolish use of the holder-in-due-course doctrine on sales credit paper. Many commentators, however, have noted that the UCCC, by permitting easy entry into the consumer loan business and by permitting other operations to occur at the place of business of a consumer loan office, would merely cause the holder-in-due-course doctrine to be maintained, because credit sales would become, in effect, consumer loans, in which negotiable notes are permitted.

Perhaps no other issue (aside from loan rate ceilings) arouses consumer groups as much as the holder-in-due-course doctrine. Ziegel notes, "As in the United States, few problems in the consumer credit field have fostered as much litigation in Canada as the attempt by finance companies, as assignees of retail finance paper, to isolate themselves from buyer-dealer disputes by the use of cut-off clauses and promissory notes.''[64] It is argued that this doctrine causes the rights of consumers who receive defective or otherwise unsatisfactory merchandise to be abrogated as soon as the sales note changes hands. Proponents of the doctrine argue that the consumer credit market cannot afford to hold the third party responsible for defective merchandise. This responsibility would necessitate that the third parties become inspection agents, vastly increasing the cost of credit and restricting its availability. Speaking for the American Bankers Association, Vaughn has argued that creditors are simply in no position (that is, do not have the staffs or expertise) to maintain a policing function. The new effect would be a decrease in credit, especially consumer credit, through small offices or smaller banks.[65] Greer's study supports this view, with the qualification that creditors surveyed do not frequently use or value the holder-in-due-course doctrine as a remedy.[66]

Kripke agreed with this conclusion, noting, ''Part of this [support of holder-in-due-course removal] is based on the folklore that financiers dominate the dealers, who become mere agents of the financiers. As a generalization, this view is completely erroneous, as anyone who has seen the reality of financier competition for dealer business in the field of automobile credit and other favored types of credit knows.''[67]

Ziegel pointed out, however, that creditors in England cannot use the holder-in-due-course doctrine, and ''. . . the British companies continue to survive successfully and the only practical effect . . . has been to make them more selective in their choice of dealer contracts.''[68] The studies by Barth and Benston found a similar situation in the United States.[69] Much would depend on both the market structure for consumer credit within a locality and upon the perceptions of consumer paper purchasers of their risk position without the doctrine of holder in due course.

Equal Opportunity Reform

All three reform packages propose that the states maintain the provisions of the federal Equal Credit Opportunity Act. The MCCA goes farther, proposing that credit rights be extended without discrimination on account of income sources or political affiliation. Forbidding discrimination because of political affiliation should have no effect whatsoever on the supply, price, and quality of credit, except to those individuals who were previously discriminated against on this basis. MCCA undoubtedly had in mind those affiliated with radical political groups, whose numbers are small.

Opponents of the income source provision argue that income sources are indeed a valid proxy in determining credit delinquencies. Prohibiting the use of this measure would make credit less available and/or more expensive across the board, because creditors would have to subsume a greater share of risk than if they could make use of this proxy. Proponents argue that the same is true for any of the provisions of antidiscrimination legislation; even if it is a valid proxy for credit status, discrimination according to income source is still a denial of the basic human rights of privacy and equal treatment. Moreover, since income source is often a proxy for race and sex, which are prohibited as bases for granting credit by all three regimes and by federal law, the use of income sources is discriminatory in effect and should be outlawed. This argument clearly can be applied to other socioeconomic factors (length of employment, income, asset holdings, and so forth) currently used by creditors to rank credit risk. It then becomes a question of how far creditors must go to reverse historical discriminatory processes.

Summary

There is great similarity among the reform packages, and national legislation has been drafted based on recommendations of the Hunt Commission, the National Commission on Consumer Finance, and the "Discussion Principles" of the Financial Institutions in the Nation's Economy. Although several legislative hearings were held on these reforms, many have yet to be implemented. One primary goal of the three packages is increasing competition within financial markets in order to create allocative efficiency in the markets and provide price and quality benefits to consumers. Although there is some difference in detail, the reform packages generally propose that rate ceilings on deposits be removed, reserve requirements be made uniform across institutional and geographic lines, entry restrictions into consumer credit markets be eased, and thrift institutions be permitted to accept demand deposits.

Both explicitly and implicitly, the three packages call for increased uniformity in market regulation. This implies a larger federal role and a smaller role for state legislators and regulators. Because of historical, market, and demographic differences among the states, it is likely that a price will be paid for this uniformity. The long-term effects of these reforms may well include a net decrease in competitive activity. If this is the case, then the goals of the three packages will be violated.

NOTES

1. *The Report of the President's Commission on Financial Structure and Regulation* (Washington, D.C.: U.S. Government Printing Office, December 1971), p. 9.
2. For further detail see Karl Schriftgiesser, *The Commission on Money and Credit: An Adventure in Policy Making* (New York: Prentice-Hall, 1974). Schriftgiesser was the assistant director of information for the commission.
3. Douglas Greer, "Rate Ceilings, Market Structure, and the Supply of Finance Company Personal Loans," *Journal of Finance* 29 (December 1974): 1363–1382. See also Greer, "An Econometric Analysis of the Personal Loan Credit Market," in *Technical Studies*, vol. IV, National Commission on Consumer Finance (Washington, D.C.: U.S. Government Printing Office, 1972).
4. George Kaufman, "Bank Market Structure and Performance: The Evidence from Iowa," *Southern Economic Journal* 32, no. 4 (April 1966): 429–439.
5. Franklin Edwards, "Concentration in Banking and Its Effects on Business Loan Rates," *Review of Economics and Statistics*, no. 46 (August 1964): 294–300.
6. Paul Meyer, "Price Discrimination, Regional Loan Rates and the Structure of the Banking Industry," *Journal of Finance* 22, no. 1 (March 1967): 37–40.
7. Franklin Edwards and Arnold Heggestad, "Uncertainty, Market Structure, and Performance in Banking: The Galbraith-Caves Hypothesis and Managerial Motives in Banking," *Quarterly Journal of Economics* 87, no. 3 (August 1973): 455–473.
8. F. Thomas Juster and Robert Shay, *Consumer Sensivity to Finance Rates: An Empirical and Analytical Investigation*, Occasional Paper no. 88 (New York: National Bureau of Economic Research, 1964); E.A. Nagata, "The Cost Structure of Consumer Finance Small-Loan Operations," *Journal of Finance* 28, no. 5 (December 1973): 1327–1337.
9. Ralph Nader, testimony. Hearings before the Subcommittee on Finan-

cial Institutions, U.S. Senate Banking, Housing, and Urban Affairs Committee, *Financial Institutions Act of 1973* (Washington, D.C.: U.S. Government Printing Office, 1973), pp. 917-925.

10. Ross Robertson, "Discussion," in *Policies for a More Competitive Financial System* (Boston: Federal Reserve Bank of Boston, June 1972), p. 40.

11. Edward Herman, "Discussion," in *Policies*, p. 66. What makes this quote especially interesting is that General Motors did enter the mass transit market in the late 1940s, effecting a monopoly position in bus and trolley lines in many cities. The company then eliminated trolley services, in favor of the more profitable bus lines. For an illuminating discussion of this example, see Barry Commoner, *The Poverty of Power* (New York: Knopf, 1976).

12. National Commission on Consumer Finance, *Consumer Credit in the United States* (Washington, D.C.: U.S. Government Printing Office, December 1972), p. 3.

13. Albert Cox, "Regulations of Interest on Deposits: An Historical Review," *Journal of Finance* 22, no. 2 (May 1967): 295.

14. Edward Kane, testimony, Hearings before the Subcommittee on Financial Institutions, House Banking, Currency and Housing Committee, *FINE Discussion Principles* (Washington, D.C.: U.S. Government Printing Office, 1975), p. 113.

15. Tom Scott, *FIA 75*, p. 179.

16. Ray Fair and Dwight Jaffee, *Policies*, pp. 99-148; Paul Anderson and Robert Eisenmenger, *Policies*, pp. 149-172; and Patrick Hendershott, "The Impact of the Financial Institutions Act of 1975," reprinted in *Housing Goals and Mortgage Credit: 1975-1980*, Hearings before the Subcommittee on Housing and Urban Affairs of September 22, 23, and 25, 1975.

17. Craig Swan, *FINE*, pp. 138-142; Kenneth Thygerson, testimony, *Housing Goals and Mortgage Credit*.

18. Embree Easterly, testimony, Hearings before the Subcommittee on Financial Institutions, U.S. Senate Banking, Housing and Urban Affairs Committee, *Financial Institutions Act of 1973* (Washington, D.C.: U.S. Government Printing Office, 1973), p. 345.

19. Fairfax Leary, *FINE*, p. 889.

20. Paul Smith, "Fricing Policies on Consumer Loans and Commercial Banks," *Journal of Finance* 25, no. 2 (May 1970): 517-525.

21. The Carter administration's proposals generally follow their recommendation.

22. Irving Schweiger and John McGee, "Chicago Banking," *Journal of Business* 34 (July 1961): 203-366.

23. Robert Eisenbeis, "The Allocative Effects of Branch Banking Restrictions on Business Loan Markets," *Journal of Bank Research* 6, no. 1 (Spring 1975).

24. See Stanley Black, Glenn Canner, and Robert King, *The Banking System: A Preface to Public Interest Analysis* (Washington, D.C.: The Public Interest Economics Center, February 1975).
25. H. Prescott Beighley and Alan McCall, "Market Power and Structure and Commercial Bank Installment Lending" (Chicago: Banking Research Center, Northwestern University, August 1973), mimeograph.
26. Fredrick Bell and Neil Murphy, *Costs in Commercial Banking: A Quantitative Analysis of Bank Behavior and Its Relation to Bank Regulation*, Research Report no. 41 (Boston: Federal Reserve Bank of Boston, April 1968).
27. Donald Jacobs and H. Prescott Beighley, "The Changing Dimensions of Banking Structure," *Journal of Bank Research* 5, no. 3 (Autumn 1974): 145-155.
28. Greer, "Rate Ceilings."
29. Paul Smith, "The Status of Competition in Consumer Credit Markets," in *Technical Studies*, vol. VI.
30. Black, Canner, and King, *The Banking System*.
31. Bell and Murphy, *Costs in Commercial Banking*.
32. George Benston, "An Analysis of Maine's '36 Month Limitation' on Finance Company Small Loans," in *Technical Studies*, vol. II.
33. Jack Guttentag, *FINE*, pp. 485-488.
34. S. 1540, p. 11; reprinted in *FIA 75*, p. 441.
35. Philip Klein, *The Cyclical Timing of Consumer Credit*, Occasional Paper no. 113 (New York: National Bureau of Economic Research, 1971).
36. Maurice Mann and Harris Friedman, "Controlling Lender Behavior: Asset and Liability Restraints," in *Credit Association Techniques and Monetary Policy* (Boston: Federal Reserve Bank of Boston, 1973), p. 35.
37. See Bernard Gelb, *Mortgage Debt for Non-Real-Estate Purposes* (New York: The Conference Board, 1971); and John Kain and John Quigley, *Housing Markets and Racial Discrimination: A Microeconomic Analysis* (New York: National Bureau of Economic Research, 1975).
38. *A Business Report on Consumer Credit*, National Business Council for Consumer Affairs, November 1972, mimeograph.
39. See Erma Angevine, Edward Berlin, and George Brunn, testimony, Hearings before the Subcommittee on Consumer Affairs, House Committee on Banking and Currency, *Consumer Credit Regulations* (Washington, D.C.: U.S. Government Printing Office, 1968), pp. 5-6, 49-50, and 11-16, respectively.
40. *Model Consumer Credit Act*, National Consumer Law Center, 1973, pp. iv-v, mimeograph.
41. See, for example, the hearings held by the Senate Banking Committee on the National Commission on Consumer Finance, May 17, 1973.
42. For example, see John Chapman and Robert Shay, *The Consumer*

Finance Industry: Its Costs and Regulation (New York: Columbia University, 1967).

43. George Brunn, *Consumer Credit Regulations,* pp. 11–16.
44. Robert Shay and Milton Schober, "Consumer Awareness of Annual Percentage Rates of Charge in Consumer Installment Loans: Before and After Truth in Lending Became Effective," *Technical Studies,* vol. I.
45. George Day and William Brandt, "A Study of Consumer Credit Decisions: Implications for Present and Prospective Legislation," *Technical Studies,* vol. I.
46. Terry Deutscher, "Credit Legislation Two Years Out: Awareness Changes and Behavioral Effects of Differential Awareness Level," *Technical Studies,* vol. I.
47. Edward Berlin, *Consumer Credit Regulations,* pp. 49–50.
48. Benny Kass, "S. 2589 and the UCCC: A Comparison of Consumer Protection," *George Washington Law Review* 37 (1969): 1131.
49. Erma Angevine, *Consumer Credit Regulations,* p. 150.
50. Paul Douglas, *Consumer Credit Regulations,* p. 141.
51. See Robert Shay, "The Impact of State Legal Rate Ceilings Upon the Availability and Price of Consumer Installment Credit," *Technical Studies,* vol. IV; and Greer, "Rate Ceilings."
52. Robert Johnson, "The Uniform Consumer Credit Code and the Credit Problems of Low Income Consumers," *George Washington Law Review.*
53. William Proxmire, "Separate Statement," and "Additional Separate Views," in *Consumer Credit Regulations.*
54. See Meyer, "Price Discrimination"; Edwards, "Concentration in Banking"; and Dwight Jafee, *Credit Rationing and the Commercial Loan Market: An Econometric Study of the Structure of the Commercial Loan Market* (New York: John Wiley and Sons, 1971).
55. David Fand and Ronald Forbes, "On Supply Conditions in Consumer Credit Markets," *Paper in Quantitative Economics* (Lawrence, Kansas: University of Kansas Press, 1968).
56. Robert Shay, "Factors Affecting Price, Volume and Credit Risk in the Consumer Finance Industry," *Journal of Finance* 25, no. 2 (May 1970): 503–515.
57. Douglas Greer, "Creditors' Remedies and Contract Provisions: An Economic and Legal Analysis of Consumer Credit Collection," *Technical Studies,* vol. V.
58. Henry Bailey, "The Substantive Provision of the UCCC," *Ohio State Law Journal* 29 (1968): 597–623.
59. Kripke, "Consumer Credit Regulation: A Creditor-Oriented Viewpoint."
60. Jacob Ziegel, "Consumer Credit Regulation: A Canadian Consumer-

Oriented Viewpoint," *Columbia Law Review* 68 (1968): 505–506.

61. George Benston, "The Costs to Consumer Finance Companies of Extending Consumer Credit," *Technical Studies*, vol. II; and James Barth et al., "The Impact of Credit Regulation," studies prepared for the Federal Trade Commission, 1973, mimeograph.

62. Robert Jordan and William Warren, "A Proposed Uniform Code for Consumer Credit," *Boston College Industrial and Commercial Law Review* 8 (1967): 457.

63. Greer, "Creditors' Remedies."

64. Ziegel, "Consumer Credit Regulation: A Canadian Consumer-Oriented Viewpoint," p. 497.

65. Walter Vaughn, testimony for the American Bankers' Association, Subcommittee on Consumer Protection and Finance, House Committee on Consumer Protection and Finance, August 31, 1976.

66. Greer, "Creditors' Remedies."

67. Kripke, "Consumer Credit Regulation: A Creditor-Oriented Viewpoint."

68. Ziegel, "Consumer Credit Regulation: A Canadian Consumer-Oriented Viewpoint."

69. Barth, "The Impact of Credit Regulation"; and Benston, "The Costs to Consumer Finance Companies."

FIVE
The Economic Impact of Deposit Rate Ceilings*
John J. Mingo

Introduction

Legal ceilings on deposit interest rates, including a prohibition of interest payments on commercial bank checking accounts, have been a fact of American life for over forty years. The various effects of deposit ceilings on consumers and financial institutions have been well documented in an extensive literature. Nevertheless, several important questions have not been answered and are the subjects of analysis in this chapter. Those findings will have implications for the likely effects of the phasing out of rate ceilings by 1986, as embodied in the Depository Institutions Deregulation and Monetary Control Act (DIDMC) of 1980.

Under the terms of the Banking Act of 1933, the Federal Reserve was empowered to limit, by regulation, rates paid on time and savings accounts by member banks. In addition, interest payments on demand deposits were expressly prohibited. The Banking Act of 1935 extended rate ceilings to cover the deposits of nonmember,

*The views expressed herein are those of the author and not necessarily those of the Federal Reserve Board or its staff. Contributions to this paper by Anthony Santomero, Charles Haywood, Arnold Heggestad, and the Abt Associates Advisory Board are greatly appreciated.

federally insured banks as well.[1] Two major concerns apparently led to the enactment of the 1933 legislation. First, for some time the New York "money center" banks had been competing for demand balances from the smaller banks in the interior. These so-called bankers' balances would move freely from bank to bank in response to changes in the interest rate being offered—much like the modern-day flow of federal funds and negotiable certificates of deposit. Bankers' balances, it was argued, were responsible for a diversion of credit away from needy local businesses toward the money center banks. In addition, the large New York banks were using their newly acquired bankers' funds to make loans to stock and commodity market speculators—a group widely held to be responsible for the crash of 1929. Finally, liquidity crises at the New York banks had resulted when non-New York banks withdrew their bankers' balances and the New York banks were hard pressed to liquidate assets to pay for the withdrawals. By 1933 New York could pay for bankers' balances, in order to control their spread.[2]

The second concern that led to the 1933 act stemmed from the rapid growth of time and savings accounts at commercial banks. The ratio of savings and time deposits to total deposits rose from .26 in 1914 to .40 in 1929.[3] Federal Reserve member banks, especially, were induced to compete for time and savings accounts, because reserve requirements on such accounts were lower than on demand accounts. As competition pushed up interest rates on time accounts, it was feared that the higher cost of deposit funds would force banks to seek riskier, higher yield investments, thus threatening the solvency of individual banks and perhaps the system as a whole. Indeed, by 1933 several states already had passed legislation limiting the rates that state-chartered banks could offer on time and savings accounts.[4]

For some years, the rationale behind the deposit rate ceilings enacted in 1933 remained unchallenged. Indeed, until the 1950s, deposit rate ceilings were largely redundant, since market rates of interest appeared to be below the ceilings. The average rate on time and savings accounts was only .85 percent in 1945 and 1.36 percent in 1955.[5]

During the late 1950s, however, rising rates brought the ceilings' rationale into question, and in the 1960s several scholarly studies attacked the original justifications for the rate ceilings as unsound. Cox pointed out that stock market speculation was carried out by individuals who had credit alternatives other than bank financing.[6]

Hence, creation of the Securities Exchange Commission and other reforms were more effective in curbing speculative excesses than were the imposition of the rate ceilings on commercial bank deposits. Besides, as Cox pointed out, rates paid on bank deposits were not especially high in 1929 prior to the crash, averaging about 2 percent—some four percentage points below the average rate of return on loans.

Cox's important contribution was to examine the degree of statistical correlation between interest rates paid on bank deposits and the quality of bank assets or the probability of bank failure. He found no evidence that high deposit rates led to investment in risky (high-rate) assets, as proponents of the 1933 act had claimed. Benston's work, which predates Cox's work slightly, supported the general conclusion that competitive bidding for deposit funds did not lead to excessive risk taking.[7] Using two separate samples of banks (New York state banks in the 1923–1934) period and all national banks in the 1928–1933 period), Benston found no statistically significant relation between interest rates paid on bank deposits and various measures of risk taking (such as gross return to assets or incidence of loan losses). In addition, Benston was the first to corroborate the notion that banks could use nonprice methods to attract deposits (such as increased services and conveniences) instead of explicit interest payments. He found that in the pre-1934 period banks paying relatively high rates on deposits incurred relatively low costs for salaries and other expenses, and those paying low rates incurred high costs. Hence, interest payments and customer conveniences are treated as substitutes by bank management.

Re-examination of the rationale for deposit ceilings was prompted also by a phenomenon occurring with regularity through the 1960s—the process of "disintermediation." During periods of rising interest rates, banks suffered deposit withdrawals as customers switched to market instruments with higher yields than the deposit ceilings would allow. Consequently, liquidity crises, and even failures, occurred at some institutions. Prior to 1966, thrift institutions were not generally subject to deposit rate ceilings and were able to bid freely for deposit funds. However, during periods of rising rates, the cost of deposit funds rapidly outstripped the return to the thrifts' mortgage portfolios, often leading to severe earnings problems. Deposit ceilings were extended to thrifts in 1966, largely to protect thrift viability during periods when rates were increasing. However, deposit rate ceilings were responsible for thrift disintermediation in the late 1960s, leading to illiquidity and earnings problems similar to those occurring in the early 1960s. Moreover, thrift disintermediation has been responsible for severe cyclical restrictions in the flow of mortgage funds in recent years.

The disintermediation problem, while potentially severe, represents only one of several recent arguments for removing deposit rate ceilings. The main argument against the ceilings, of course, has been that they treat the unsophisticated, small-deposit customers unfairly—since presumably only the wealthier large-deposit customers can afford to circumvent the ceilings by transferring funds to higher yielding market instruments. Another argument against ceilings is that they create inefficiencies and lead to a suboptimal allocation of resources. The prohibition against interest payments on checking accounts, for example, has led to more resources being used in the processing of checks than would otherwise be the case: to compete for checking funds, banks have offered free or low-cost checking services in lieu of prohibited interest on checking accounts. With free checking, there is little incentive for consumers to economize on the writing of checks (for example, by carrying more cash, by consolidating bills on credit cards, or by switching to electronic methods of funds transfer). As a result, consumers send or receive about 19 billion checks per year, at a cost of $6 billion.[8] If checks were explicitly priced at a level close to the true costs of producing them, there would probably be a decline in check usage and a switch to other, cheaper means of payment.[9]

Deposit rate ceilings may also contribute to reduced bank earnings and greater probability of institutional failure—occurrences against which the ceilings were originally intended to guard. In the absence of deposit interest ceilings, bankers would choose the combination of interest and noninterest payments (such as more customer conveniences or remission of check fees) that would minimize the cost of deposit funds. When a deposit interest ceiling is set too low, bankers must rely too heavily on noninterest devices to attract deposit funds, perhaps at a greater overall cost. In effect, the deposit customer may value the noninterest convenience at less than it costs the bank to produce the convenience, thereby making the noninterest method of attracting customers more costly than the interest payment method.

In addition, deposit ceilings may reduce bankers' flexibility and increase the inherent riskiness of the intermediation process. For example, deposit rate ceilings may hinder bankers in bidding for interest-sensitive funds whenever profitable investment opportunities arise (an argument that parallels the disintermediation argument). Also, during times of economic contraction, reductions in costs may be easier to achieve by reducing deposit interest rates than by reducing customer conveniences (for example, by closing branches or reducing hours of operation). Low or zero deposit interest ceilings clearly reduce management options.

Several study groups have examined the arguments favoring removal of ceilings. However, as late as 1963, the Heller Commission, supporting the traditional arguments, did not recommend repeal. In 1971 the Hunt Commission recommended a phased withdrawal of ceilings on time and savings accounts but continuation of the prohibition on checking account interest. The Financial Institutions Act of 1973 (also 1975 and 1976) and the Financial Reform Act of 1976 would have phased out all deposit rate ceilings; both measures were defeated. NOW accounts (similar to interest-bearing checking accounts) have been allowed in New England and New York, and commercial banks have been allowed to offer their customers automatic transfers (overdrafts) from savings to checking accounts. Such transactions closely approximate explicit interest on demand deposits. DIDMC allows for a phaseout of Regulation Q ceilings and permits all federally insured depository institutions to offer interest-bearing NOW accounts, which would still be subject to a rate ceiling during the six-year phaseout of deposit rate ceilings.

Clarification of the benefits and costs associated with deposit ceilings is hindered by the uncertainty surrounding several issues:

1. In recent years an argument supporting ceilings has been based on the notion that repeal would raise bank costs, thus leading to institutional instability. The existence of deposit ceilings, the argument goes, allows financial institutions to maintain monopoly power in the pricing of deposits. Repeal of ceilings would make bank customers better off, but as banks began to bid up deposit interest rates, costs would rise and some institutions would fail—a socially undesirable by-product of reform. Failure would occur especially because banks would be forced to purchase high-yield, high-risk assets as deposit costs rose. However, recent research has not measured the likely long-run effect on bank risk, one way or the other, if repeal were to take place.[10]

2. What would be the distributional effects of removing rate ceilings? For example, removal of the prohibition on checking account interest is likely to lead to explicit charging for check services. Which class of consumers would benefit from interest on

demand deposits plus per-check charges? Which classes might suffer? If explicit charging for checks reduces depositors' use of checks, how large is the potential social savings from such a reduction?

3. How would removal of deposit rate ceilings affect aggregate economic conditions?

4. How would removal of ceilings, which would eliminate the interest rate differential accorded to thrift institutions, affect the supply of mortgage funds?

The first two issues are examined here. The interested reader will find an analysis of the third, as well as a closer look at the effect of deposit rate ceilings on bank costs, in the interim and final reports by Abt Associates Inc. to the National Science Foundation.[11] The impact of ceilings on mortgage flows is not discussed here.

The Effect of Deposit Rate Ceilings on Bank Risk

As noted earlier, deposit rate ceilings were imposed largely because of the concern that competition for deposit funds would push up the cost of such funds, banks would be forced to offset the increased cost by seeking higher yielding, riskier investments, and more bank failures would result.

This notion—that the bidding up of deposit rates would lead to excessive risk taking on the asset side of the balance sheet—should have been laid to rest with the publication of Benston's study in 1964. Using two separate samples of banks (New York state banks in the 1923–1934 period and all national banks in the 1928–1933 period), Benston found no statistically significant relation between interest rates paid on bank demand deposits and various measures of bank risk taking (such as gross return on assets or incidence of loan losses). In conducting his study, Benston posed the 1930s argument as a "profit target hypothesis"—that is:

> ...without restrictive legislation, at least some bankers would offer higher interest on demand deposits to attract more deposits. Their competitors would have to raise the interest rates they offer to avoid losing deposits. Since costs would be increased, bankers would shift their investment portfolio to assets with higher gross yields. Since higher gross yields almost always are purchased at the cost of greater risk, *ceteris paribus,* bankers would engage in unsafe investment activities.[12]

In effect, the bankers were attempting to maintain a "targeted" level of earnings, and increased deposit costs would force them to seek higher investment yields (assume greater risk).

Benston offered an alternative to the profit target hypothesis—the profit maximization hypothesis:

> The willingness of a banker to invest in assets bearing any perceived degree of risk is a function of the expected returns from the investment and the inclination of the banker toward risk-taking. Thus, the interest rate on deposits offered by a banker is a function of the investment possibilities (and their associated risks) available to the banker, rather than the reverse.[13]

Thus, the possibility of receiving high rates of return on assets could cause bankers to bid up deposit rates; the much maligned interest payments on demand deposits could be a *result*, not a *cause*, of risk (return) on assets.

In addition to questioning the direction of the causal relationship between deposit interest and asset returns, Benston (indirectly) broached two important reasons why deposit rate ceilings could cause increased risk in banking. First, deposit rate ceilings may lead to increased costs in the long run, since bankers will compete for scarce funds using nonprice means (for example, free checks, extensive advertising). Such nonprice means of competing may be less efficient than direct price competition if consumers do not value the nonprice devices at (at least) their true marginal costs of production. Hence, price (interest) ceilings will prevent bankers from minimizing costs for any level of deposit funds "purchased" from depositors; and increased cost moves the risk-yield frontier inward, leading to a position of increased risk and reduced return. Second, too great an emphasis on nonprice competition may reduce bankers' flexibility. By purchasing deposit funds via high fixed costs (for example, impressive bank buildings, numerous branches), bankers cannot respond as readily to changes in investment opportunities as they can by altering deposit rates. Hence, rate ceilings should result in greater earnings variance.[14]

Despite the empirical evidence in the Benston study (and in the 1966 Cox study)[15] and despite the strong theoretical arguments to the contrary, the notion that unbridled rate competition leads to increased bank risk appears to persist to this day.[16] The empirical evidence discussed below is provided in an effort to clarify the relationship between interest rate competition and bank risk. The evidence is based on (1) more recent and more extensive data than those used in the Benston and Cox studies, and (2) a more multivariate approach to isolating the relationship between deposit interest and bank risk.

Methodology

Out of necessity, Benston used pre-1933 data on demand deposit interest to conduct his study. Since 1933, of course, no interest has been allowed on demand deposits, and time and savings accounts have been subsequently limited to payment of Regulation Q ceiling rates. Since the early 1960s, however, banks have had considerable room, within the confines of Regulation Q, to alter the mix of interest versus noninterest devices with which they compete for deposit funds. First, large negotiable certificates of deposit (CDs), sold mostly to corporate depositors, have grown in importance as a source of funds. At times during the 1960s and after 1970, when Regulation Q ceilings were lifted on such CDs, bank rates on large CDs were competitive with rates on market alternatives. Second, interbank deposits (federal funds) and nonbank deposits in the form of securities repurchase agreements have not been subject to rate ceilings; by June 1977, federal funds purchased and repurchase agreements had aggregated to more than $90 billion for all banks. Third, various changes in Regulation Q ceilings by maturity of deposit have given banks the flexibility to structure their deposits toward those (generally longer) maturities for which ceiling rates are less likely to be binding and/or nonprice forms of competition are less important for attracting deposit customers. In fact, in some local markets, household depositors are so insensitive to market alternatives to bank deposits that Regulation Q ceilings have often not been binding.[17]

Hence, because of the structure of rate ceilings (including their absence in the case of some liabilities) and because of local market insensitivity to deposit alternatives, bankers in recent years have had some degree of flexibility in choosing to purchase loanable funds by offering either interest payments or noninterest devices to attract depositors. For this reason, we may use cross-sectional data to test for the ceteris paribus relation between banks' relative use of interest versus noninterest means of purchasing funds and the degree of bank risk. Some bankers have chosen, or have been allowed by local market conditions, to circumvent deposit rate restrictions and hence have relied largely on interest competition for funds. The profit maximization hypothesis says that, for these bankers, the relatively greater interest costs should lead to *reduced* risk.[18] The target hypothesis says that the greater interest costs should lead to *increased* bank risk.

To test the relation between the use of interest payments to attract deposits and bank risk, we drew on research conducted by Edwards and Heggestad and by Crew and Stewart.[19] These authors hypothesized that risk depends on several things: market characteristics (for example, concentration and the firm's market share), firm size, and degree of leverage (that is, capital-asset ratio). They found that risk (which they measured by earnings variance or the coefficient of variation of earnings) decreased as a firm's market power or size increased and as leverage decreased. Presumably, the size variable captures the beneficial effects of diversification and/or economies of scale. Market power, however defined (for example, high concentration or large share), has often been found to increase earnings, and also decrease the earnings variance ceteris paribus. The positive correlation between leverage and earnings variance is probably explained by the influence of management (firm) preferences—for example, conservative managers will strive both for low earnings variance and high capital-asset ratios, while aggressive managers will seek high earnings variance and low capital-asset ratios.

To test the relation between the firm's choice of price versus non-price payments and its degree of realized risk, we extended the above framework to include a variable describing the bank's use of interest payments. That is, we used regression analysis to test for a statistical correlation between risk and the following variables: market characteristics, firm size, capital-asset ratio, and degree of usage of interest payments.

Data

The data consist of a combination of cross-section and time-series information about insured commercial banks in standard metropolitan statistical areas (SMSAs). The SMSA was chosen as a convenient definition of a local "market" for which ample demographic and financial data are readily available. The sample was restricted to SMSAs in limited branching states. This restriction is necessary in order to use market-based data (for example, concentration indices, per capita income) that bear some reasonable relationship to the actual geographic market of the bank. In an unlimited branching state, although a bank may be represented (by its branches) in several SMSAs, bank financial data are available only at the aggregated level (that is, financial data are summed over all the bank's branches throughout the state). A further requirement was that financial data be available for each bank over a long period of time and on a consistent basis (that is, such that year-to-year changes in a bank's financial status are not due to mergers, failures, and so forth), so that we could calculate various measures of earnings variance. The Federal Reserve has constructed a data set that meets these requirements; the set consists of observations made of 1,864 banks over the period year-end 1961 to year-end 1972.[20]

Analysis

To analyze the data, we tested for a statistically significant relation between "risk" (defined five different ways) and the relative reliance on interest payments to attract funds. A regression was run for each definition of risk.[21]

The traditional target hypothesis says that unbridled interest rate competition leads to increased risk; hence, support for this hypothesis requires a *positive* coefficient for the interest variable, other things being held constant. However, in the five regressions run on the study data, the sign for the interest variable was negative in each case and statistically significant in three cases. This means that, depending on the definition of risk, a bank's reliance on interest payments to attract funds is either uncorrelated with risk or negatively correlated, other things being equal.

However, Benston's point that increased rate competition for deposit funds may *result from* higher asset yields (the profit maximization hypothesis) implies nothing about the sign of the relation between interest and risk—risk will still depend on bankers' risk preference, market conditions, and so forth. Hence, a nonpositive sign for the interest variable provides support for the profit maximization hypothesis. Finally, the notion that reliance on noninterest competition for funds is inefficient and/or inflexible implies a negative relation between risk and interest—that is, relative reliance on interest payments to attract funds will reduce risk. Thus, no matter which definition of risk is used, the results tend to overturn the traditional notion that interest rate competition for funds is risky. By implication, Regulation Q ceilings either do not affect bankers' risk positions or affect them adversely.

Distributional Effects of Interest on Checking Accounts and Explicit Pricing of Checks

With the prohibition on checking account interest for personal accounts repealed, in the long run we can expect banks (or in some cases thrifts) to pay market rates of interest on checking accounts while pricing check services in relation to actual costs. Which classes of deposit customers will be helped or hurt as institutions move from nonprice to price forms of competition? Also, what social savings will result from consumers' reduced use of checks? The answers to these questions require knowledge of how the demand for payment services and the demand for payment balances vary by check fee, by interest rate, and by income level. That is, if we know the level of demand balances a given income class will hold and the number of checks it will write (at given per-check fees and given interest rates on checking balances), we can calculate the gain or loss that class will incur in the move from zero-interest free checking to positive-interest, explicitly priced checking.

Methodology and Data

To examine the household's decisions regarding size of checking balance and number of check transactions, we relied on the earlier work of Santomero and Keen.[22] In the Santomero-Keen formulation, household demand for checking balances is based on transaction costs, and the level of checking balances will be a function of transaction fees (that is, check fees and costs of holding currency), alternative rates of return on liquid balances, and income. The number of checking transactions will also depend on transaction fees, income, and the level of transaction balances. In our study, then, we tried to find the statistical determinants of (1) the level of transaction balances, and (2) the number of transactions (checks) per month. We wanted to see how sensitive these variables are to variation in interest rates on the one hand and check fees on the other. Historical data are available for only one type of household deposit account that pays interest *and* allows "checks" to be written—the negotiable order of withdrawal (NOW) account offered in the New England states—hence, we used NOW data to examine household behavior with respect to transaction balances.

The sample consists of 190 banks and thrifts in Massachusetts and New Hampshire that offered NOW accounts in June 1976. This sample allowed use of countywide household income data and institutional financial data to test our hypothesis, because in 1976 Massachusetts and New Hampshire were limited banking states (basically, banks could not branch across county lines). Thus, the institutional financial data conform to the specific banking market (county) for which household income data are available.[23]

We expected that the levels of NOW balances would rise with income and with a higher effective NOW rate. As transaction costs rise (that is, as the per-draft fee increases), other financial assets should look more attractive to the household customer and NOW balances should fall. In addition, transactions should fall as check fees rise and as incomes fall.

We ran regressions on two equations.[24] The first explored the relationship between the average NOW balance at the offering institution and the per-draft fee, the interest rate (APR) paid by the bank on NOW accounts, and household income in the county for 1975. The second looked at the relationship between the number of NOW drafts per month per account and the per-draft fee charged, household income in the county for 1975, and average NOW balances at the offering institution.

Regression Results

Contrary to our expectations, higher fees charged per draft correlated positively with higher average NOW balances. Presumably, this does not mean that higher fees attract NOW customers, however. Rather, it is likely that NOW draft fees are positively correlated with an omitted variable which we cannot accurately observe—the nonprice and convenience aspects of competition between NOW institutions. That is, institutions charging high draft fees may also be those that offer more convenience (longer hours, automated tellers, and so forth). Another possible explanation is that variation of income within the county is more important than income difference across counties. For example, high-income groups within a given county may demand greater average NOW balances at any given fee; thus, both the equilibrium fee charged in that locality and the average NOW balances may be higher than in low-income localities. However, many institutions require a minimum NOW balance; if the account level falls below the minimum, the customer must pay a service charge. The higher this service charge, the higher the customers will keep their average balances to avoid paying the charge.[25]

Similarly, our finding that income and average NOW account balances are negatively correlated was also counterintuitive. Again, this may be due to our use of countywide income data; that is, the "true" relation between the two (as found in, say, the Keen study) may be obscured by within-county income variation. However, the finding does make intuitive sense to the extent that higher income families are more likely than lower income families to be sensitive to market rates of return and, thus, may be more likely or able to economize on their transaction balances.

Finally, analysis of the first regression equation showed that, other things being equal, average NOW balances are $1,100 higher at banks than at thrift institutions. This finding may reflect the non-price elements of competition between banks and thrifts (for example, banks may still enjoy the traditional "one-stop" advantage over thrifts), and, of course, banks may require greater minimum NOW balances than other institutions. Unfortunately, our data do not allow us to delve further into the important differences between banks and other institutions in the nonprice area of competition.

Analysis of the regressions run on the second equation showed that the average number of NOW drafts declines as fees increase, and increases as average balances rise. These two results confirm our initial expectations—people economize on NOW drafts when charged a higher fee, and a higher average balance implies a greater need for transactions, hence greater numbers of NOW drafts are written. Nevertheless, the fee sensitivity of NOW draft usage is not great. For example, for a household with an income of $13,678 (the sample county minimum), a $.10 increase in *fee* (say, from zero to $.10) implies only a .71 per month decline in NOW draft usage. For a household with an income of $17,244, the $.10 increase in fee would not reduce NOW draft usage at all! Presumably, the number of monthly transactions that must be undertaken by households does not vary noticeably by income level and these transactions would not be affected by an increased draft fee. Also, a per-draft fee does not appear to alter a household's decision to use "checks" to purchase one or more items not on the monthly list of purchases.

To summarize, we find that lower NOW fees and higher NOW

interest do *not* result in higher average NOW balances. In fact, counterintuitive results are obtained for the average balance equation, perhaps due to unobserved nonprice elements of interinstitutional competition for NOW account balances or to minimum balance requirements, which were not part of our data. With respect to NOW draft usage, the number of drafts per month declines with check fees and increases with average balance size and household income. However, the sensitivity of draft usage to draft fees, as well as to balance size and income, is not very great.

What, then, are the distributional implications of NOW accounts—the effects on various income classes of explicit interest and explicit fees on checking accounts? Without knowing the actual combination of interest on checking and per-draft fee that the financial system will ultimately adopt, we cannot answer the question accurately. However, we can use the results from the second equation to compute the gains (or losses) to NOW account holders with various balances of a hypothetical move from zero-interest, "free" checking to, say, a NOW account at 5.09 percent interest (the sample mean) and a NOW draft fee of $.08 (again, the sample mean). These results are presented in Table V-1 for five values of average NOW balances—the minimum, maximum, and quartile breakpoints.

The calculations in Table V-1 indicate that most account holders would gain under the hypothesized scenario but that the percentage gains (relative to account size) rise as account size rises. Obviously, very small account holders could lose absolutely under the scenario, and even modestly large account holders could lose if the equilibrium NOW fee were higher. For example, at a $.20 draft fee, the $474 account loses an estimated $1.01 a year.

One further note: to the extent that low-income families would be hurt by the move to explicit pricing of checks, they would continue to demand free or low-cost checking and zero- or low-interest accounts. Hence, some financial institutions may continue to have incentives to offer such accounts. For example, in New England free checking accounts coexist with NOWs, and almost one-half of the household checking accounts eligible for switching to NOWs have not been converted. Therefore, low-income families may not be hurt at all by repeal of the prohibition of interest on checking, especially if it takes the form of nationwide NOWs, with increased competition for transaction balances between thrifts and banks preserving several options for the depositor.

TABLE V-1 Predicted NOW Draft Usage for Various NOW Balance Levels*

NOW Balance Category	$ NOW Balance	Predicted Monthly NOW Drafts	NOW Draft Cost (yearly)	NOW Interest (yearly)	Net Gain (loss)	Gain or Loss as % of NOW Balance
Sample minimum	$ 474	11.33	$10.88	$ 24.12	$ 13.24	2.79
1st quartile	796	11.78	11.31	40.52	29.21	3.67
Sample midpoint	1,067	12.17	11.68	54.31	42.63	3.99
3rd quartile	1,993	13.10	12.58	101.44	88.86	4.45
Sample maximum	8,870	19.28	18.51	451.48	432.97	4.88

*Assuming a 5.09 percent APR rate and $.08 draft fee on NOW accounts.

Summary and Conclusions
Deposit Rate Ceilings and Risks

The traditional notion, dating back at least to the passage of the Banking Act of 1933, is that, in the absence of deposit rate ceilings, banks will bid up deposit interest rates, which will cause banks to seek out higher yielding, riskier assets to justify the high deposit rates. Thus, placing ceilings on deposit rates will lead to safer and sounder banking institutions. The counter arguments are that (1) rate ceilings will cause banks to substitute for interest payments possibly less efficient nonprice means of competing for deposits; (2) when opportunities arise for purchasing high-yielding assets, banks will be hindered by rate ceilings in the attempt to purchase profitable deposits (in the extreme, ceilings will cause disintermediation); and (3) when asset returns fall, banks that have relied heavily on nonprice means of competing for deposits will have trouble reducing liability costs because of the relative inflexibility associated with branch networks, deposit-related services, and other nonprice devices. In short, these arguments suggest that deposit rate ceilings could lead to greater, not lesser, bank risk.

Our test of these opposing views was an *indirect* test of the bank risk associated with deposit rate ceilings. Within the confines of modern-day Regulation Q ceilings (and the prohibition on demand deposit interest), there remains considerable variation in the degree to which banks are willing or able to use interest payments, rather than nonprice devices, to attract deposit funds. The possibilities include (1) using large negotiable CDs, federal funds, and repurchase agreements; and (2) structuring deposits toward those maturities for which Regulation Q ceilings are less likely to be binding and/or nonprice forms of competition are less important. To some extent, use of interest payments to attract funds will depend on the bank's size (whether it can issue substantial amounts of $100,000 CDs) and/or the structure of its market (whether its customers are sensitive to rates and whether they are composed largely of households); to some extent management preferences play a role. The test was to find out whether a bank that is able (or willing) to compete for funds by offering explicit interest payments will, ceteris paribus, enjoy greater or less risk. To the extent that imposition of rate ceilings reduces a bank's ability to compete via interest payments, the test used is an indirect test of the effect of ceilings on bank risk.

Our approach was to test for a statistically significant relation between risk (variously defined) and the relative reliance on interest payments to attract funds (interest expense/total expense). According to the regression analysis, risk and interest expense/total expense are either significantly and negatively correlated, or uncorrelated. The lack of significant, positive correlation tends to refute the traditional hypothesis that interest competition for deposits leads to increased risk. The significant, negative correlations provide support for the hypothesis that use of interest payments to attract funds (which would occur to a greater extent if Regulation Q were repealed) can lead to greater flexibility, reduced cost, and hence reduced bank risk.

Explicit Pricing of Checks and Interest on Checking Accounts

First, the social savings from a move toward explicit pricing of checking services would probably be small. In the case of NOWs, at least, the degree of fee elasticity in the demand for checking-type services appears to be quite low (and nonexistent as income rises). Hence, nationwide use of NOWs and explicit pricing of Federal Reserve services to banks on the processing of checks and other means of payment (which could induce banks to begin charging their customers higher prices for checks) are not likely to lead to a large reduction in the multibillion dollar yearly cost of the nation's payment mechanism.

Second, the statistical results can be interpreted to mean that low-income classes *could* be hurt absolutely and/or relative to high-income classes, if free checking were replaced by interest-bearing checking accounts with explicitly priced checks. Absolute losses to depositors would occur, however, only for the lowest income households (those with average deposit balances below the sample data minimum of $474) or if financial institutions charged much more than the $.08 per-draft average in our NOW sample. Finally, to the extent that the lowest income (deposit-level) classes continued to benefit from free checking, some institutions would probably continue to offer such accounts (as long as competition among financial institutions continued).

NOTES

1. The 1935 act empowered the FDIC to set regulations paralleling the Federal Reserve Board's Regulation Q. The Federal Credit Union Act of 1934 empowered the Bureau of Federal Credit Unions (later the NCUA) to set deposit rate ceilings for federally chartered credit unions. Federally insured savings and loan associations were subjected to rate ceilings by the Federal Home Loan Bank Act as amended in 1966.
2. In an excellent capsulized history of the 1933 act, Haywood and Linke point out that five banking "panics," between 1857 and 1907, were initiated by withdrawals of bankers' balances from New York banks. The Federal Reserve in the 1913–1920 period had tried, through moral suasion, to maintain informal ceilings on rates paid on such balances. Charles F. Haywood and Charles M. Linke, *The Regulation of Deposit Interest Rates,* prepared for the Trustees of the Banking Research Fund, Chicago, 1968.
3. Ibid., p. 13.
4. As Haywood and Linke point out, it is interesting that neither of the two major concerns preceding the 1933 Act—the concerns for bankers' balances and for the growth of time accounts—explains the outright prohibition of interest on checking accounts. Why was the ceiling extended to business and consumer demand balances, in addition to bankers' balances, and why was the rate ceiling on demand accounts set at zero?
5. Haywood and Linke, *Deposit Interest Rates,* p. 29.
6. Albert H. Cox, Jr., "Regulation of Interest Rates on Bank Deposits" (Ann Arbor, Michigan: Bureau of Business Research, University of Michigan, 1966).
7. George J. Benston, "Interest Payments on Demand Deposits and Bank Investment Behavior," *Journal of Political Economy* 72 (October 1964): 431–439.
8. Arthur D. Little, Inc., "The Consequences of Electronic Funds Transfer" (Cambridge, Mass.: Arthur D. Little, Inc., June 1975).
9. The savings that would result have not been estimated, because we have no information on the degree to which consumers and businesses would cut back on check usage as check prices rose. Estimation of the "check demand function" is part of the approach discussed below.
10. Both Chase and Cates and the Federal Reserve have "measured" earnings losses associated with repeal under very stringent assumptions. (See Samuel B. Chase, Jr. and David Cates, "The Payment of Interest on Checking Accounts," report to the South Carolina Bankers Association, February 1976; and Federal Reserve System, "The Impact of the Payment of Interest on Demand Deposits," prepared by the staff of the

Board of Governors, January 31, 1977.) However, these studies have not been able to predict the extent to which explicit pricing of bank services (checks, and so forth) would offset higher interest payments, because the studies have not estimated the demand for bank services.

11. See Arnold Heggestad and John Mingo, eds. *Public Regulation of Financial Services: Costs and Benefits to Consumers,* Phase I Interim Report to the National Science Foundation (Cambridge, Mass.: Abt Associates Inc., 1977; and idem, *The Costs and Benefits of Public Regulation of Consumer Financial Services,* Final Report to the National Science Foundation (Cambridge, Mass.: Abt Associates Inc., 1978).

12. George Benston, "Interest Payments," p. 432.

13. Ibid., p. 433.

14. Perry Quick, "Interest-Bearing Demand Deposits and Bank Portfolio Behavior: Comment," *Southern Economic Journal* (September 1977): 349–401.

15. Cox, "Regulation of Interest Rates."

16. For a restatement of the traditional view, see John Paulus, "Effects of 'NOW' Accounts on Costs and Earnings of Commercial Banks in 1974–75," Staff Economic Studies, no. 88, Board of Governors of the Federal Reserve System, 1977.

17. Benston recognized that bankers' preferences and/or local market conditions could lead to variation in rates paid on deposits. Further, the finding of "a negative or insignificant correlation [between deposit rates and risk] is not inconsistent with the [profit] maximization hypothesis...[because] some banks may find payment for funds with services or other indirect means more advantageous than direct payment with interest. Or banks may be in different markets for the purchase or sale of funds, causing some banks to pay more for funds and to receive lower gross yields on assets than do other banks. And banks that are in the same market for funds may be in different markets for other factors of production."

18. Recall that "circumvention" of rate ceilings will (1) reduce long-run deposit costs by allowing optimal choice of interest versus noninterest devices, (2) allow the firm to bid for more deposit funds when asset rates rise, and (3) allow the firm to cut deposit costs more easily when asset rates fall.

19. Franklin R. Edwards and Arnold A. Heggestad, "Uncertainty, Market Structure, and Performance: The Galbraith-Caves Hypothesis and Managerial Motives in Banking," *Quarterly Journal of Economics* 87, no. 3 (August 1973): 455–473; and Michael A. Crew and David B. Stewart, "Fixed Costs, Uncertainty and the Firm: Theoretical and Empirical Considerations" (unpublished paper), 1974.

20. All financial data are from Reports of Income and Condition; condi-

tion reports are for June and December of each year, income reports for December of each year.

21. For a detailed discussion of the five definitions of risk and the equations used in the regression analysis, see Heggestad and Mingo, *The Costs and Benefits of Public Regulation.*

22. Howard Keen, Jr., "Banking Pricing and the Demand for Demand Deposits: The Case of Special Checking Accounts" (Philadelphia: Federal Reserve Bank of Philadelphia, Department of Research, January 1977); and A.M. Santomero, "The Role of Transaction Costs and Rates of Return in the Demand Deposit Decision," Federal Reserve Bank, Working Paper, Philadelphia, 1976.

23. An important caveat should be issued at this point in the discussion. The "theory" underlying the examination procedure pertains to the behavior of individual households; however, the data on NOW accounts are available only for average account balances and activity at offering institutions, and corresponding household income data are available only as an average for the banking market (county). Hence, the results we obtained must be generalized with caution, because the effects stemming from variation of household income *within* counties may be masked by variation of average household income across counties.

24. See Heggestad and Mingo, eds. *The Costs and Benefits of Public Regulation.*

25. See John H. Boyd, "Household Demand for Checking Account Money," *Journal of Monetary Economics* 2 (1976): 81–98.

SIX
An Evaluation of Interinstitutional Competition for Consumer Financial Services

Arnold A. Heggestad

Introduction

Although competition among consumer financial institutions has been limited by numerous regulations, market forces continually erode the barriers between banks and other financial firms. Many of the current regulatory reform proposals are directed at increasing competition in the markets for demand deposits, time deposits, and consumer credit. These reforms could lead to increased competition and correspondingly lower interest rates on loans and higher deposit rates, especially since Regulation Q is being lifted. This chapter analyzes the nature and extent of competition among the diverse firms that offer these consumer financial services. Applying the market structure-conduct-performance model to the consumer credit and consumer deposit markets, we use rates of charge on deposits and consumer loans to estimate the impact of market structure and measure the effects of differing degrees of interinstitutional competition.

The Institutional Setting

The numerous consumer financial services are

provided by a wide range of financial institutions, some specialized and some offering many products. The industry is dominated by commercial banks, which offer most services and have traditionally been the only type of firm to offer demand deposits, although this position is being eroded by recent changes in market structure and regulations. Commercial banks compete, to varying degrees, with specialized institutions, such as credit unions, savings and loan associations, and mutual savings banks. Table II-2, in Chapter Two, shows the amount of deposit and loan services provided by each type of institution in 1975. Commercial banks continue to hold the largest aggregate share of savings deposits and consumer loans.

The other institutions, although more specialized, are also highly diversified in structure. The thrift institutions—mutual savings banks and savings and loan associations—compete with commercial banks in the savings deposit and mortgage credit markets, but not in consumer credit markets. Credit unions offer consumer loans and savings deposits. In some areas, credit union share drafts compete directly with commercial bank demand deposits. The potential for credit union growth and resulting competition in local markets are limited by regulatory restrictions, particularly the requirement that all credit union members have a common bond. Retailers and finance companies offer only consumer loans. Their competitive strength may be limited because they do not have access to low-cost sources of deposit funds.

The distribution of market shares does not necessarily reflect the options available to individual consumers. Consumer financial service markets are local in nature, and there are substantial local differences in the market share of each type of institution and in the number of institutions within a given market. In some areas the thrifts dominate the market for savings deposits; in other areas banks or credit unions dominate. Perhaps more relevant is the variation in the degree of competition among each type in the local markets. Many markets are competitively structured in that entry is easy, and numerous finance companies, credit unions, and other types of institutions already compete. However, most banking markets are not competitively structured in terms of ease of entry and number of firms. They exhibit little or no competition for consumer loans or demand deposits. These markets may still be competitive, however, if strong interinstitutional competition exists.[1]

Studies of competition traditionally assume that all firms will maximize their profits subject to the constraints of regulation, market demand, and cost conditions. Thus, an increase in the number of firms in a market will cause an increase in rivalry and result in lower rates as market constraints become more binding. However, the existing empirical evidence suggests that this relationship may not exist in the consumer financial services industry. Brigham and Pettit found that mutual firms do not minimize costs, nor do they adjust rapidly to market changes in their investment accounts, according to Hester and Pierce.[2] Furthermore, banks may exhibit objective functions with goals beyond profit maximization. Under certain conditions, they may not minimize costs,[3] or they may act in a more risk-averse manner.[4] Thus, the direct application of a market model assuming profit-maximizing behavior may not be appropriate. In this case empirical evidence of the effect of market structure on performance becomes even more important.

Regulation of Interinstitutional Competition

A major goal of financial regulation is to promote the soundness and stability of depository institutions. For commercial banking, the basis for this regulation rests on two beliefs: (1) that commercial banks, operating to maximize the private value of their firms, would take on excessive risk resulting in an incidence of failures higher than is socially optimal; and (2) that the social costs of bank failure significantly exceed the private costs to bank owners.[5] These social costs involve changes in public expectations about the strength of financial markets, collapse of the payment system, and contractions in the money supply.

The rationale underlying soundness regulations for other types of consumer financial institutions is less clear. One recent explanation is that society takes the paternalistic view that "public capital suppliers [depository institutions] should be protected from the more serious consequences of their own propensity to normative error in the matter of risk taking [with their assets].... ."[6] Also implicit is the belief that the public is incapable of judging the safety of depository institutions. An alternate rationale is the need to provide for equity among the types of institutions relative to society's goals in credit allocation. If commercial banks are regulated to maintain soundness and are provided with government-subsidized deposit insurance, their deposits may be deemed safer by the public than deposits at other institutions.[7] In order to maximize the distributional effects of this government intervention, similar direct subsidies should be offered other depository institutions.[8]

The regulatory framework is also used to promote goals other than financial soundness. Among these goals are promotion of thrift and investment by the public;[9] promotion of a financial system that complements or at least does not hinder monetary policy;[10] and credit allocation, primarily allocation of commercial and industrial loans to disadvantaged groups, such as home buyers, small businesses, and consumers.[11] Finally, regulation attempts to protect the public from being exploited in credit transactions.[12]

These often conflicting goals are implemented via a complex network of regulations and legal requirements, including restrictions on competition between types of institutions, entry restrictions, branching restrictions, capital requirements, deposit insurance, price ceilings on loans and deposits, and direct limitations on management behavior. One important set of regulations is designed to segment financial markets by differentiating products and limiting competition among financial institutions of a particular type.

Market segmentation reduces competition for consumer products and is intended to promote soundness. Since the end result of any competitive situation is that the least efficient firms are unable to survive, one rationale behind regulations that segment the market is that they promote soundness by increasing firm profitability and thus reducing the likelihood that individual firms will be forced out of business. Alternatively, it is feared that competition for deposits will drive up costs, forcing firms to choose riskier, higher yield asset portfolios. Although the theoretical and empirical evidence does not support this view, it still remains an important rationale for regulation.[13] Market segmentation is also designed to allocate credit to specific sectors of society. The thrifts are expected to make more funds available to consumers. Presumably, in the absence of specialized financial intermediaries, these groups would receive less credit.

The most important aspect of market segmentation is the monopoly on demand deposits enjoyed by commercial banks, which can offer convenience in the competition for savings deposits—for example, "one stop" banking—and which, until 1980, had a source of inexpensive funds, since they were forbidden by law to pay interest on demand deposits.[14] When the law was changed in 1980, this monopoly was weakened. Access to inexpensive funds may also give banks an advantage in consumer loan markets.[15]

Deposit competition is also limited by rate ceilings, which will be removed by 1985. These ceilings guarantee a rate differential between commercial banks and thrift institutions that is advantageous to the thrifts. Moreover, the ceilings prohibit any type of depository institution from bidding for consumer funds in periods of high interest rates.[16] Thus, they simultaneously set the distribution of deposits by type of institution and restrict the general intensity of competition in tight credit markets.

Interinstitutional competition for deposits and loans is also limited by general chartering and entry restrictions. For example, a consumer finance company cannot be chartered as a commercial bank, even though there may be an excess of capital invested in consumer finance and a shortage in commercial banking. Charter restrictions have limited the number of new bank charters by as much as 50 percent.[17] Branching restrictions also affect the pattern of competition among institutions. Some types of firms, such as consumer finance companies, are able to branch across state lines, thereby gaining access to national advertising markets and being able to concentrate resources in geographic areas with the greatest return. Most depository institutions, however, cannot cross state lines. Even within states branching laws vary considerably. In 60 percent of the states commercial banks are prevented from branching throughout the state. Savings and loan associations with national charters are permitted to branch with considerably fewer limitations. Credit unions are effectively prevented from branching by the common bond requirement, which limits their market to a specific geographic concentration of customers. However, one group of large credit unions is able to branch nationwide (see Chapter Two).

Regulations segment asset markets in a similar manner to deposit markets. The segmentation takes two forms: limitations on the types of assets that the various kinds of financial institutions can hold, and limitations on the characteristics of consumer loans.

Credit markets are segmented by asset limitations on each type of institution. Savings and loan associations could effectively hold only mortgages and government bonds prior to 1980. Credit unions are limited to short-term notes from their members, government bonds, and mortgages. Commercial banks may hold not only consumer loans and mortgages, but also commercial and industrial loans. Mutual savings banks may hold consumer loans and mortgages in some states, as well as make equity investments. By tradition, however, mutual savings banks are not active in the consumer loan sector.

Credit markets are also segmented by differential state usury ceilings. Usury ceilings impose limits on effective rates charged by each type of institution and/or for each type of consumer loan they offer. There is considerable variation among states, with the highest ceilings on usury rates charged by consumer finance companies. The 1980 legislation may act to remove this distinction.

Usury laws tend to reduce institutional flexibility in terms of the rate and maturity set for various loans. Because profit-maximizing lenders will make loans where the net yield (gross return minus costs) is the highest,[18] the effect of usury laws may be that commercial banks, subject to low usury ceilings, will tend to make loans only to very safe customers with a low probability of default. Furthermore, given the cost of making consumer loans, they will not be able to make small, short-maturity consumer loans to any customer.[19] Although credit unions generally have a very safe clientele due to the common bond requirement,[20] their low ceiling may limit their ability to cover costs on small, low-maturity loans, especially if there is some likelihood of default. Therefore, the ultimate impact of usury legislation may be to force consumers with high-risk characteristics or consumers who desire only small loans of short maturity to seek credit at those institutions with the greatest flexibility in rate and maturity structure—the consumer finance companies. Although, legally, finance companies can always charge less than the usury ceiling and thus compete for safer, less risky customers with banks and credit unions, they cannot compete effectively for these customers, since consumer finance firms are generally not depository institutions and do not have access to low-cost, federally insured deposit funds.

Evidence of Competition Among Institutions

Although the restrictions on interinstitutional competition are extensive, they are not completely stifling. Financial firms do have the capacity to evade many of the restrictions on interinstitutional competition if it is profitable to do so or if forced by competitive pressures. For example, numerous devices have been developed to evade Regulation Q ceilings and the prohibition of interest on demand deposits.[21] These range from negotiable order of withdrawal (NOW) accounts and repurchase agreements for large companies[22] to premiums for opening savings accounts. Similarly, competition for savings deposits may be nonprice in nature, thereby avoiding the rate ceilings.[23]

Competition for consumer loans could take place even if regulations and usury ceilings had virtually segmented the markets. No segmentation scheme, especially by borrower risk characteristics, is perfect. There will always be a spectrum of consumers with characteristics that fall within limits acceptable to more than one type of institution. This competition for marginal customers could be significant and could equate net yields for all consumer loans. The degree of overlap for marginal consumers depends on local market structure and on the intensity of market regulation.

Competition for Consumer Credit

The consumer credit industry has undergone considerable structural change since World War II. As demonstrated by Haywood in Chapter Two, the shares of the major types of firms have changed dramatically. In the aggregate, credit unions have experienced extremely rapid growth; their share of the market has increased by 400 percent in the past twenty-five years. This growth has been at the expense of retailers and finance companies.[24] Changes in aggregate shares of this magnitude are consistent with extensive interinstitutional competition. On the other hand, these changes may simply reflect relative changes in the demand for credit by the particular segments of credit markets each institution serves. A disaggregated analysis of local market data is necessary to determine which forces have been operating in consumer credit.

Two approaches have been used to estimate the extent of interinstitutional competition for consumer credit. One approach is to use cross-sectional data to determine if structural differences among the different types of firms affect some measure of market performance, such as the supply of credit or rejection rates. Presumably, if differences in structure cannot be shown to affect market performance, the respective institutions are segmented by regulatory barriers. The alternate approach is to focus on borrower characteristics. Segmentation would most likely be accomplished on the basis of systematic characteristics of borrowers that are related to the size and the riskiness of loans. If markets are segmented, there should be quantifiable differences in loan size and risk characteristics of customers at different types of institutions. Presumably, companies allowed the highest rates and the greatest flexibility would offer the smallest loans and serve the highest risk customers.

The two studies that have investigated the impact of market structure on interinstitutional rivalry have produced conflicting results. Greer finds no evidence that rejection rates at consumer finance companies are influenced by the existence of alternative competitors.[25] If competition exists, rejection rates should be lower in markets with many competitors. According to Greer, the lack of any effect of market structure on rejection rates suggests that markets are effectively segmented. Consumer finance company customers are no better off when there is bank competition, since banks are not alternative sources of loans for their customers.

The only other study to use this approach was conducted by Smith. He finds some weak evidence of interinstitutional competition for consumer credit by estimating the responsiveness of demand for loans to changes in interest rates on consumer loans offered by other suppliers. Smith's research indicates that the volume of loans by finance companies is directly related to commercial bank interest rates: increased rates at banks increase the demand for finance company loans. Similarly, the volume of loans at credit unions is directly related to rates charged by finance companies. Although he could find no other similar relationship, Smith concludes from these rather weak results that credit markets are quite competitive.[26]

A major difficulty with both the Greer and the Smith study is their reliance on state data to approximate local markets. The geographic market for consumer credit is inherently local. Because of high transaction costs, firms are generally unable to extend credit beyond a fairly narrow geographic area, such as a city or standard metropolitan statistical area (SMSA). Extension beyond this area increases the costs of obtaining data on the credit worthiness of potential borrowers. Similarly, efforts to collect on delinquent loans are less expensive and easier when the borrower lives within close proximity of the lender. Therefore, the market will tend to be considerably smaller than a state.[27]

The alternate approach partially avoids the market definition problem by analyzing the characteristics of borrowers at various types of institutions. These characteristics should be constant across markets. Eisenbeis and Murphy could not distinguish among borrowers at banks, credit unions, or finance companies in Maine. They conclude, "this inability to distinguish would indicate that, in

Maine, banks, credit unions, and finance companies are real alternate suppliers and they compete in the same product market."[28]

Boczar conducted a similar test using a national sample of borrowers. Also unable to distinguish between bank and finance company customers, he concluded that substantial overlap exists between the two groups of customers, and "risk segmentation is not an effective barrier to interindustry competition. . . ."[29]

This analysis suggests that credit markets are already competitive. The results are correct, however, only if the independent demographic variables accurately capture risk characteristics, and there is considerable reason to doubt this assumption. As Boczar suggests, the same demographic data may have different meanings to the two types of firms. A high-income borrower at a bank is likely to be a safe customer. A high-income individual forced to go to a finance company, on the other hand, may have a bad credit record and have been rejected by the banks. Income, in this case, would not discriminate between customers, although true risk measures would discriminate between the customers at the two types of institutions.

In summary, the existing evidence of overlap between consumer credit institutions is not conclusive. Using the best data available, analyses of consumer attributes suggest that markets are not segmented. However, there is considerable reason to question the appropriateness of the approximations of risk attributes. The two studies that use cross-sectional data have produced mixed results. Both studies use state data to approximate markets, an approximation that has little economic merit and may have distorted the findings.

Competition for Savings Deposits

Savings deposits are a more homogeneous product than consumer loans. The primary distinguishing characteristics of consumer loans are their riskiness and their maturity. Since all deposits under $100,000 are insured by the federal government, they are all risk-free and extremely liquid. It is likely, therefore, that the market for savings deposits would be less segmented than the market for consumer loans. However, Regulation Q, which was instituted in 1966, has severely restricted competition for these deposits.

Early studies of competition for savings deposits analyzed changes

in aggregate shares in depository institutions,[30] and therefore were
not based on market concepts. They generally concluded that competition was strong prior to the adoption of Regulation Q in 1966.
Spellman found similar evidence of competition at the market
level.[31]

Deposit markets still may be considerably more competitive than
was intended under Regulation Q. Spellman finds high cross-
elasticity of deposit demand, which is consistent with competition.[32]
The higher the cross-elasticity of demand, the greater the responsiveness of one segment of the industry's demand to changes in the
price charged by another segment. High rates at savings and loan
associations attract deposits from commercial banks. In addition,
White finds evidence of nonprice interinstitutional competition.[33]
The number of bank branches in SMSAs is greater, ceteris paribus,
in markets with strong thrift competition. Thus, even with Regulation Q differentials, there may be strong competition among the
depository institutions.

Finally, interinstitutional competition for demand deposits may
occur in areas where the thrifts are permitted to offer NOW accounts. Studies of the NOW account experiment demonstrate that
the competitive reactions vary considerably.[34] Thrifts in
Massachusetts and New Hampshire used aggressive pricing and promotion of NOW accounts to gain a much larger share of total
deposits. In other New England states, however, the thrifts have
priced and marketed NOW accounts less aggressively, and banks
have experienced a smaller decline in market share.[35]

The experiment is not complete. These markets are still in dis-
equilibrium as firms attempt to develop pricing mechanisms that are
competitive and cover costs.[36] Thus, it is likely that the final
equilibrium solution in New England demand deposit markets will
differ from the present situation. Differences between the first states
to participate in the experiment (Massachusetts and New Hampshire) and other New England states suggest the process is still
under way. However, according to the existing evidence, while there
is now little interinstitutional competition for demand deposits outside New England, permitting thrifts in other regions to offer an
alternative to demand deposits will have substantial effects on rates
paid for demand deposits and, therefore, on market shares.

In summary, the empirical evidence of market segmentation is not
conclusive. It suggests that there have been some attempts to evade

restrictions. In at least some cases interinstitutional competition has led to an improvement in performance. However, the extent of competition among the various types of institutions is still unclear.

Empirical Analysis

We used two sets of data on interest rates and charges for consumer financial services to assess the impact of interinstitutional competition on consumers. The first data set was obtained from a survey of interest rates on consumer loans at randomly selected credit unions, consumer finance companies, and commercial banks in 1977. The second set consists of interest rates on consumer credit and consumer deposits at commercial banks in 1973.

Using the structure-conduct-performance model, we developed statistical tests to determine if the presence of a large number of possible substitute firms influences the pricing behavior of each industry, after accounting for other industry characteristics that would affect equilibrium prices. The structure-conduct-performance model is a general statement of the determinants of market performance. Simply stated, conduct or rivalry in a market is determined by market structure conditions, especially the number and size distribution of firms and the conditions of entry. The outcomes of this rivalry include predictable levels of prices, advertising, profits, and other aspects of market performance. Thus, the performance of firms in a market is tied to the structure of the market through the link of conduct. Everything else being equal, the more firms there are in a market, the more they will compete, and the lower consumer prices will be.

Traditional economic theory has analyzed firm and market behavior under the extreme conditions of perfect competition among a large number of firms and monopoly by one firm. In these polar cases, rational profit-maximizing behavior leads to predictable prices and other aspects of performance. Under conditions of perfect competition, all firms produce efficiently and price is forced down to the cost of production. This is the best situation for consumers. Under a monopoly, consumers are worse off, because price exceeds cost, and output is restricted to exercising profits.

Most markets do not fall neatly into the perfect competition or monopoly categories. Chamberlin and Robinson first studied imperfectly competitive markets.[37] As the structure of markets becomes more monopolistic, will performance approach the monopoly level or will it remain competitive? The answer depends on how firms interact. Chamberlin's assumption, which still seems the most reasonable, is that firms will want to achieve jointly the same price-output configuration that a monopolistic firm would, in order to maximize their joint profits. However, coordination of activities to achieve this configuration is difficult. Even though it is in the interests of the group to set the monopoly price, each firm may do better by cutting its price relative to the group. The more firms in the market, the more likely it is that aggressive price-cutting behavior will take place.

Competition in Consumer Credit

Tests of interinstitutional competition for consumer credit were conducted using a 1977 survey of interest rates on a hypothetical consumer loan in fifty-seven SMSAs. The survey was designed to give the responding firm the impression that a potential customer was calling. The interviewer said he was buying a new car and needed to borrow $1,400. (This amount was less than the legal lending limit in every area sampled.) The interviewer then requested the rate on a three-year loan.[38]

Credit unions, consumer finance companies, and commercial banks were randomly selected within each SMSA.[39] Two credit unions were chosen in each. The number of banks and finance companies chosen was proportional to the number of each type of firm operating in the city. After eliminating firms that did not report rates by telephone, firms that did not report the annual percentage rate, and firms for which other relevant data were not available, the final sample for analysis included 695 firms—403 banks, 221 consumer finance companies, and 71 credit unions, operating in a total of 57 SMSAs.[40]

ANALYTIC TECHNIQUE. The model employed in analyzing the data hypothesized that the rate of charge on a loan at a given type of firm is a function of market demand, the concentration of that particular type of firm in the market, the strength of actual or potential interinstitutional competition in the market, and control variables related to a specific type of loan (for example, maximum amount of loan, length of loan, ceiling on interest rates).

Demand conditions were measured by two variables: per capita income, which reflects the relative strength of demand for consumer credit, and growth in credit over time, which reflects the increase in demand during the period. The interest rate ceiling for loans in a given state was also added as an explanatory variable since it effectively limits the interest rate that may be charged.

The strength of interinstitutional competition—the extent of rivalry due to the presence of other types of financial firms—is proxied by the numbers of these firms. The use of numbers of firms rather than measures that reflect the number and size distribution creates problems that are well documented.[41] In general, at least in banking markets, the number of firms is as good a predictor of rivalry as the more theoretically desirable indices, such as the Herfindahl Index and the concentration ratio.[42]

There is another, more subtle problem with using the number of each type of institution to reflect differences in the intensity of competition. For firms of a particular type, such as banks or credit unions, it is safe to assume that the number of firms in a market represents the number of independent units. The antitrust laws prevent overt ties between the firms, so any cooperation must be covert. This is not the case, however, with respect to the different types of financial institutions. Herman documents that 16.6 percent of savings and loan associations have at least one director whose primary occupation is commercial banking.[43] The incidence of common directors between banks and savings and loan associations is no doubt considerably higher. A similar relationship exists between commercial banks and mutual savings banks. In fact, there are many shared office facilities in New England.[44] Finally, commercial banks act as a supplier to all other types of financial institutions. Commercial banks supply demand deposit facilities to the credit unions and the thrift associations. More important, commercial banks are a major source of credit for the consumer finance industry, especially for the smaller, independent firms. Thus, care must be taken in interpreting the measures of institutional rivalry, because it is quite possible that many of the firms are not independent.

We used two additional measures of the strength of interinstitutional competition. The first is the number of offices, which may better reflect the strength of other types of institutions in the market than the number of firms, because the number of offices is more sensitive to branch networks. The second additional measure of competitive strength is the numbers equivalent, which is based on the Herfindahl Index and indicates the number of firms of equal size that would generate a Herfindahl Index comparable to the actual Herfindahl Index in the market.[45] The numbers equivalent is based on deposits of the thrift institutions. The results for equations using these measures did not differ substantially from the results of the equation using number of firms.

EMPIRICAL RESULTS. The rate charge on a hypothetical loan was estimated separately for each type of financial institution: banks, credit unions, and finance companies.

The results of our tests of interinstitutional competition in consumer credit markets suggest that commercial banks have greater competitive strength and are more isolated from interinstitutional competition than other credit-granting institutions. Strong bank competition within a local market tends to force down credit union and finance company rates, whereas consumer finance companies and credit unions do not affect bank rates. This result is consistent with the hypothesis that credit markets are not segmented by risk class. Commercial banks are able to compete effectively for most consumer loan accounts. The segmentation that does occur is probably attributable to the advantage of low-cost demand deposits. Other types of firms are not able to compete effectively with commercial banks because their costs are significantly higher.

Some care must be taken in interpreting these results. Statistical estimation problems make precise estimates of the strength of interinstitutional competition difficult to obtain.

The Impact of Interinstitutional Competition on Bank Performance

Data on 1973 bank prices were employed to test further the effect of interinstitutional competition on bank pricing behavior. Two analyses of these data demonstrated that bank market structure affects local market competition.[46] In markets with high bank concentration, loan rates and demand deposit service charges at commercial banks are higher, ceteris paribus. Time deposit rates and certificate of deposit rates are weakly inversely related to concentration of bank deposits. These studies did not include a full analysis of interinstitutional competition. However, they did separate and analyze the markets where thrifts had either demand deposit accounts or consumer loan powers. The presence of thrift institutions with consumer loan powers did not affect bank loan rates. On the other hand, the presence of thrift institutions with NOW account powers reduced demand deposit service charges substantially—$1.56 per month on the average.

We used two analytic approaches to test the impact of interinstitutional competition on demand deposit service charges, savings rates, rates on certificates of deposit, and new automobile loan rates. The first paralleled the test on consumer credit—variables were added to explanatory equations to reflect directly the number of nonbank financial intermediaries in the bank market. The second approach involved redefining concentration ratios or the Herfindahl Index to reflect the difference in the relative market powers of nonbank financial institutions. All depository institutions were treated as if they were full competitors of commercial banks. If they are, in fact, full competitors, explanatory equations using this approach should perform in a superior manner and explain price differences across markets.

Our sample consisted of five banking offices selected at random from each of sixty-nine SMSAs. In the sample SMSAs the Herfindahl Index ranged from .0465 to .4471, compared to a range of .0465 to .5759 for all SMSAs. There was also wide variation in bank size (less than $20 million in deposits to over $1 billion) and in market shares (less than 2 percent to over 75 percent).

EMPIRICAL RESULTS. A general regression model was used to analyze the determinants of prices within banking markets. Our analysis of the 1977 sample of interest rates on consumer credit indicated that the only measurable nonbank competition came from mutual savings banks. The 1973 results on loan rates are similar: loan rates are inversely related to the number of savings and loan associations in the bank's market, even though savings and loans generally do not offer consumer loans. They are not related to the numbers of mutual savings banks or credit unions. This is further evidence of market segmentation by commercial banks.

The impact of interinstitutional competition on savings deposit rates is not as hypothesized. A priori, greater numbers of competitors are expected to increase average savings rates, as it becomes more likely that banks will succumb to competitive pressure and pay the ceiling rates. Rates do increase with the number of credit unions, suggesting direct competition, but are inversely related to greater thrift activity. This is consistent with market segmentation in savings markets.[47] In markets with active thrift competition, given the Regulation Q differential, commercial banks do not even attempt to compete. They pay a lower rate, and the only advantage they can offer customers is convenience. In the markets for certificates of deposit, a similar relationship exists. In general, banks pay less for these certificates when confronted with active mutual savings banks. Again, this may reflect market sharing.

To summarize, our analyses provide some evidence of interinstitutional competition, but the competition is not strong. However, with regulatory barriers removed, as they were for credit unions in 1978 and for savings and loan institutions in 1980, markets are likely to become significantly more competitive.

NOTES

1. For an analysis of local banking market structure, see Arnold A. Heggestad and John J. Mingo, "The Competitive Condition of U.S. Banking Markets and the Impact of Structural Reform," *Journal of Finance* (June 1977).

2. E. Brigham and R.R. Pettit, "Effects of Structure on Performance," in *Study of the Savings and Loan Industry*, ed. I. Friend, vol. 3 (Washington, D.C.: Federal Home Loan Bank Board, 1969); D. D. Hester and J. C. Pierce, *Bank Management and Portfolio Behavior* (New Haven: Yale University Press, 1975).

3. Franklin R. Edwards, "Managerial Motives in Regulated Industries: Expense Preference Behavior in Banking," *Journal of Political Economy* (January–February 1977): 147–162.

4. Franklin R. Edwards and Arnold A. Heggestad, "Uncertainty, Market Structure, and Performance: The Galbraith-Caves Hypothesis and Managerial Motives in Banking," *The Quarterly Journal of Economics* 87 (August 1973): 455–473.

5. A. Santomero and R. Watson, "Determining an Optimal Capital Standard for the Banking Industry," *Journal of Finance* XXXII, no. 4 (September 1977): 1267–1282.

6. R. Clark, "The Soundness of Financial Intermediaries," *The Yale Law Journal* 86 (November 1976): 23–24.

7. W. F. Sharpe, "Bank Capital Adequacy, Deposit Insurance, and Security Values," Working Paper No. 209, National Bureau of Economic Research, 1977.

8. In a recent study Tucillo found differential subsidies to thrifts and banks, with commercial banks receiving the largest subsidy. See John Tucillo, "Taxation by Regulation: The Case of Financial Intermediaries," *Bell Journal of Economics* 8, no. 2 (1977).

9. Benton Gup, *Financial Intermediaries* (Boston: Houghton Mifflin, 1976).

10. John Mingo, "The Economic Impact of Deposit Rate Ceilings," in *Public Regulation of Financial Services, Costs and Benefits to Consumers*, eds. Heggestad and Mingo, Phase I Interim Report to the National Science Foundation (Cambridge, Mass.: Abt Associates Inc., 1976).

11. E. J. Kane, "Good Intentions and Unintended Evil: The Case Against Selective Credit Allocation," *Journal of Money, Credit, and Banking* 9 (February 1977): 55-69.

12. N. N. Bowsher, "Usury Laws: Harmful When Effective," Federal Reserve Bank of St. Louis, *Review* (August 1974): 16-23.

13. See George J. Benston, "Interest Payments on Demand Deposits and Bank Investment Behavior," *Journal of Political Economy* 72 (October 1964): 431-439; and Mingo, "Deposit Rate Ceilings."

14. Tucillo argues that the convenience advantage is worth .5 percent in interest in competing for savings deposits. See Tucillo, "Taxation by Regulation."

15. Hester and Pierce, *Bank Management*.

16. E. J. Kane, "Short-Changing the Small Saver: Federal Government Discrimination Against the Small Saver During the Vietnam War," *Journal of Money, Credit, and Banking* 2 (1970): 513-522.

17. S. Peltzman, "Entry into Commercial Banking," *Journal of Law and Economics* (1965): 163-177.

18. Douglas F. Greer, "Rate Ceilings, Market Structure, and the Supply of Finance Company Personal Loans," *Journal of Finance* 29 (December 1974): 1363-1382.

19. High fixed rates make the break-even amounts of loans very high.

20. M. S. Flannery, "Credit Unions as Consumer Lenders in the United States," Federal Reserve Bank of Boston, *New England Economic Review* (July-August 1974): 3-12.

21. For a thorough survey, see Kane, "Good Intentions."

22. Repurchase agreements are a procedure whereby banks buy and sell government bonds for depositors with accounts exceeding a negotiated minimum. Using this procedure, banks can offer large depositors interest payments on their demand balances.

23. For a discussion of nonprice competition, see Arnold A. Heggestad and John J. Mingo, "Prices, Nonprices and Concentration in Commercial Banking," *Journal of Money, Credit, and Banking* 8 (February 1976): 107-118.

24. The share of retailers in total credit outstanding is misleading, since much of the credit is ultimately sold to commercial banks or is financed by borrowing from commercial banks. For this reason and because they are not directly involved in the reform proposals, retailers are excluded from this discussion.

25. Douglas F. Greer, "Rate Ceilings and Loan Turndowns," *Journal of Finance* 30 (December 1975): 1376-1383.

26. See Paul F. Smith, "The Studies of Competition in Consumer Credit Markets," *Technical Studies*, Vol. VI, National Commission on Consumer Finance, 1973. Smith attributes the generally weak results to measurement error (p. 2).

27. The SMSA is used as an approximation of banking markets. A substantial portion of most banks' business is locally oriented. For an analysis of market definition in banking, see Ralph H. Gelder and G. Budzeika, "Banking Market Determination: The Case of Central Nassau County," Federal Reserve Bank of New York, *Monthly Review* (November 1970); and R. A. Eisenbeis, "A Study of Geographic Markets for Business Loans: The Results for Local Markets," in *Proceedings of a Conference on Bank Structure and Competition* (Chicago: Federal Reserve Bank of Chicago, 1970). Relevant case law is presented in *U.S. v. Philadelphia National Bank* 374 U.S. 321 (1967) and *U.S. v. Connecticut National Bank* 94 Ct. 2788 (1974).

28. R. A. Eisenbeis and N. B. Murphy, "Interest Rate Ceilings and Consumer Credit Rationing: A Multivariate Analysis of a Survey of Borrowers," *Southern Economic Journal* 41 (July 1974): 122.

29. Gregory E. Boczar, "Competition Between Banks and Finance Companies: A Cross-Section Study of Personal Loan Debtors," *Journal of Finance* 23 (March 1978): 255.

30. J. Vernon, "Competition for Savings Deposits: The Recent Experience," *The National Banking Review* 4 (December 1966): 181-182.

31. L.J. Spellman, "Competition for Savings Deposits: 1936-1966," *Journal of Financial and Quantitative Analysis* (November 1975).

32. Ibid.

33. L. White, "Price Regulation and Quality Rivalry: A Profit Maximizing Model," *Journal of Money, Credit, and Banking* VIII, no. 1 (February 1976): 97-106.

34. See Mingo, "Deposit Rate Ceilings."

35. Ralph C. Kimball, "Impacts of NOW Accounts and Thrift Institution Competition on Selected Small Commercial Banks in Massachusetts and New Hampshire, 1974-76," *New England Economic Review* (January-February 1977: 22-38.

36. This is not a simple matter; it involves unbundling a large number of services that traditionally have substituted for the payment of interest on demand deposits.

37. See Edward H. Chamberlin, *The Theory of Monopolistic Competition* (Cambridge, Mass.: Harvard University Press, 1933); and Joan Robinson, *The Economics of Imperfect Competition* (London: Macmillan, 1933).

38. If asked, the interviewer described himself as a thirty-two-year-old, married schoolteacher. The car was a 1978 Toyota with a purchase price of $3,869.

39. The selection procedure is described by Robert Shay and William Batko in "Credit Disclosure Legislation and Consumer Shopping Behavior," In *Public Regulation of Financial Services,* pp. 353–400.

40. There are at least three possible sources of error in obtaining rates in this manner. First, there may be a systematic relation between rates actually charged and the firms that refuse to divulge rates over the telephone. Second, some firms may not comply with the Truth in Lending Act, reporting rates in a form other than the average percentage rate. These may be the firms that typically charge the highest rates. They were deleted from the sample. Finally, firms may tend to quote lower rates over the telephone than those actually charged customers. Again, those that charge the highest rates are most likely to follow this practice.

41. For a thorough discussion of alternative measures, see F. M. Scherer, *Industrial Market Structure and Economic Performance* (Chicago: Rand McNally, 1970).

42. See Peter S. Rose and Donald R. Fraser, "The Relationships Between Stability and Change in Market Structure: An Analysis of Bank Prices," *Journal of Industrial Economics* 24 (June 1976): 251–266.

43. Edward S. Herman, "Conflicts of Interest in the Savings and Loan Industry," in *Study of the Savings and Loan Industry,* ed. I. Friend (Washington, D.C.: Federal Home Loan Bank Board, 1969).

44. R. A. Eisenbeis and A. D. McCall, "Some Effects of Affiliations of Mutual Savings Banks and Commercial Banks," *Journal of Finance* 27 (September 1972): 875–877.

45. The Herfindahl Index is the sum of the squared market shares of each firm on the market.

46. See Heggestad and Mingo, "Prices, Nonprices and Concentration"; and idem, "The Competitive Condition of U.S. Banking Markets."

47. These results are consistent with those reported earlier by Eisenbeis and McCall in "Some Effects of Affiliations."

SEVEN
Regulation, Structure, and Technological Change in the Consumer Financial Services Industry
Charles F. Haywood

Studies of the effects of regulation in electric power generation and distribution, communications, and air and surface transportation indicate that the pace and character of technological change in these industries have been affected by regulation. Little attention has been given to the effects of regulation on technological change in the financial services sector of the U.S. economy. Over the past thirty years, the production and distribution of financial services have been significantly affected by technological improvements in data processing, communications, transportation, and organization, as well as by innovations in financial services and instruments. At the same time, financial services, particularly consumer financial services, have increased. Now that the consumer financial services industry is undergoing radical change with the development and regulation of electronic funds transfer systems, a study of the effects of regulation on technological change in this industry is especially timely. The purpose of this chapter is to stimulate interest in further research on the subject by reporting on the incidence of computer technology among commercial banks. Examining data obtained from the 1975 National Operations and Automation Survey, conducted by the American Bankers Association, the analysis seeks to identify factors that may explain, for example, why 722 of the respondent banks offered credit cards and 896 did not. The analysis also examines data on such "computer-based services" as the incidence of cash-dispensing machines, automatic teller machines, automated services (for example, installment loan accounting), and automated check clearing.

Bank size was found to be the most influential factor affecting the incidence of computer-based services; that is, large banks are somewhat more likely than small banks to offer computer-based services.

Affiliation with a bank holding company was also found to be significantly associated with the incidence of computer-based services. The survey data, unfortunately, did not differentiate between one-bank and multibank holding companies. The most that can be said, therefore, is that banks owned by either one-bank holding companies or multibank holding companies are somewhat more likely to offer computer-based services than banks that are not owned by such companies.

Since the surveyed banks were identified by the state in which they were located, it was possible to test for the effects of state regulations governing the multioffice operation of commerical banks. To give dimension to the analysis of this type of regulation, the states were grouped into five categories: (1) states prohibiting branching and multibank holding companies; (2) states prohibiting branching but permitting multibank holding companies; (3) states permitting limited branching but prohibiting multibank holding companies; (4) states permitting limited branching and multibank holding companies; and (5) states permitting statewide branching. The likelihood that a bank would offer computer-based services was found to increase with the degree of liberality in state regulations governing multioffice banking; that is, banks in category 1 states were least likely to offer such services, while banks in category 5 states were most likely to do so.

The significant differences appeared to be as follows: The incidence of computer-based services in category 1 states was significantly lower than in category 2 states, suggesting a positive influence by multibank holding companies in unit banking states permitting this form of multioffice operation. Incidence in category 3 states was higher than in category 2 states but not significantly so. Limited branching without multibank holding companies thus showed about the same results as unit banking with multibank holding companies. Category 4 states were found to have a significantly higher incidence of computer-based services than category 3 states; that is, the incidence of limited branching with multibank holding companies was higher than the incidence of limited branching without multibank holding companies. Interestingly, the incidence of computer-based services in category 5 states—statewide branching—was the highest but was not significantly higher than the incidence in category 4 states. Limited branching with multibank holding companies thus appears to be about as favorable as statewide branching with respect to the diffusion of computer-based services among banks.

These results are affected by interaction among bank size, holding company affiliation, and state multioffice categories. Banks affiliated with holding companies tend to be larger than unaffiliated banks. Small banks are more numerous in states that prohibit branching than in states that permit limited branching, and are more numerous in limited branching states than in statewide branching states. The lower incidence of computer-based services in category 1 states reflects, in part, the lower incidence of such services among small banks. At the other extreme, the higher incidence in category 5 states reflects, in part, the high incidence of such services among large banks.

Several observations can be made as a result of trying to sort out the interaction among bank size, holding company affiliation, and state multioffice categories. First of all, bank size is clearly the most influential factor affecting the incidence of computer-based services. Holding company affiliation is less important than bank size but more important than state restrictions governing multioffice banking. However, when banks not affiliated with holding companies are grouped by size and analyzed by themselves, rather significant differences are found in the incidence of computer-based services among the state multioffice categories. Incidence increases with the degree of liberality of state multioffice regulation.

These findings suggest that state restrictions on multioffice banking have inhibited, both directly and indirectly, the diffusion of computer-based services among commercial banks. Restrictions on multioffice banking pose a barrier to the entry of new participants in local banking markets, and thereby tend to reduce competitive pressure for improvements in technology and expansion of services. By constraining bank size, such restrictions also work indirectly against technological improvements, which are more likely to be undertaken by large banks than by small banks. Thus, regulation directly affects technology by influencing competitive conditions and indirectly affects it by influencing banking structure (the relative size of market participants).

Technological change may also affect regulation and structure. Technological improvements may pose a need for changes in regulation, as electronic funds transfer technology is doing today. Changes in technology may also be conducive to changes in the relative size and/or organizational form of banks. The application of computer technology to banking, beginning in the late 1950s, led to predictions in the 1960s that the number of commerical banks would decline by at least several thousand. These predictions have not been realized, but the number of banking organizations declined after 1966 as the formation of multibank holding companies accelerated in certain states. To what extent did improvements in technology facilitate the expansion of multibank holding companies? Clearly, the main factor was relaxation of restrictions in certain states, as well as revisions in federal law, but regulatory change may have been prompted by technological improvements affecting the prospects of successful banking over more extensive geographic areas.

In studying the effects of regulation on technology in the financial services sector, one should recognize that the effects are not all in one direction. Regulation, structure, and technology interact, each exerting direct and indirect influences on the other. The regulation of commercial banking, though, has been very much oriented to the determination of banking structure. This orientation is evident in policies governing the chartering, branching, and merging of commerical banks. It is also reflected in policies governing the powers of commercial banks and in supervisory standards relevant to bank performance and soundness. Much the same is true, but in varying degree, of regulations concerning savings and loan associations, credit unions, mutual savings banks, and consumer finance companies. Hence, it can be said that regulation in the consumer financial services industry in general has had a strong structural orientation. Much of the effect of regulation on technology has apparently been indirect: regulation has affected structure, which in turn has affected the pace and character of technological change.

Although our findings suggest that state restrictions on multioffice banking have impeded the diffusion of computer-based services, this is not sufficient reason to argue for relaxation of such restrictions. Further analysis is needed to measure the effect of technology on concentrating banking resources in relevant market areas. If a high level of concentration is found to be unfavorable to the diffusion of computer-based services, it might be argued that the favorable effects of relaxing state restrictions could be offset by the higher concentration of resources that might result from more liberal regulation of multioffice banking.

It should also be noted that, despite the constraining influence of state multioffice restrictions, the diffusion of computer-based services has been relatively rapid. Based on its triennial surveys, the American Bankers Association has estimated that the proportion of banks using computers for one or more major functions increased from 16 percent in 1963 to 92 percent in 1977. In a period of about twenty years the industry went from experimentation in the application of computers to check processing to virtually industrywide adoption of computer processing.

The state multioffice categories used in this study provide only a broad measure of regulation. This approach was not only dictated by the availability of data but also was consistent with the structural orientation of regulation, as discussed above. Regulations imposed over the past decade, however, impinge more directly on the performance of financial institutions, particularly banks. This recent type of regulation may have different implications for technological change than past regulation, impinging somewhat more on structure than on the performance of individual banks. Also, regulation of electronic funds transfer systems may directly influence the development of this type of technology. Studies of other regulated industries indicate that the strongest effects of regulation on technology tend to occur where regulation impinges directly on the performance of individual units and their choice of technology. It can be demonstrated theoretically that such regulation tends to limit output below levels that would be attained in the absence of regulation. One of the costs of regulation may therefore be lower productivity. Quantification of this cost of regulation is difficult, and provides a challenging topic for research.

EIGHT
Public Regulation of Financial Services: The Truth in Lending Act

Robert P. Shay and
William K. Brandt

Introduction

The Truth in Lending (TIL) Act represents one of the first large-scale attempts by the federal government to mandate the disclosure of accurate cost information in a clear and consistent manner. The law was passed in the belief that consumers armed with information about credit costs would make better decisions regarding credit use.

This chapter examines the initial assumptions and the resultant effectiveness of TIL a decade after its implementation on July 1, 1969. At the present time, when alteration of TIL is being considered, it is pertinent to review what the research has uncovered concerning the use of information about credit costs and its relation to consumer decision making. In the following sections of this chapter we review the empirical research dealing with consumer awareness of, and sensitivity to, interest rates and finance charges, and we assess the effectiveness of TIL in light of its initial objectives, tracking the pattern of changes in consumer awareness and behavior from 1969 to the present. We also discuss the results of a national survey examining the links between consumer awareness and behavior.

Consumer Awareness of Credit Charges
Before Enactment of the Truth in Lending Act

Four empirical studies examined consumer awareness of rates and/or dollar charges for installment credit before enactment of TIL.[1] These early studies—two were local and two were national—provided the first clues to consumers' lack of knowledge of both rates of charge and dollar charges for credit.

The local studies were (1) an analysis by Due of the most recent installment purchase made by a random sample of 311 families in Champaign and Urbana, Illinois, during the first quarter of 1954;[2] and (2) a study by Hoskins covering rates of charge only for new and used car installment purchases, based on interviews with 105 purchasers in the San Francisco Bay area in the fourth quarter of 1957 and the first quarter of 1958.[3] Two-thirds of Due's sample knew neither the rate nor the dollar charges, while about 70 percent of Hoskins's respondents could not estimate rates of charge and the other 30 percent estimated rates that were less than half the rates actually paid. The Due study found that a higher proportion of families in the lower income classes than in the upper income classes knew the dollar carrying charges. The opposite was true of knowledge of rates of charge.[4]

In a 1959 national survey conducted by the Survey Research Center at the University of Michigan, respondents were asked to estimate the charges they thought they would pay to finance the purchase of a car on credit. (Interviewers converted responses into effective rates.) Thirty-nine percent did not know or gave vague answers. The remaining answers varied widely, but again, on balance, respondents underestimated rates of charge substantially.[5]

Juster and Shay, working at the National Bureau of Economic Research, tested both rate knowledge and rate sensitivity among respondents in a national sample of Consumers Union subscribers in May 1960. Compared to the general population, the sample was biased upward with respect to education, income, and propensity to shop. Even so, rate knowledge and sensitivity to differences in levels of charges were low. Comparison of mean *reported* rates with mean rates *calculated* from payment information given on installment purchase during the previous two years revealed the following:
1. Even though estimates of rate levels were poor, mean estimated rates fell with the size of the loan, suggesting that respondents

knew small installment purchases cost more to finance than large ones.

2. Only 6.6 percent of respondents reported rates which fell within 2.2 percentage points above and below rates calculated from payment details. If it were assumed that rate knowledge included those who reported add-on or discount rates (at about half effective rate levels), another 11.3 percent could be regarded as possessing some rate knowledge. Under both assumptions, however, 82.1 percent of the respondents did not meet the criteria for rate knowledge.

3. A large minority (28 percent) of respondents reported that the rate paid was 6 percent, irrespective of calculated rates, which ranged widely but mostly above that level. This reinforced the then-current view that consumers believed in the ''6 percent myth.''[6]

It was widely believed that consumers were insensitive to rates of charge but sensitive to the size of the monthly payment when formulating their demands for credit. Juster and Shay tested two hypotheses about consumer behavior, using a hypothetical question that specified alternative ways of financing the purchase of an automobile costing $1,500 after trade-in allowance. According to one hypothesis, borrowers were totally insensitive to interest rate differences other than their potential effect on monthly payments; according to the other, borrowers were sensitive to interest rates. Alternative finance plans with varying down payments, monthly payments, maturities, and finance rates (some disclosed, some not) were sent to sixteen groups selected randomly from the Consumers Union sample. Demand elasticities were computed with respect to finance rates (when disclosed and when not disclosed) and maturities. Demand elasticities predicted by the first (monthly payments) hypothesis were compared with those calculated from consumer responses to the question.

Calculated demand elasticities were low, suggesting little sensitivity to interest rates, but observed elasticities were more than double those that would have been predicted by the monthly payments hypothesis. Also, elasticities were considerably greater when finance rates were disclosed among alternatives than when they were not disclosed. However, this result should not be regarded as strong evidence that disclosure would add significantly to rate sensitivity, because the hypothetical question on the survey did not reflect a likely situation under a disclosure regulation. Nonetheless, Juster and Shay concluded that their results ". . .clearly indicate the necessity for qualification of the widely held view that consumer borrowing decisions are unresponsive to changes in finance rates, aside from their effect on monthly payments."[7]

After Enactment of the Truth in Lending Act

The Truth in Lending Act had three clear goals:[8]

1. To assist and encourage consumers to shop among credit sources.
2. To describe the terms of credit so that consumers can choose between (1) using liquid assets or credit to finance purchases, and (2) using credit or postponing consumption expenditures.
3. To help stabilize the economy by preventing overindebtedness and offering cyclical movements by deterring consumption during periods of prosperity, when interest rates are high, and encouraging consumption when economic activity and interest rates are low.

Although pockets of rate-sensitive consumers might be found in the borrowing public, rate knowledge and sensitivity to interest rates were considered to be low prior to enactment of the Truth in Lending Act. Thus, to accomplish its goals, TIL would have to raise consumer awareness of rates of charge. If, as a result, consumers were sensitive to rates, they would be expected to shop differently and to substitute liquid assets for credit in making expenditures or postpone expenditures. It was expected that such changes in consumer behavior would decrease the cyclical fluctuation of credit expenditures on purchases of durable goods and lower the proportion of overindebted households in the general population.

Several empirical studies tested the impact of TIL fifteen months after its passage,[9] and in one of these studies respondents were interviewed a second time nine months later.[10] The research focused primarily on consumer awareness of credit costs and shopping behavior, since changes in both were considered prerequisites to other aspects of the consumer's decision to incur expenditures and to pay for them on credit or in cash.

Shay and Schober conducted a study for the National Commission on Consumer Finance (NCCF) in which data from national samples collected by the Board of Governors of the Federal Reserve System just prior to TIL's effective date in mid-1969 were compared with data from a survey of other respondents fifteen months later.

Awareness gains in the interval between the two surveys varied widely according to education level, income, race, residence area (poverty versus nonpoverty area) and credit source (bank, finance company, credit union, retailer, other). The greatest awareness gains and the highest levels of awareness were found among nonblack respondents with higher educational levels and incomes who lived outside of poverty areas. Awareness gains were generally observable for all credit sources and all types of credit.

One interesting finding from the Shay-Schober study was that the highest levels of unawareness could be ranked according to various combinations of type of credit source, type of product, and characteristics of the borrower. Among the categories associated with high levels of unawareness were dealers in used cars, appliances, home improvements, and personal loans and, with respect to borrower characteristics, race, poverty area, and education or income.[11] A 1970 Federal Trade commission (FTC) survey of compliance by type of retailer indicated that used car dealers and jewelry stores were the poorest in terms of compliance with regulations while home improvement companies were highly varied in compliance.[12] This rough parallel between problem areas in awareness of annual percentage rates (APRs), ranked by Shay and Schober, and problem areas in compliance, noted by the FTC, suggests a possible link between the two: consumer awareness may not have improved because compliance with TIL was poor. Based upon these and other findings, the NCCF distinguished between the "general" market, where TIL gains in awareness might be considered effective, and the "high-risk" market, where the potential for disclosure is limited.[13]

To understand the high-risk market better, the NCCF sponsored a study by Durkin, who looked at the market for loans of $100 or less to low-income borrowers by "small loan companies" in Texas. A special statute permitted such loans to be made on an unsecured basis at rates ranging from 108.75 percent to 240 percent per annum.[14] Durkin's sample of 500 borrowers, all personally interviewed, was drawn from the lowest economic and social classes, and most borrowers belonged to one of the two largest minority groups—blacks and Mexican-Americans. The level of awareness of rates was very low, but the level of awareness of dollar finance charges was very high (64.3 percent); in fact, these respondents demonstrated greater awareness of charges (on closed-end installment contracts) than any of those previously surveyed. Not only were borrowers aware of the dollar cost of their loans, but a large proportion of the respondents (85 percent) felt that their loans were worth the cost. Significant predictors of awareness in this market were race (white), sex (male), income ($3,600–$5,900), and occupation (low-level production and service workers). Although Durkin's findings were based on a regional survey and therefore cannot be generalized to all low-income segments of the population, they confirm earlier findings from the Due study and add credence to the notion that awareness of finance charges is widespread among the lowest income and educational classes, at least with regard to very small loans.

In another study Mandell used Survey Research Center data to construct an index of accuracy for APR awareness, which he calculated based on auto credit buyers' answers to a hypothetical question about the cost of financing a car for twelve months. The answers were then related to actual rates, calculated from payment details supplied by the respondents.[15] The mean index of accuracy rose from .45 to .53 after enactment of TIL—a finding that was statistically significant and in line with the Shay-Schober findings. Mandell also found that the amount borrowed and total nonmortgage debt were related to APR awareness, as were age, income, and education.

A third major empirical study was conducted for the NCCF by Day and Brandt at the same time as the Shay-Schober study. Findings from the Day-Brandt study and a sequel NCCF study by Deutscher[16] coincided closely with the Shay-Schober results.

Day and Brandt asked respondents to specify the APR they would be likely to pay on a one-year retail installment loan for a $500 television set, with payments in equal monthly amounts. Education, sex (male), family status (family head over forty-five, with or without children), number of credit sources used in the past (more sources), and ratio of monthly payments to income (low ratios) were significantly related to rate awareness.[17] Respondents showed a strong tendency to overestimate the total costs, resulting in unusually high finance charge estimates. While 51 percent of the respondents estimated APRs with reasonable accuracy, only 20 percent accurately estimated dollar finance charges.

Day and Brandt developed a hypothesis that awareness of rates of charge could lead to confusion and overestimation of dollar finance charges if consumers, used to calculating finance charges by applying add-on and discount rates to the amount borrowed, applied the APR to the amount borrowed in order to estimate the finance charge. They concluded that many consumers "misunderstood the proper procedure for relating finance charges and interest rates for installment contracts. It is ironic that TIL's requirement to provide APR instead of the discount and add-on methods that were formerly used may have encouraged some of the current confusions."[18]

Deutscher, interviewing the same respondents nine months later, found that while APR estimates had improved, dollar finance charge estimates were less accurate.[19] This finding implies that improvements in knowledge of APRs were likely to be accompanied by decreases in knowledge of dollar finance charges. Reinterviewing the Day-Brandt respondents to determine whether or not gains in awareness of APRs were permanent, Deutscher found that further gains in awareness were muted by "forgetting," so that awareness gains were partially offset by awareness losses. While continued experience with credit reinforces people's knowledge of credit costs and tends to keep them aware of the general level of APR, experience with credit does not appear to play a significant role in the initial process of becoming aware of APRs. Demographic variables, particularly education and income, appear to be most important in this process.[20]

In addition to examining consumers' awareness of rates of charge and actual finance costs, the Day-Brandt study examines the background of credit decisions. The findings are an important precursor to the research reported in the rest of this chapter.[21] First, Day and Brandt found that credit-related decisions for a particular purchase were highly dependent on product-related questions, the consumer's attitude toward credit, and perceptions of the quality of services provided with credit.

Second, most consumers were methodical in their purchase decisions. For household or auto purchases of more than $100, 80 percent of the respondents had planned the purchase for several weeks or more, and 70 percent shopped several days or more before buying. An attempt to measure the number of credit sources consulted was not very successful. The results showed that 20 percent of credit users visited more than one type of credit source (23 percent for car purchases and 17 percent for household durables), but this result was probably biased downward because of deficiencies in the questionnaire. A second query sought to measure the extent of shopping for credit information before the purchase. Among the 246 credit buyers, only 27 percent indicated any kind of search for credit information of the following forms: talked with friends or relatives (12 percent); noticed a television, radio, or newspaper advertisement (7 percent); visited banks, credit unions, or loan companies (11 percent); read mailings from credit sources (5 percent).[22]

Third, consumer attitudes were found to reflect cautious approval of the use of credit. Three-fourths of all credit buyers did not have sufficient cash available to make a major purchase. Families with the greatest need for credit were those that had young children, earned low incomes, were already heavily indebted, and lacked savings or the capacity to save for large purchases. Credit-needy families did not behave much differently from families with available cash. Although they tended to search more widely among types of credit sources, they generally exhibited similar shopping behavior.

Fourth, most credit users did not find the credit-related decision difficult to make, and credit-related decisions were less significant than other aspects of the purchase decision.

With regard to the high-risk market for credit, Day and Brandt noted a sharp difference in the criteria used to make credit decisions. Seventy percent of low-income minority families listed low installment payments as very important, while only 38 percent of low-income whites and 32 percent of middle- and high-income whites listed that criterion as very important. Since easier terms are generally available through dealers than through direct loans, Day and Brandt found that low-income and minority buyers relied more heavily on dealer-arranged credit than on loans. The hypothesis that low-income consumers lacked mobility and were forced to shop at neighborhood stores was not true of the low-income classes in this California-based study, who were found to travel somewhat farther than others to make purchases.[23]

The multivariate analysis conducted by Day and Brandt revealed that race and income were highly significant in explaining perceptual differences in access to credit (difficulty in obtaining credit). Most of these California consumers were able to discriminate realistically among the general rates of charge for various types of credit. Respondents ranked finance companies as having above-average rates, while credit union and bank single-payment loans were ranked as below average. These differences in the ability to discriminate by credit source types were most closely associated with income (positive), credit experience (positive), and sex (male).

Finally, Day and Brandt found it paradoxical that, while over 80 percent of the respondents recognized that differences in credit costs justified shopping around, most buyers simplified the credit decision process by allowing the dealer to make the credit arrangements and allocating more of their own time and effort to decisions about the product purchased. Thus, Day and Brandt concluded:

> Until the credit-related decisions become a more important part of the overall decision process, there is little likelihood that major changes can be expected in consumer credit buying patterns. And since the finance charge represents only a part of the total purchase outlay there is little likelihood that credit shopping and comparison activities will assume greater importance in the future.[24]

Summary:the First Fifteen Months Under TIL

Empirical studies of the impact of TIL upon consumer knowledge of and sensitivity to rates of charge indicate that the goals of TIL were only partly fulfilled during the first fifteen months following its enactment. During that period, awareness of rates of charge expressed as annual percentage rates increased markedly during the first fifteen months of regulation, although the distribution of awareness levels among middle- and high-income groups was a source of concern to some proponents. However, given the fact that APRs were never generally quoted before TIL in non-mortgage consumer credit, it must be considered reasonable that such information would be absorbed and retained by those who had both the greatest capacity and incentive to utilize it. Yet the finding that rate awareness gains were accompanied by losses in finance charge awareness raises the question of whether the rate disclosure legislation would add to the confusion of lower income and/or minority groups, who are primarily aware of dollar finance charges rather than rates of charge.

There was little evidence that credit shopping was affected by TIL in the one study that looked into the question. However, without further information concerning the number of credit outlets visited, it could not be assumed that TIL had no effect upon shopping habits. There was only minor evidence that rate awareness was associated with a more extensive search for credit information or sources.

Given these findings and until further studies were made, it was difficult to believe that rate sensitivity of credit purchasers increased appreciably during the first fifteen months of TIL.

Changes in APR Awareness Levels, 1969–1977

It was not until the fall of 1977 that improvement in consumers' awareness and use of TIL disclosure was again the subject of major research. At that time, two large-scale surveys addressed these issues in some detail. The first, sponsored by the Board of Governors of the Federal Reserve System and conducted by the Survey Research Center of the University of Michigan, was analyzed by Thomas A. Durkin of Pennsylvania State University.[25] The survey consisted of lengthy personal interviews with a national sample of 2,563 households.

The second survey, conducted for the National Science Foundation by Abt Associates Inc. under the direction of Robert P. Shay and William K. Brandt of Columbia University, focused only on consumers who had purchased a major consumer durable, such as a car or household appliance, costing $200 or more within the twelve months preceding the interview. In addition to surveying a national probability sample of 813 households, the researchers interviewed two separate samples; one consisted of 54 female heads of households, and the other included 100 inner-city consumers (who qualified only if they were a minority, 62 years or older, female head of household, or earned under $10,000 a year as a household).[26] Inclusion of three different samples made it possible to study purchase decisions—and the role of credit in the decisions—in a rigorous manner and to focus as well on the particular problems of disadvantaged consumers and those protected by the Equal Credit Opportunity Act.

The remainder of this chapter reports primarily on the findings from the Shay-Brandt study. However, where appropriate, the results of the Durkin study and those of two studies sponsored by the Federal Reserve System in 1969 and 1970 are discussed as well.

Each of the early studies of TIL observed significant gains in APR awareness for all types of credit after the law was passed, but a majority of borrowers gave unrealistic estimates of rates and charges. It is possible to assess the changes in APR awareness levels for actual credit purchases using data from the three nationwide surveys sponsored by the Federal Reserve System in 1969, 1970, and 1977, since they are reasonably consistent in method and scope. Using Shay and Schober's definitions of awareness,[27] Table VIII-1 shows the dramatic gains in awareness from June 1969 (just before enactment of TIL) to September 1970 (fifteen months after enact-

TABLE VIII-1 Changes in Awareness of Annual Percentage Rates on
Actual Purchases, by Type of Credit Used, 1969–1977

	NUMBER OF CASES			LEVEL OF APR AWARENESS		
Type of Credit	1969	1970	1977	1969	1970	1977
All closed-end credit	5,248	4,021	1,092	14.5%	38.3%	54.5%
Retail revolving credit	5,183	4,478	1,305	35.2	55.5	64.7
Bank credit cards	2,587	1,782	921	26.6	63.4	71.3

*Source: Thomas Durkin and Gregory Elliehausen, The 1977 Consumer Credit Survey
(Washington, D.C.: Board of Governors of the Federal Reserve System, 1978), Table
2-1.*

ment) to September 1977. For all forms of closed-end indebtedness,
awareness increased from 14.5 to 54.5 percent among respondents
from 1969 to 1977; for retail revolving credit, the corresponding
figures are 35.2 and 64.7 percent, and for bank credit cards, 26.6
and 71.3 percent. Despite these impressive increases in awareness,
in 1977—more than eight years following enactment of TIL—almost
one-half of closed-end credit borrowers, one-third of retail revolving
account holders, and about 30 percent of bank card users were still
unable to provide reasonable APR estimates for their accounts.

Based on earlier predictions, are these levels of *un*awareness high
or low? Using a panel survey in 1970 and 1971, Deutscher forecast
a finite limit on the potential for awareness levels because of the
trade-offs between "learners" (unaware consumers who become
aware) and "forgetters" (aware consumers who become unaware).[28]
For closed-end credit, Deutscher predicted that awareness might
peak at about 67 percent in 1973, a level deemed acceptable for
legislation in the NCCF report.[29] By this standard, the 55 percent
awareness level observed in 1977 remains far short of the 1973 peak
level predicted by Deutscher.

The Shay-Brandt survey shows that awareness levels for actual
purchases are comparable to the figures reported in Table VIII-1,
even though the items in each category are specified somewhat differently (see Table VIII-2). For closed-end credit purchases of autos
and other expensive durable goods (over $1,000), reasonably ac-
curate APR estimates were provided by 55 percent of the borrowers.
This component of durable goods credit purchases matches the 54.5

percent figure for closed-end credit observed in the Durkin study.

For closed-end credit purchases of less expensive durable items, less than one-third of the respondents were reasonably aware of the APR in 1977. Previous studies have likewise observed lower levels of awareness on closed-end accounts for less expensive durable items. When bank credit cards and retail revolving accounts were used for such purchases, however, awareness levels were sharply higher: 65 percent in 1977 (Table VIII-2) and 64.7 to 71.3 percent (Table VIII-1). Since the consumer received a disclosure notice on every monthly statement, it is not surprising to observe higher levels of awareness on open-end accounts.

Not unlike earlier studies of APR awareness, the Durkin survey indicates that education, income, race, and the type of creditor and credit had a strong influence on awareness levels (see Table VIII-3). Gains in APR awareness were large among all classes of borrowers shown, and the impact of TIL disclosure was clearly not limited to well-educated and affluent whites. Awareness among blacks, for example, rose from 9 to 38 percent. Still, the gains have been markedly greater among some groups of consumers (awareness among whites, for example, rose from 15 to 56 percent) relative to others, and in some cases the disparities in APR awareness between groups of consumers have actually increased since passage of the Truth in Lending Act.

Links Between APR Awareness and Its Effect on Purchase Behavior

These dramatic increases in the overall levels of APR awareness suggest that TIL has achieved its initial goal, at least for certain segments of society. Knowledge of awareness levels alone, however, does not explain why certain segments become aware while others remain unaware, nor does it indicate whether being aware of interest rates influences purchase decisions and shopping behavior.

In the Shay-Brandt study, the links between gaining APR awareness and its effect on purchase behavior were addressed in four ways: (1) whether the disclosed information was noticed and, if noticed, whether it affected shopping behavior; (2) which groups were aware either of rates or finance charges or both; (3) what criteria were used in making a purchase decision; and (4) how consumer shopping behavior was affected by any of the above. The

TABLE VIII-2 Changes in Awareness of Annual Percentage Rates for
Actual Purchases, 1970 to 1977, National Sample

	AUTOS & HSHD >$1,000* NON- REVOLVING CREDIT		DURABLES ≤$1,000** NON- REVOLVING CREDIT		DURABLES ≤$1,000 REVOLV- ING CREDIT	
	1970	*1977*	*1970*	*1977*	*1970*	*1977*
Number of Cases	1,626	279	1,206	61	6,260	37
Aware	33%	55%	35%	31%	58%	65%
Unaware	39	22	24	38		19
Don't Know	28	23	41	31	42	16

*In 1970 household durable purchases greater than $500 in price were combined with autos.
**In 1970 this category included only furniture and appliances, in contrast to a wider array of
items purchased in 1977.
Source for 1970 data: R. Shay and M. Schober, "Consumer Awareness of Annual
Percentage Rates of Charge in Consumer Installment Credit," Technical Studies,
vol. 1, National Commission on Consumer Finance, 1972, Tables 1 and 2.

findings from the Shay-Brandt study are summarized here; a more
detailed report on the study appears in *The Costs and Benefits of Public
Regulation of Consumer Financial Services.*[30]

Notice and Use of Disclosed Information

The first step toward changing consumer aware-
ness of APRs is to require that the credit grantor provide APR information in a uniform and consistent manner. A compliance survey
of cash loan sources in November 1977, conducted by Batko for Abt
Associates Inc., indicates that well over 90 percent of the 1,080 institutions interviewed were in compliance with TIL with respect to
oral APR disclosure.[31]
    Whether information disclosed on the credit contract or monthly
statement constitutes actual notice which might lead to improved
APR awareness is another matter.[32] Tables VIII-1 and VIII-2 indicate higher awareness levels for revolving (open-end) accounts
than for closed-end credit. One possible explanation for the difference is the frequency of disclosure notices: for closed-end credit,
a singular disclosure is made at the contract signing, whereas for

open-end credit the APR must also be disclosed on each monthly statement. Bank cards are used more frequently than individual retail revolving accounts, and the receipt of monthly bank card statements increases the likelihood of APR notice and, in turn, APR awareness. Thus, the highest levels of APR awareness are found for items purchased with a bank credit card.

To investigate the association between respondents noticing APR information and awareness levels, the Shay-Brandt study asked a series of questions about notice and use of credit information. The questions were designed to determine whether or not TIL disclosure information had been noticed, and, if so, what was noticed and how the credit decision was affected by the information. Each credit purchaser was asked:

1. Did you notice any information on the credit agreement or the monthly statements which tells you anything about the cost of borrowing this money?
2. If so, did this information indicate the:
   a. Terms of credit; that is, interest rate and finance charges?
   b. Disclosure of penalties for late payment?
   c. Saleman's commissions?[33]
   d. Credit insurance charges?
3. Did the information affect your decision to use credit in any way?
4. If so, how did the information affect your decision?

In the national probability sample, 58.4 percent of credit purchasers claimed that they had noticed information about the cost of borrowing money (see Table VIII-4). Among those who noticed, virtually everyone reported observing the terms of credit; three-fourths, the late payment penalties; and two-thirds, the credit insurance charges. When asked whether the information affected their decision to use credit, only 5.3 percent of credit users responded affirmatively. Among credit users in the inner-city sample, fewer than one-third reported having noticed the information, and none indicated that the disclosed information had influenced the decison to use credit.

Another breakdown in Table VIII-4 considers the differences between credit users protected by the ECOA and those who were not protected. A protected household in the Shay-Brandt survey is defined as one that is headed by a single female or single male, a minority group member, a person sixty-two years or older, an im-

TABLE VIII-3 Changes in Awareness of Annual Percentage Rates by Item Purchased, Credit Outlet, and Selected Borrower Characteristics, 1969 and 1977.

	Level of APR Awareness—1969	Level of APR Awareness—1977
Type of Closed-End Credit		
New automobiles	18%	70%
Home improvement	15	67
Personal loans	20	55
Appliances and furniture	12	45
Used automobiles	7	38
Type of Creditor (Closed-End Credit)		
Credit unions	8	66
Finance companies	17	58
Banks	13	52
Retail dealers	9	42
Education		
Closed-end credit:		
Some college or more	18	65
High school	18	53
Some high school or less	9	41
Open-end, retail revolving credit:		
Some colleges or more	48	76
High school	32	61
Some high school or less	20	45
Open-end, bank credit card:		
Some college or more	39	80
High school	19	66
Some high school or less	16	52
Income		
Closed-end credit:		
$17,500 or more	18	64
$12,500–$17,499	16	57
$ 7,500–$12,499	15	49
Less than $7,500	6	32
Open-end, retail revolving credit:		
$17,500 or more	43	77
$12,500–$17,499	37	59
$ 7,500–$12,499	28	55
Less than $7,500	19	42

Open-end, bank credit card:

$17,500 or more	33	78
$12,500–$17,499	29	67
$ 7,500–$12,499	23	61
Less than $7,500	11	58

Race (Closed-End Credit)

Caucasian (non-Hispanic)	15	56
Black (non-Hispanic)	9	38
Hispanic, American Indian, Asian	18	57

Source: Thomas Durkin and Gregory Elliehausen, The 1977 Consumer Credit Survey *(Washington, D.C.: Board of Governors of the Federal Reserve System, 1978), Tables 2-2, 2-3, and 2-4.*

---

migrant, or a person receiving public welfare payments. Compared to unprotected respondents, those who were protected were somewhat less inclined to notice credit information, but among those who did notice, a higher proportion reported that their decision was affected by the information.

Considering the fact that less than 60 percent of credit users even remembered noticing the information and that only one in twenty claimed to use it in some way, the impact of TIL might seem meager. From another perspective, however, these results appear more positive. First, among consumers whose decisions were affected by the disclosed information, almost one-half indicated that it had helped them decide to use credit, and some noted that they simply felt more confident knowing the credit terms. It can be argued that even a small proportion of credit buyers who use the disclosed information to find a better deal will help to "police" the market in terms of encouraging competition among credit grantors.

A second reason for optimism is the strong association between noticing the information and APR awareness. Among those who had noticed the disclosed information, 61.7 percent provided a reasonably accurate estimate of the APR, whereas only 38.1 percent of those who had not noticed the disclosure could estimate the APR accurately. Although there is always a question of causal direction in a survey of this kind, it seems plausible to assume that information was noticed prior to awareness of the APR. This issue will be treated more fully later in this chapter.

TABLE VIII-4 Consumer Notice and Use of Credit Information Disclosed on Contracts and Monthly Statements, 1977

			COMBINED SAMPLE	
	National Sample	*Inner-City Sample*	*Unprotected Classes*	*Protected Classes* *
Number of Credit Purchasers	415	48	255	224
Credit Users Who: Notice information about cost of borrowing money	58.4%	31.3%**	58.8%	52.2%
If noticed, type of information				
Terms of credit-interest rates and charges	96.1	100.0	97.3	94.8
Late payment penalties	77.0	84.6	77.0	76.7
Credit insurance charges (installment and cash loan users only)	65.4	44.4	67.5	58.8
Credit decision affected in some way by information	5.3	0	3.8	6.1

*Respondents who were members of one or more of the following groups were classified as protected: unmarried male or female head of household, minority race, head 62 years of age or older, head receives public assistance or is an immigrant to U.S.
**Differences in group means significant at $p < .05$.

Awareness of APRs

Some early critics of Truth in Lending contended that the impact of wider dissemination of rates would be minimal because credit buyers were already well aware of the costs of credit and could appraise the impact of its use on their budget. The validity of this criticism may depend on the meaning of being "well aware" of the costs of credit, but the results from the Shay-Brandt survey indicate that fewer consumers were able to make realistic estimates of the dollar cost of borrowing, than they were about interest rates. Furthermore, consumers did not appear to understand the basic relationship between annual percentage rates and dollar charges.

Tables VIII-5 reports that for an actual credit purchase within the preceding year, 31 percent of respondents who bought an auto or other expensive household durable ($1,000 or more) were able to estimate a finance charge which, when converted to an APR, fell within the reasonably accurate range (8 to 25 percent). For less expensive household items, only 11 percent fell within a comparable range of 12 to 25 percent.[34] "Don't know" responses were appreciably higher for autos and higher priced durables (42 percent) than for less expensive durables (26 percent). The tendency to overestimate finance charges was substantially greater for purchases of less expensive durable goods than for autos and higher priced items.[35]

Comparison of these results with the Day-Brandt findings must be regarded as tentative, but it suggests that awareness levels for finance charges have not improved since 1970;[36] if anything, consumer awareness might have declined. The reasons for this lack of improvement are explored below.

Evaluating the effectiveness of TIL disclosure based on APR awareness levels for actual credit purchases has two limitations. First, the conclusions are applicable only to the subsample of recent credit buyers, thereby precluding any generalization to the total population. Second, respondents may be unaware of the APR because they did not participate in the financial aspects of the purchase decision.

To minimize these problems, the entire sample in the Shay-Brandt study was asked the following hypothetical questions:

> Suppose the price of a color TV were $500, and you were to pay the dealer in 12 monthly installments. How much would you pay *in total* for the color TV after *one year—including* interest and finance charges? (IF RESPONDENT DOESN'T KNOW, PROBE WITH: Well, just give me your best estimate.)

> About what percent of interest per year do you think this would be? (IF RESPONDENT DOESN'T KNOW, PROBE WITH: Well, just give me your best estimate.)

The first question elicited the respondent's estimate of dollar

TABLE VIII-5 Estimates of Finance Charges Converted to Annual
Percentage Rates, National Sample, 1977

APR Estimate	AUTOS AND OTHER EXPENSIVE DURABLES ($1,000)		LESS EXPENSIVE HOUSE- HOLD DURABLES ($1,000)	
	Number	Percent	Number	Percent
0-7.9	56(34)*	23.0(15.4)*		
0-11.9			26(4)*	40.6(9.3)*
8-25.0	75	30.9(33.9)		
12-25.0			7	10.8(16.3)
Over 25.0	11	4.5(5.0)	15	23.1(34.9)
Don't know	101	41.6(45.7)	17	26.1(39.5)
Subtotal	243(221)	100.0(100.0)	65(43)	100.0(100.0)
Cannot estimate	45		62	
Total	288		127	

*Figures in parentheses represent cases and percentages when responses of zero finance charges are
excluded.

finance charges and the second, an estimate of the APR for the
hypothetical purchase. The accuracy range used for reported interest
rates was identical to that used for actual credit purchases costing
$1,000 or less: estimates of 12 to 25 percent were classed as
reasonably accurate. Using this range, 52.9 percent of the APR
estimates were reasonably accurate; that is, over one-half of the
respondents in the national sample, whether or not they had actually
made a recent credit purchase, were generally aware of interest
rates.

Awareness of Finance Charges

In contrast to the generally high level of APR
awareness, respondents tended to overestimate finance charges.
Only 14.3 percent of the respondents provided a dollar estimate that
fell within a reasonably accurate range when calculated to an
equivalent APR. Less than 1 percent gave an estimate that might be
considered too low, whereas nearly two-thirds offered estimates
above the probable charges for retail installment credit.

The inaccuracy of estimated finance charges raises important
questions about how APR information is being used by consumers.

If respondents actually believed that finance charges were as high as their estimates indicated, it would appear that TIL disclosure of APRs and finance charges might discourage the use of credit, rather than encourage it.

Before drawing any conclusions from the data, we need to examine possible misunderstandings of APR and finance charge information. In their 1970 study Day and Brandt also observed that many respondents apparently did not understand the basic relationship between APRs and finance charges for installment credit.[37] Whereas before TIL was enacted consumers were accustomed to multiplying the 9 percent add-on rate by the amount borrowed to approximate the finance charge, the current disclosure of approximately 18 percent APR requires that they multiply the APR by about one-half of the amount borrowed to provide a reasonable approximation of the finance charges.[38] For example, the finance charge for an 18 percent APR for a $500 one-year contract is approximately $45 ($250 x 18 percent), not $90 ($500 x 18 percent). The average finance charge estimated in this study, $99.75, represents an average APR of 36 percent—twice the 18 percent rate prevalent in most states—suggesting that many respondents might have been familiar with interest rates but did not understand the conversion of rates to finance charges.

A cross-tabulation of the APR and finance charges (converted to an APR) in Table VIII-6 shows that only 4.3 percent of respondents in the national sample apparently understood the basic relationship between APR and equivalent finance charges. Even here the range of acceptable answers is sufficiently broad that some guesses are probably included in this range. If we divide the estimate of finance charges by two, however, nearly one-fifth of the responses fall within the acceptable range of correspondence between APR and finance charges. Allowing for some guessing in this instance also, the results suggest that a large number of respondents might have attempted to calculate the finance charges from an estimated interest rate by multiplying the APR times the $500 purchase price.

The comparison of differences in awareness levels of California respondents between 1970 and 1977 reinforces the plausibility of the Day-Brandt-Deutscher hypothesis that consumer gains in awareness of APR levels will be accompanied by losses in awareness of finance charges.[39] With disclosure of both required by law, it is not clear why this is the case. In view of the greater attention paid to APR in advertising direct loan rates and publicity by consumer advocates, it

TABLE VIII-6 Correspondence Between Estimates of Annual Percentage Rates and Finance Charges for a Hypothetical Television Purchase, National Sample, 1977 (N = 813)

	Actual Estimate of Finance Charge	Actual Estimate of Finance Charge Divided by Two
General correspondence between estimates of APR and finance charge*	4.3%	18.8%
APR estimated higher than finance charge	.1	16.8
Finance charge estimated	47.2	16.0
Could not provide one or both estimates	48.4	48.4

*APR estimates were converted to an equivalent finance charge. Both estimates were then grouped in categories within a range of $20.

seems likely that dollar cost disclosure has been underemphasized, except for mortgages.

Graduated Awareness Levels for APRs and Finance Charges

When measuring awareness levels for APRs or finance charges, the question arises as to whether particular consumer characteristics are related to awareness of interest rates and charges. Table VIII-7 shows graduated levels of awareness of rates and charges by respondent characteristics. Responses are assigned to one of five levels of awareness, according to the respondent's estimates of APR and finance charges for the hypothetical television purchase.[40] These five levels are:

1. Estimates that fall within the acceptable ranges for both the APR and finance charges.
2. Estimates that are reasonable (12 to 25 percent) for the APR but are incorrect or "don't know" for finance charges.
3. Estimates that are reasonable ($40 to $50) for finance charges but incorrect or "don't know" for the APR.

TABLE VIII-7 Levels of Awareness of Rates and Charges for a Hypothetical Television Purchase, by Respondent Characteristics, Combined Sample, 1977*
(N = 967)

Characteristic	1 Accurate APR and Finance Charges	2 Accurate APR but Incorrect or Don't Know Finance Charges	3 Accurate Finance Charges but Incorrect or Don't Know APR	4 Incorrect APR and Finance Charges	5 Don't Know APR and Finance Charges
Number of cases	67	418	67	230	185
Percent of cases	7%	43%	7%	24%	19%
Household income ($000)	$ 21.2	$ 19.5	$ 18.0	$ 15.6	$ 15.7**
Nonmortgage debt	$2,109.0	$2,053.0	$2,154.0	$1,767.0	$1,332.0**
Number of loans in 3 years	2.7	2.2	2.1	1.8	1.3**
Education (years of schooling)	14.5	13.9	13.0	12.7	12.2**
Age	42.8	40.1	38.9	40.1	46.8***
Sex (female)	39%	55%	58%	68%	72%
Race (minority)	12%	12%	23%	22%	19%
Marital status (unmarried)	40%	27%	32%	42%	41%

*All figures represent means of respondent characteristics within the five categories of knowledge.
**Differences between groups using one-way analysis of variance, significant at p ∨ .01.

4. Estimates that fall outside the acceptable ranges for both the APR and finance charges.
5. "Don't know" responses for both the APR and finance charges.

The columns in Table VIII-7 are arranged in order of decreasing awareness, with column 1 representing awareness of APR and finance charges, columns 2 and 3, partial awareness, and columns 4 and 5, unawareness. The second row of the table indicates that 7 percent of the respondents in the combined sample were aware of both the APR and finance charges, 50 percent were aware of either rates or charges (columns 2 and 3), and 43 percent were unaware of both (columns 4 and 5).

The data in this table suggest a strong association between awareness and the respondent's demographic and socioeconomic characteristics. For income, loan experience, education, and sex, there is almost a straight-line relationship between the characteristic and the five levels of awareness. In each instance higher income, more years of schooling, and greater loan experience are associated with better understanding of rates and charges.

It is noteworthy that column 3, knowledge of finance charges but incorrect or "don't know" responses for the APR, showed the highest means for debt level and minorities and the lowest means for age. One could hypothesize that these groups (minorities, young families, and those with high debt levels) have the greatest need or desire for credit, but limited income forces them to pay close attention to the out-of-pocket dollar charges of a credit transaction.[41]

Among the five categories, it is apparent that the means shown in column 1 differ significantly on most dimensions from those in columns 2 and 3. Between the latter two categories (columns 2 and 3), however, the differences are relatively minor, except for race and education. Again, respondents who were aware of interest rate levels but not finance charges tended to be well educated, affluent, and not from a minority, in comparison to respondents aware of finance charges but not the APR. Between columns 4 and 5, the differences were also relatively minor, except for age—older respondents were less inclined to provide any estimate of rates or charges.

Having viewed the relationship between awareness and consumer characteristics, considered one at a time, we can now consider the influence of relationships among the characteristics. For example, what is the relationship between education and awareness, after differences in race, age, and income have been taken into account? This question is best answered by multiple regression analysis—in this instance to identify the characteristics associated with APR awareness for a hypothetical television purchase.[42] As noted earlier, the respondent was considered to be aware (a value of one) if his or her estimate fell within a range of 12 to 25 percent and was considered unaware (a value of zero) if the answer was "don't know" or outside the range specified.

The characteristics chosen to explain differences in awareness levels are grouped into four classes:

1. Socioeconomic characteristics indicating the household's financial or demographic status and not protected by the provisions of ECOA: income, education, total level of nonmortgage debt.
2. Demographic characteristics protected by ECOA: sex, marital status, race.
3. Whether or not the respondent noticed information about credit rates and charges on the contract or monthly statements.
4. Market conditions measuring creditor compliance with TIL disclosure regulations and the degree of market concentration by major types of depository cash-lending institutions within an SMSA.[43]

Because the question about noticing the credit information applied only to credit purchasers, the data analyzed do not include responses from buyers who paid cash for their items.[44] The characteristics and other elements related to APR awareness do not differ appreciably, however, between cash and credit buyers.

The results of this analysis are almost identical to those observed by Day and Brandt in 1970,[45] with education and sex showing the strongest correlation with APR awareness: respondents who were either male and/or better educated showed greater awareness of interest rates. Respondents who had never married displayed less awareness of rate levels, but those who were widowed, separated, or divorced were indistinguishable from married respondents, after other differences were taken into account. Part of the difference for single respondents may be attributed to the fact that a few young respondents, although over eighteen and involved in making the purchase decision, were still living at home and perhaps were less experienced with credit transactions. Minorities also indicated less awareness, when other characteristics were taken into account, but the effect was not as strong as those already noted. No other characteristic (such as income, family size, age, debt level, employment stability, or receipt of public assistance), whether protected by ECOA or not, showed any linkage with APR awareness.

Two other conditions *were* related to awareness levels, however: (1) respondents in market areas where credit institutions demonstrated greater compliance with TIL regulations showed higher levels of awareness,[46] and (2) those who noticed the disclosure information on credit contracts and statements had much higher awareness levels. Although cause and effect between noticing information and awareness cannot be distinguished by this study, it seems plausible to assume that noticing information, at least over time and with accumulated experience, leads to awareness.[47] As we noted earlier, for revolving credit plans, where the opportunity to notice information is typically more frequent and regular, relative to closed-end credit, awareness levels are higher.

Thus, in addition to the finding that education, sex, and marital status continue to have a definite and predictable bearing on APR awareness, the study offers evidence for the first time that TIL disclosure also plays an important role, which over time appears to improve consumer awareness of interest rates.[48]

Important Criteria in the Credit Decision

It has frequently been suggested that credit source decisions, especially by low-income minorities, are based on credit availability (where they can get credit) and obtaining the lowest monthly payment. Advocates of TIL might argue, however, that with increased awareness of APRs and finance charges, the interest rate itself or the dollar cost of credit will become more salient in choosing a credit source or deciding whether to use credit.

The Shay-Brandt survey included two questions designed to ascertain the relative importance of various criteria in the credit decision. Each credit purchaser was asked:

> In choosing a way to finance the (ITEM PURCHASED), which of the following features was most important to you? Would you say it was the:
> amount of credit granted,
> rate of interest charges,
> size of the down payment,
> size of the monthly payment, or
> total finance charges?[49]
> Which feature was second most important?

Table VIII-8 reports that credit users in the national sample ranked monthly payment size as the most important criterion,

TABLE VIII-8 Decision Criteria Considered by Credit Users in Financing a Credit Purchase, National Sample, 1977
(N = 375)

Decision Criterion*	Most Important	1st or 2nd in Importance
Size of monthly payment	34.9%	61.4%
Rate of interest charge	31.5	53.1
Amount of credit granted	14.1	23.1
Total of finance charges	10.1	35.2
Size of down payment	6.7	22.4
Other	2.7	4.8

*Respondents were asked the following question:
  In choosing a way to finance the [ITEM PURCHASED], which of the following features
  was most important to you? Would you say it was the:
  amount of credit granted,
  rate of interest charges,
  size of the down payment,
  size of the monthly payment, or
  total finance charges?
  Which feature was second most important?
  The sequence of the criteria was chosen randomly.

followed closely by the rate of interest charged. Nearly one-third of the sample indicated that the interest rate was the most important feature, and over half noted that it was either first or second in importance. Although the majority of respondents considered total finance charges much less important than the first two criteria, 10.1 percent of the respondents believed that this was the most important feature and 35.2 percent ranked it first or second in importance.

The study had postulated that a consumer's decision criteria are influenced by his or her awareness of interest rates and charges. Consumers who are more knowledgeable about credit costs are expected to rank these criteria higher when considering the financing components of a major purchase.

The findings in Table VIII-9 confirm this hypothesis: the APR awareness levels for those who considered interest rates and finance charges important were significantly above the levels for those who ranked these criteria as unimportant. To illustrate, 56.8 percent of the respondents who ranked the interest rate charged as the first or second most important criterion provided reasonably accurate APR estimates, compared with 46 percent of those who did not rank interest rates as important. In contrast, respondents who considered

TABLE VIII-9 Association Between APR Awareness and Decision Criteria Considered in Financing a Hypothetical Television Purchase, Combined Sample, 1977

Decision Criterion	RESPONDENTS PROVIDING REASONABLY ACCURATE APR ESTIMATES IF DECISION CRITERION WAS:	
	1st or 2nd in Importance	Unimportant
Interest rate charged	56.8	46.0*
Amount of finance charges	58.9	47.4*
Size of monthly payment	45.7	56.9*
Size of down payment	39.4	53.7*
Amount of credit granted	53.6	50.1

*Differences between proportions significant at p < .05.

the size of the down payment or monthly payment more important showed significantly lower levels of APR awareness.

Again, it is not possible to separate cause and effect in these relationships, but for the first time we have observed a positive association between APR awareness and the relevant decision criteria—the interest rate charged and amount of finance charges.[50]

The next question raised by these findings is whether APR awareness is still important in "determining" the decision criteria if we take other characteristics into account. In their 1970 study, Day and Brandt observed, for example, that the consumer's race and income level had a definite bearing on the importance of various criteria, namely, that low-income minorities showed a strong preference for low monthly payments, low down payments, and long maturities (which typically permitted lower monthly payments).[51] The respondent characteristics most closely associated with each decision criterion were analyzed in this study also to determine whether particular characteristics of consumers, including being aware or unaware of APRs, appear to influence the use of the interest rate charged or the size of monthly payment as criteria in the credit decision process.

For respondents who felt that the interest rate charged was important, credit was most commonly used to purchase a car or other expensive household durable. Higher income respondents and those who were employed three years or longer with the same organization were also concerned about interest rates. Awareness of the APR was positively associated as well, but the relationship was weaker than expected, given the results reported in Table VIII-9.

Awareness of APRs exhibited the strongest association of all variables explaining respondents' concern with total finance charges: APR-aware respondents were most inclined to consider the finance charges criterion important.[52] Respondents with long tenure on the job (three years or more) and minorities were more concerned with finance charges, whereas women and higher income households were less concerned, relative to other groups.

For the other three criteria, the results are less than dramatic but are generally consistent with what might be expected. Characteristics that were positively associated with the interest rate and finance charges criteria were either unassociated or negatively associated with the other criteria (size of monthly payment, down payment, and credit granted). Of particular interest are the associations with APR awareness—positive for the interest rate and finance charges criteria and negative for the size of down payment and monthly payment criteria. This suggests that APR awareness might have enhanced consumer sensitivity to interest rate and finance charges and dampened concern for size of monthly payment (and down payment), as early TIL proponents had contended. Again, the direction of causality is unclear, but awareness can be viewed as one possible precursor of changes in the criteria used to make credit decisions, a hypothesis supported by the evidence in this study.

Shopping Behavior Incidental to Credit Purchase

Having traced the positive effects of noticing disclosed information on APR awareness and the impact of awareness on credit decision criteria, we can now consider the influence of these criteria on shopping behavior. Shopping can take many forms prior to a major purchase: visits to retail stores or dealers; visits to cash-lending outlets; telephone requests for information; perusal of catalogs, mailings, ads, and consumer periodicals (such as *Consumer Reports*); and recommendations from friends.

Although our primary interest is in the link between credit decision criteria and credit shopping, determining a direct relationship is difficult. A potential credit buyer who visits a store customarily investigates the cost of the item and credit terms during the same visit, as they are joint products offered by the seller in virtually all instances. Visits are made to more than one store to compare alternative goods and/or credit arrangements. Since the credit feature of the sale is intertwined with the purchase at the store location, distinguishing between the two forms of shopping is generally impossible.

Nevertheless, it is feasible to measure the extent of shopping for each type of activity. Table VIII-10 indicates that respondents in the national sample visited an average of 3.49 retailers and .94 cash loan sources before making a credit purchase. A comparison of these results with those for inner-city respondents shows a dramatic difference in activity, with the latter group shopping significantly less. If we combine the samples and compare respondents who are protected by ECOA guidelines with those who are not protected, the differences are even sharper, particularly for retailer shopping: 3.73 retailers were visited by unprotected shoppers, 3.01 by those who were protected.

These comparisons suggest that while all groups shopped to some extent, lower income and ECOA-protected consumers (who, theoretically at least, have the most to gain from additional shopping) chose or were forced to limit their shopping. The characteristics associated with shopping at retailers or cash-lending outlets are noted below.

CREDIT DECISION CRITERIA AND SHOPPING ACTIVITIES.   Before exploring the influence of personal characteristics on shopping behavior, it is important to examine the intervening effects of credit decision criteria on actual shopping. The expectation of TIL advocates and a hypothesis used in this study is that consumers who rank interest rates and finance charges high in their decision priorities will also shop more than other consumers.

The results shown in Table VIII-11 generally confirm this hypothesis. For each relationship, the proportions of respondents who ranked the credit cost criteria as first or second in importance were higher among those respondents who shopped widely. For example, among credit users who visited no cash loan outlets, only 31 percent considered the interest rate charged an important consideration. Among those who visited two or more sources, however, 58 percent considered this criterion important. As might be expected, concern over interest rates was not associated with extensive retailer

TABLE VIII-10 Average Number of Visits to Stores and Cash Loan Sources by Credit Purchasers, 1977

			COMBINED SAMPLE	
Shopping Activity	*National Sample*	*Inner-City Sample*	*Unprotected Classes*	*Protected Classes*
Number of credit purchasers	415	48	263	230
Visits to retailers	3.49	3.03	3.73	3.01*
Visits to cash loan sources	.94	.79	.97	.90

*Differences in group means significant at p < .05.

TABLE VIII-11 Association Between Credit Decision Criteria and Credit Shopping, Combined Sample, 1977

	RESPONDENTS WHO CONSIDERED DECISION CRITERION 1ST OR 2ND IN IMPORTANCE	
Shopping Activity	*Interest Rate Charges*	*Total Finance Charges*
Visits to retailers * (N = 422)		
1 or 2	42.9%	23.8%**
3 or 4	47.8	29.7
5 or more	44.7	43.9
Visits to cash loan outlets (N = 489)		
0	31.0**	23.4**
1	50.9	31.7
2 or more	58.0	35.8

*Purchases not made from retailers excluded from analysis.
**Chi-squared differences between categories significant at p < .05.

shopping. These respondents apparently realized that retail rates are relatively homogeneous and shopping for better rates therefore requires visits to cash loan sources.

INFLUENCES ON SHOPPING ACTIVITIES.   To expand the analysis beyond the decision criteria, multiple regression was used to examine the influence of the following four sets of variables on the two shopping measures (visits to retailers and to cash loan outlets):
1. Conditions surrounding the purchase decision, such as type of item purchased, amount borrowed, and prior experience at the retail outlet or lending institution.
2. Important criteria related to the credit decision—the singular or combined importance of interest rates charged and the amount of finance charges.[53]
3. Socioeconomic characteristics not protected by ECOA: income, education, family size, and level of nonmortgage debt.
4. Characteristics protected by ECOA: sex, marital status, and race.

Prior retailer experience and concern about the amount of finance charges were the principal influences on retailer shopping. Prior purchase experience at the store or dealer was associated with fewer visits, but sensitivity to finance charges spurred shopping activity. In this case, the average respondent who was concerned about finance charges but not interest rates visited one more retail outlet than the respondent concerned about other aspects of credit terms (taking into account differences in other characteristics). The results also show that larger families visited more retailers (perhaps reflecting the budgetary constraints often imposed by having several children) and that senior citizens and recipients of public welfare visited fewer retailers.

The findings for visits to cash loan outlets are much stronger than those for retailer shopping because of one variable, the type of item purchased. Purchasers of cars and other expensive household durables visited one more cash loan outlet, on average, than those who bought less expensive items. This makes sense in that consumers typically rely more heavily on retailer plans or revolving accounts for less expensive purchases.

Respondents with higher incomes shopped at significantly fewer cash loan outlets. In this instance, income may represent a surrogate for the value of time, implying that the marginal benefits of additional shopping are less than the costs in terms of incremental time and effort expended.

We also find that respondents with more nonmortgage debt visited more cash loan outlets than those with less debt. This might indicate that some purchasers had already borrowed to the limit of their credit worthiness at lower cost sources and were now being forced to find other (high cost) outlets, or that budgetary constraints forced them to seek savings by shopping widely.

Sensitivity to finance charges but not to interest rates showed a strong positive association with credit shopping. Concern about interest rates but not finance charges also correlated positively (though not as strongly) with the dependent measure; however, respondents who considered both credit cost criteria important behaved no differently from those who found other criteria to be important.[54]

Although the latter finding may appear curious, the other results suggest that sensitivity to one of the credit cost criteria was sufficient to spur shopping among cash loan outlets. (It should be noted that less than 10 percent of the sample was sensitive to both the interest rate charged and the amount of finance charges.) The finding that shopping activities are more strongly associated with concern about finance charges than with interest rate sensitivity (when other factors are taken into account) indicates that budgetary considerations may still be more real in the minds of consumers than a fraction represented by an APR.

Summary: Truth in Lending After Eight Years

The Truth in Lending Act was predicated on two assumptions: (1) consumers were not knowledgeable about APRs and finance charges, and (2) the availability of such information would lead to more informed credit decisions by facilitating the identification and comparison of credit terms. Underlying these broad assumptions were specific questions regarding the types of people who were knowledgeable, their sources of information, and their willingness or ability to use the information.

Eight years after enactment of TIL, consumer awareness of APRs continued to show dramatic improvement in all segments of society. Depending on the type of credit being considered, between one-half and three-fourths of consumers possessed at least a general awareness of the APR being charged. Notice of the disclosed information on credit contracts and monthly statements was linked to awareness of APRs, suggesting that TIL disclosure was working.

Despite these widespread gains, the level of APR awareness among less advantaged consumers was still far below the level of awareness among other groups, and in percentage terms the gap appeared to be widening. Women, minorities, unmarried and widowed consumers with less credit experience and particularly those with less education remained significantly less aware of APRs than consumers without these attributes.

Furthermore, growing awareness of interest rates was not accompanied by corresponding changes in knowledge of finance charges. Awareness levels for finance charges appeared to have declined since 1970. Considering the marked changes in APR awareness, this finding reinforces the conclusion reached in 1970 by Day and Brandt that awareness of APRs weakens awareness of finance charges, because consumers use APR information to compute finance charges incorrectly.

Unlike the 1970 Day-Brandt study, which found little or no linkage between awareness levels and actual shopping behavior, after eight years of TIL disclosure there was some evidence that awareness of interest rates and finance charges does, in fact, stimulate shopping for credit. Empirical support for the model tested linked awareness of rates and charges with financial decision criteria related to the choice and use of credit. Thus, consumers who were aware of APRs were also more concerned about the rate of interest charged and amount of finance charges; that is, they were more sensitive to credit costs. These concerns led to more extensive shopping at retailers and cash loan sources prior to the final credit purchase. In addition, interest rate awareness was directly linked to more shopping for cash loans to finance the purchase of automobiles and expensive durable goods. Credit-related decisions are known to be only one subset of the broader decision process involved in the purchase of durable goods, and credit costs only one element of this subset; thus, encountering significant empirical support for this model of credit-shopping behavior is encouraging.

To conclude that TIL has achieved its objectives after eight years would be a vast overstatement. Awareness levels have risen and shopping behavior shows signs of change, but problems persist—problems that until solved will limit the usefulness of TIL to the less advantaged in our society. But on the other hand, we have found that groups already regard finance charges as an important criterion in the credit decision. Furthermore, respondents who are aware of finance charge levels and not the APR shop more than respondents who are unaware of both, as well as consumers aware of APRs alone. This finding suggests that the less privileged have a reasonable basis of concern for credit costs and that they might be receptive to special counseling in credit use.

Policy Proposals: Implications for Change

Because TIL alone can do little to alter actual behavior in the marketplace, most of the suggestions for change presented here focus on the need to discover ways to (1) increase the likelihood that the disclosed information will be noticed and understood, and (2) reach those segments of society that have not benefited from TIL even in terms of increased awareness.

Simplified Disclosure Notice

Unlike APR awareness, whether or not a credit user notices the disclosed credit information is not strongly linked with any particular personal characteristic. This finding should make it easier to increase the proportion of consumers who notice the disclosure, since a simpler array of information should lead to more effective notice across the board. A proposal currently being reviewed by Congress is intended to alleviate much of the misunderstanding, confusion, and disinterest attending the current disclosure notices.

We would add two recommendations to those changes in TIL now under consideration. First, require borrowers to initial the disclosure section of the credit contract containing the "Annual Percentage Rate (APR)" and "Finance Charge." Second, require that the APR and finance charges be included on payment forms or coupon booklets in closed-end credit arrangements.

The first recommendation is intended to reach groups still unaware of APRs and finance charges on the theory that a person is more apt to notice a number when he or she initials the section that contains the relevant information. The second recommendation would increase the frequency of notice given to consumers signing closed-end credit agreements. The consumer who regularly uses a revolving credit plan receives a monthly notice containing the APR and finance charge, whereas the only written notice for a closed-end plan is typically included in the original credit agreement. A procedure could be designed which specifies the original APR and finance charges on the monthly payment forms used in closed-end credit transactions. With more frequent notice of the APR and finance charges, consumers would be reminded of the cost of the credit established in the original credit agreement.

Consumer Education

To increase both the awareness and use of the APR and finance charges in credit decision making, we recommend that an educational booklet explaining how TIL information can be used by consumers be distributed to customers signing agreements to finance purchases. The booklet should also warn consumers that retailers advertising "free credit" or "easy credit terms" may be selling inferior goods or using high markups to hide finance charges. The booklets need not be distributed everywhere. Instead, distribution could be pinpointed to inner-city areas and/or to types of credit transactions where awareness of APRs is low, for example, used auto, appliance, and furniture purchases.

For inner-city residents, providing booklets may not be enough. Since education levels are more frequently low among these consumers, and the high-risk credit market rate ceilings are subject to evasion by some creditors,[55] we suggest a two-pronged approach. First, stricter enforcement of TIL is recommended. Second, since inner-city residents possess an abundance of characteristics associated with low awareness levels, we urge implementation of special educational programs in these areas.

Special educational programs for consumers can be carried out most effectively by consumer organizations at the grass roots level. Federal, state, and local authorites can supply literature, but unless the lessons contained in the educational programs are disseminated widely to the appropriate groups, they will be of little use. Clearly, organizations with constituencies that would benefit from further implementation would be the logical sponsors. Such organizations include the Consumer Federation of America, AFL-CIO, National Urban League, Parents Without Partners, Inc., National Organization for Women, Public Interest Research Groups, Consumers Union, National Foundation for Consumer Credit, and Legal Aid.

In addition to educational literature, a range of activities should be planned and executed by organizations concerned with the welfare of consumers. Such activities could include magazine articles in diverse publications ranging from *Family Circle* to *Consumer Reports*; public service radio commercials pinpointed to inner-city areas; and meetings of tenant groups, church organizations, and local chapters of national consumer organizations. Local and state government could contribute to these meetings, but to be effective, they should be instigated by the local organizations that serve the particular constituencies in need of consumer education.

To accomplish longer-run goals, consumer organizations should advocate effective treatment of installment credit mathematics in junior high and high school mathematics texts. In adult education courses dealing with budgeting, shopping, and consumer economics, the use of TIL disclosure information should be integrated with family financial management, rather than simply describing the law's provisions, as is frequently the case at present.

NOTES

1. For a more detailed review of these and other studies discussed in this section, see Wallace P. Mors, *Consumer Credit Finance Charges: Rate Information and Quotation* (New York: National Bureau of Economic Research, 1965), chapter 5.
2. J.M. Due, "Consumer Knowledge of Installment Credit Charges," *Journal of Marketing* (October 1955): 164.
3. Lois S. Hoskins, "Interest Rates Paid for Automobile Credit by San Franciso Bay Area Families," Master's thesis, 1958.
4. Mors, *Consumer Credit Finance Charges,* pp. 80–82.
5. Ibid., pp. 83–84.
6. F. Thomas Juster and Robert Shay, *Consumer Sensitivity to Finance Rates: An Empirical and Analytical Investigation,* Occasional Paper 88 (New York: National Bureau of Economic Research), pp. 55–61.
7. Ibid. Juster and Shay hypothesized that the universe in the monthly payments model would be composed solely of "rationed" consumers, whose preferred debt levels are greater than those available from their primary (lowest cost) credit source. The second model, called the marginal borrowing cost model, included rationed and "unrationed" consumers, the latter being those whose preferred debt level and actual debt level (available from the primary credit source) are the same. For rationed consumers, preferred debt levels are higher than actual debt, and the monthly payment size represents the price of credit. The interest rate is the price of credit for unrationed consumers. The empirical bases for classifying consumers in these categories were three in

number: (1) marital status-income (fewer years married and lower income = rationed, others = unrationed; (2) liquid asset holdings (less than $2,000 = rationed, $2,000 or more = unrationed; (3) attitude toward credit (intend to use credit in the future = rationed, do not intend = unrationed).

8. National Commission on Consumer Finance, *Consumer Credit in the United States* (Washington, D.C.: U.S. Government Printing Office, December 1972), pp. 173–174.
9. See Board of Governors of the Federal Reserve System, *57th and 58th Annual Reports* (Washington, D.C.: 1970, 1971); and the following studies published in *Technical Studies* (Washington, D.C.: National Commission on Consumer Finance, 1973): George S. Day and William K. Brandt, "A Study of Consumer Credit Decisions" (vol. I); Thomas A. Durkin, "A High Rate Market for Consumer Loans" (vol. II); T. Deutscher, "Credit Legislation Two Years Out" (vol. I); Robert P. Shay and Milton W. Schober, "Consumer Awareness of Annual Percentage Rates of Charge in Consumer Installment Loans: Before and After Truth-in-Lending Became Effective" (vol. I).
10. Deutscher, "Credit Legislation Two Years Out."
11. See *Consumer Credit in the U.S.*, p. 178; or Shay and Schober, "Consumer Awareness," p. 16.
12. "Report of the Federal Trade Commission on Surveys of Creditor Compliance With the Truth-In-Lending Act," 2nd draft, mimeograph, April, 1971, p. 3.
13. *Consumer Credit in the U.S.*, pp.176–179.
14. Durkin, "A High Rate Market," Table 1, p. 11, and Table 5, p. 17.
15. Lewis Mandell, "Consumer Perception of Incurred Interest Rates" *Journal of Finance* (December 1971): 1145–1146.
16. National Commission on Consumer Finance, *Technical Studies*. The sample is described at length in Robert Shay, "Antidiscrimination Laws in Consumer Credit Markets," in *Public Regulation of Financial Services: Costs and Benefits to Consumers*, eds. A. Heggestad and J. Mingo, Phase I Interim Report to the National Science Foundation (Cambridge, Mass.: Abt Associates Inc., 1977), p. 329.
17. Ibid., p. 54. Characteristics in parentheses are those positively related to awareness.
18. Ibid., p. 56–57.
19. Deutscher, *Technical Studies*, p. 21.
20. Ibid., pp. 33–34.
21. These findings are reported in Day and Brandt, "Consumer Credit Decisions," chapter 7.
22. Ibid., p. 67.
23. See David Caplovitz, *The Poor Pay More: Consumer Practices of Low Income Families* (New York: Free Press, 1967).

24. Day and Brandt, "Consumer Credit Decisions," p. 103.
25. Thomas A. Durkin and Gregory G. Elliehausen, *The 1977 Consumer Credit Survey* (Washington, D.C.: Board of Governors of the Federal Reserve System, 1978).
26. In the analysis which follows, national sample is used to refer to data from the national probability sample, inner-city sample refers to the 100 interviews with inner-city respondents, and combined sample refers to the entire group of 967 households.
27. Shay and Schober, "Consumer Awareness," p. 5.
28. Deutscher, "Credit Legislation Two Years Out," p. 23.
29. National Commission on Consumer Finance, *Consumer Credit in the U.S.*, p. 180.
30. Arnold A. Heggestad and John J. Mingo, eds. *The Costs and Benefits of Public Regulation of Consumer Financial Services*, Final Report to the National Science Foundation (Cambridge, Mass.: Abt Associates Inc., 1978).
31. William Batko, "Compliance with the Truth-In-Lending Act," in *The Costs and Benefits*, pp. 275–291.
32. Oral disclosure of the APR is only one aspect of the disclosure requirement. For closed-end credit, the disclosure notice must be given to the applicant before the credit contract is signed. Legally this requirement can be met by incorporating the mandated information into the credit agreement. For revolving accounts, the APR is disclosed on each monthly statement, as well as on the application.
33. The question concerning saleman's commissions was included to detect the possibility of "yea-saying," a bias that occurs when respondents believe that an affirmative answer is probably the correct one and will make them appear more intelligent in the eyes of the interviewer. Of the credit buyers who reported having noticed information about credit charges, 8 percent indicated having seen salesman's commissions on the contract or statement. To the degree that these represent a "yea-saying" bias, it is possible that the responses for terms of credit, late payment penalties, and credit insurance charges in Table VIII-4 are overstated by up to 8 percent.
34. Virtually no financing plans for small purchases are available at APRs below 12 percent.
35. Because a large number of respondents reported zero estimates for finance charges on revolving credit plans, some of which may have been correct if they paid within thirty days, the figures shown in parentheses in Table VIII-5 accentuate the disparity between the two groups of purchases showing a greater tendency to overestimate finance charges for less expensive items.
36. Day and Brandt, "Consumer Credit Decisions," p. 59.
37. Ibid., p. 56.

38. A simplified conversion procedure is being used merely to illustrate the basic relationship between APR and finance charges for installment contracts.

39. Comparing the Day-Brandt survey of 461 California respondents in 1970 with the current survey, which included 105 California respondents, shows that the proportion who provided a reasonably accurate estimate of finance charges dropped from 21.8 percent in 1970 to 8.6 percent in 1977. During the period the proportion of reasonably accurate APR estimates rose from 51.5 to 69.5 percent.

40. A corresponding evaluation for actual credit purchases was less successful because of complications in determining a "reasonable" APR or finance charges given the purchase of multiple items, use of revolving accounts, and greater incidence of refusal to answer.

41. For earlier supporting evidence, See Due, "Consumer Knowledge"; and Juster and Shay, *Consumer Sensitivity.*

42. Attempts to identify characteristics associated with awareness of finance charges was generally unsuccessful. This suggests either that the measure of awareness was inappropriate or that awareness was not systematically linked with the socioeconomic variables included in the model.

43. These include commercial banks, savings banks, savings and loan associations, and credit unions. Concentration ratios were supplied by A. Heggestad. See Chapter Six, "An Evaluation of Interinstitutional Competition for Consumer Financial Services."

44. When cash buyers were analyzed using the same variables, except for the notice-of-credit-information variable, education and sex showed the strongest correlation with APR awareness.

45. Day and Brandt, "Consumer Credit Decisions," p. 54.

46. See Batko, "Compliance with the Truth-In-Lending Act," for an explanation and results of the TIL compliance study.

47. The question can be asked as to whether the consumers who notice information are also those who tend to be more aware of interest rates. If so, notice and awareness might be associated but not in a causal way. Analyses to identify who notices information showed that education was the only personal characteristic even modestly related to notice of information. This suggests that, except for a slight effect from education, notice of information occurs randomly throughout the population. This finding strengthens our argument that notice is an independent event that generally precedes, although through repeated experiences, awareness of interest rates.

48. See George Parker and Robert Shay, "Some Factors Affecting Awareness of Annual Percentage Rates on Consumer Installment Credit Transactions," *Journal of Finance* 29 (March 1974): 217–225; Mandell, "Consumer Perceptions"; Day and Brandt, "Consumer

Credit Decisions,"Durkin,"High Rate Market," and the Shay-Brandt study in Heggestad and Mingo, *The Costs and Benefits.*

49. The sequence of asking the questions was assigned randomly for each respondent.

50. Correlations between awareness of finance charges for a hypothetical purchase and decision criteria were generally much weaker than those between APR awareness and decision criteria. The 14 percent of respondents who were aware of finance charges were less distinguishable in many ways than those who were aware of APRs. In part this might reflect the fact that many of those who provided reasonable estimates did so by guessing.

51. Day and Brandt, "Consumer Credit Decisions," p. 78.

52. A multiple regression analysis was also conducted using awareness of finance charges instead of APR awareness. As noted above, the results were generally less striking and consistent, compared with the APR awareness variable.

53. Because some respondents felt that both interest rates and finance charges were important, it was necessary to create four values in order to avoid double counting: respondents who considered interest rate and finance charges first or second in importance (value = 1); interest rate but not finance charges (value = 10); finance charges but not interest rate (value = 01); and neither interest rate nor finance charges (value = 00). The fourth category served as the base value from which to interpret the other coefficients.

54. A significant positive association was found between APR awareness and shopping at cash loan outlets for autos and household durables costing over $1,000. No relationship was observed for less expensive household durables.

55. See Federal Trade Commission, *Economic Report on Installment Credit and Retail Sales Practices of District of Columbia Retailers* (Washington, D.C.: U.S. Government Printing Office, 1968), p. 14.

NINE
Public Regulation of Financial Services: The Equal Credit Opportunity Act

Robert P. Shay,
William K. Brandt, and
Donald E. Sexton, Jr.

Introduction

The Equal Credit Opportunity Act (ECOA) is
both a consumer protection statute and a civil rights statute, sharing
a heritage with the Equal Employment Opportunity Act,[1] as well as
the Consumer Credit Protection Act of 1968,[2] to which it is attached
as Title VII. Although partly a consumer protection measure, the
ECOA is primarily an antidiscrimination statute.[3] Its requirements
for disclosing the reasons for adverse action on a credit application
are consistent with the disclosure requirements of the Truth in
Lending Act; however, inclusion of the "effects test" as a criterion
for determining whether a procedure used to screen applicants is
discriminatory is drawn directly from Supreme Court decisions on
employment discrimination.

ECOA defines credit discrimination as occurring when a creditor
treats one applicant less favorably than other applicants on any of
the bases prohibited by the statute: sex, marital status, race, color,
religion, national origin, age, receipt of income from public
assistance programs, and good faith exercise of rights under the
Consumer Credit Protection Act of 1968 (which includes, among

other titles, Truth in Lending, Fair Credit Billing, Fair Credit Reporting, and Consumer Leasing Acts). The specific constraints of the ECOA, enacted in 1974[4] and amended in 1976,[5] prevent discrimination based on any of the following characteristics:[6]

sex,

marital status,

race and color,

national origin,

public assistance income,

good faith exercise of consumer credit rights.

The ECOA definition of discrimination and the analytical framework for its application offer an opportunity to test a theory of discrimination in credit granting under the assumption of competition. Furthermore, recent analyses of the modern corporation and greater recognition of the transactions costs of acquiring accurate information (to correct misinformation) offer more leeway for discrimination by acknowledging that (1) firms may seek other objectives along with profits; (2) individuals within organizations may seek to satisfy their own preferences by discriminating, despite the firm's objectives; or (3) firms and/or individuals within them may seek to maximize expected profits by narrowing credit opportunities for the protected classes because they believe them to be less qualified and less able to repay their debts than other debtors, all other factors being equal.[7] Thus, there are plausible grounds for expecting discrimination to exist in consumer credit, whether intended or not.

With respect to the first two types of behavior, hereafter called intended discrimination, corporations may seek to cultivate an image to attract particular segments of the population as their clientele, and a strategy may be designed to discourage others (in the protected classes) from patronizing their offices. Corporate managers or officers may also seek to establish their own office image, independent of the corporation's general policies. Finally, employees may initiate or carry out discriminatory policies on their own volition, perhaps in direct contradiction to corporate policies.

The question also arises as to whether consumers in protected classes search for alternative opportunities if they encounter discriminatory treatment, either real or perceived. When a person is rejected as a credit applicant, the reason given, if any, is rarely attributed to the applicant's association with any of the protected classes.[8] If these applicants fail to seek credit from alternative sources, the discriminatory effect of a single rejection will be greater among the protected class applicants.

The research efforts described below deal with three types of possible discrimination against credit applicants from protected classes: (1) that which may occur when managers wish to forego profits in order to pursue discriminatory practices; (2) that which may occur because most managers believe it is profitable; and (3) that which may occur when the protected classes are less informed, shop less, or otherwise exhibit demand characteristics that mitigate against their chances of finding alternative sources of credit. In the following sections we discuss various aspects of discrimination from the consumer's perspective and investigate the likelihood of discrimination if two large creditors had used empirically derived credit systems before ECOA was enacted.

Our research efforts focus on three questions:

1. Did consumers reporting discriminatory treatment in 1977 perceive that credit was more difficult to obtain and if so, were they denied credit more often than others, or did they obtain less nonmortgage debt than others after differences in socioeconomic characteristics related to credit worthiness were taken into account?

2. Did consumers in classes protected by ECOA perceive that credit was more difficult to obtain, were they denied credit more frequently than others, or did they obtain less nonmortgage debt than others after socioeconomic characteristics related to credit worthiness were taken into account?

3. Did preregulation samples drawn from the accounts of a large national retailer or a large finance company indicate that discrimination existed, and would empirically derived, statistically sound credit-scoring systems have discriminated against consumers protected by ECOA on the bases of sex, marital status, and age?

The ECOA Legislation: Scope and Intent

Since Congress has already accepted the proposition that credit discrimination exists and has legislated against it, it is appropriate to review the intent and coverage of the statutes before attempting to assess their impact on the credit market.

Congress left the definition of discrimination to the Board of Governors of the Federal Reserve System, which was empowered to promulgate regulations to implement the law. In Sec. 202.4 of Regulation B the relevant provision reads: "A creditor shall not discriminate against an applicant on a prohibited basis regarding any aspect of a credit transaction."[9] Sec. 202.2(n) states, "Discriminate against an applicant means to treat an applicant less favorably than other applicants."

The ECOA law is in part a civil rights law, because its principal provision deals with a ban on discrimination.[10] This aspect of the law has particular relevance to the questions investigated here. The consumer protection aspect of the law (that is, the requirement that all credit applicants be notified of actions taken and the reasons for unfavorable action) are relevant only as they apply to actions taken by creditors to deal with the protected classes under ECOA.

The most controversial segment of the ECOA is the so-called effects test, a judicial doctrine originated in *Griggs v. Duke Power Company*,[11] brought under Title VII of the Civil Rights Act of 1964. The U.S. Supreme Court's decision prohibits not only discrimination based upon policies motivated by discriminatory intent, but also practices that have the effect of discriminating against the protected classes, irrespective of the motive or intent of the employer. According to a footnote to the legislative history of the act, Congress intended that an "effects test," such as that developed in application of equal employment opportunity law, be applicable in determining whether a creditor's judgment of credit worthiness is or is not discriminatory.[12] In addition to citing *Griggs v. Duke Power Company*, the footnote cites *Albermarle Paper Company v. Moody* and two congressional reports to bear out its contention.[13]

Regulation B does not fully define an effects test because the courts have not yet fully dealt with the application of the effects test to areas not closely related to employment discrimination. However, there are signs emanating from *General Electric v. Gilbert* that the Supreme Court may modify its effects test in the future.[14] Noting this possibility, a recent *Federal Reserve Bulletin* article prepared by the Division of Consumer Affairs of the Board of Governors of the Federal Reserve System offers a three-step analysis of possible future court applications of the effects test when dealing with credit cases: In step 1, the plaintiff would attempt to show that, although consideration of a particular credit standard—homeownership, for instance—does not appear to discriminate on the basis of sex, reliance on this standard of credit worthiness results in rejection of credit applications by women, who are members of a class

protected by the law, and that such rejections occur at a
significantly higher rate than rejections of applications by men.
Such a showing would present a prima facie case of illegal
discrimination by the creditor.

In step 2, to rebut the plaintiff's prima facie case, the creditor would
have to show that this credit standard is customarily applied to
all applicants and that the standard has a manifest relationship
to credit worthiness.

The plaintiff then would have the option of going to step 3, in which
she would attempt to prove that an alternative credit standard
that would have a lesser adverse impact on women does exist
and that the alternative would serve the creditor's legitimate
business interests at least as well as the criterion of homeownership. If the plaintiff made such a showing, the creditor—to
prevail—would have to demonstrate that the alternative practice
would not have a lesser adverse impact or that it would not
serve the creditor's interests at least as well as the consideration
of homeownership.[15]

The application of the effects test to credit-granting policies raises
some fundamental questions about procedures now in use by
creditors, and, in addition, incorporates unintended discrimination,
as well as intended discrimination, into the law. During the past two
decades, the larger creditors have turned away from judgmental
systems of evaluating credit applicants to empirically derived systems
of predicting the probability of an applicant defaulting on a credit
application. These systems allocate points according to a weighting
scheme based upon the past performance of credit applicants, using
generally accepted statistical techniques for sampling and validation.
Such systems, on their face, would appear to be lacking in any
discriminatory intent, but they may result in effects that would present a prima facie case of illegal discrimination. To deal with such a
contingency, Regulation B contains an absolute prohibition against
considering a person's sex, race, religion, or other attributes, except
age, in the credit-granting decision. Thus, credit-scoring systems
cannot use these attributes even if past experience indicates that they
are the best predictors of credit worthiness. In the case of age, if a
credit-scoring system has met the regulation's test of being
demonstrably sound and empirically derived, Section 701(b)(3) of
the amended act permits age to be considered, but, whenever the
applicant is 62 years or older, forbids the assignment of a point
value that is less than that allotted to any other age group.

The law's prohibition on considering characteristics attributable solely to the classes protected under ECOA does not automatically assure that persons falling within those classes will fare better under empirically derived credit-scoring systems. In fact, some research has shown that the protected classes fare *less* well when the prohibited characteristics score *more* favorably relative to the remainder of the population,[16] or when the prohibited characteristics are replaced by other characteristics that militate more strongly against applicants in the protected classes. Furthermore, any decline in the efficiency of the scoring system would bring higher collection costs and losses and thus would result in higher rates of charge or lower credit availability to credit users generally.[17] The fact that Regulation B does not propose guidelines for creditors to comply with the effects test portends greater dependence upon the courts, with consequently increased legal expenses, before creditors can find out exactly how they may grant credit—whether they choose to use "demonstrably and statistically sound, empirically derived scoring systems"[18] or a "judgmental system of evaluating applicants."[19]

Perceptions of Credit Discrimination and Reported Behavior of Durable Good Purchasers
Perceptions of Credit Discrimination

In the past the question of credit discrimination against particular groups of customers has been investigated largely through anecdotal evidence. During the fall of 1977, two large-scale surveys addressed this issue in some detail. The first was the Durkin survey, sponsored by the Board of Governors of the Federal Reserve System and conducted by the Survey Research Center of the University of Michigan.[20] The survey consisted of lengthy personal interviews with a national sample of 2,563 households. The second survey was conducted for the National Science Foundation by Abt Associates Inc., under the direction of Robert P. Shay and William K. Brandt.[21]

The Shay-Brandt study differs from the Durkin study in two important ways. First, it considered only consumers who had purchased a major consumer durable, such as a car or household appliance costing $200 or more, within the twelve months preceding the interview. Second, in addition to a national probability sample of 813 households, the Shay-Brandt study included interviews with a separate sample of 54 female heads of households and with another

TABLE IX-1 Perceptions of Credit Discrimination, National and
Combined Samples, 1977*

Perceived	NATIONAL SAMPLE		COMBINED SAMPLE	
Discrimination	Number	Percent	Number	Percent
Yes	87	11.8	109	12.6
Might have been	3	0.4	5	0.6
Subtotal	90	12.2	114	13.2
No	646	87.8	754	86.8
Total**	736	100.0	868	100.0

*The national sample of households was designed to be representative of metropolitan area
residents in the United States. The combined sample consisted of the national sample plus 54
households headed by single, divorced, separated, or widowed women plus 100 respondents from
four metropolitan areas who qualified if they satisfied any of the following criteria: 62 years of
age or older; nonwhite; household income under $10,000; unmarried, if female. For further in-
formation about the sample design, see Arnold A. Heggestad and John J. Mingo, The Costs
and Benefits of Public Regulation of Consumer Financial Services, Final Report to the
National Science Foundation (Cambridge, Mass: Abt Associates Inc., 1978), pp. 167–182.
**The total excludes 71 respondents in the national sample and 91 in the combined sample who
claimed that they did not seek credit during the prescribed period.

sample of 100 inner-city consumers who qualified if they satisfied
any of these criteria: minority, 62 years or older, female head of
household, or household earnings under $10,000 a year.[22]

The following discussion relies primarily on the findings from the
survey conducted by Shay and Brandt. This investigation of consumers' perceptions was undertaken two years after ECOA was first
implemented to prohibit discrimination based on sex and marital
status in October 1975. Only six months had elapsed since the
amendments to the regulation were passed (in March 1977) prohibiting the other bases of discrimination.

To gain some measure of consumer perceptions about credit
discrimination, each respondent was asked: "Whenever you tried to
get credit in the past two years or so, do you think you were treated
less favorably than others in getting the credit because of your age,
sex, marital status, race, or nationality?" Twelve percent of the
respondents in the national and combined sample said they believed
they had been treated less favorably than others, and about another
.5 percent said that they might have been (see Table IX-1). Since a
respondent's perception of discriminatory treatment cannot be
regarded as proof of discriminatory practices, the responses indicate
that about one out of every eight credit purchasers perceived that he

TABLE IX-2 Reason for Perceived Credit Discrimination, National and Combined Samples, 1977

Reason Reported	NATIONAL SAMPLE		COMBINED SAMPLE	
	Number	Percent	Number	Percent
Age*	20	25.3	25	23.8
Sex	19	24.1	25	23.8
Marital status	11	13.9	21	20.0
Race	3	3.8	4	3.8
Nationality	1	1.3	1	1.0
Other	25	31.6	29	27.6
Total**	79	100.0	105	100.0

*In this table and those that follow, 23 respondents who were less than 62 years of age and who reported age as the only kind of discrimination encountered were eliminated from the combined sample (21 from the national sample). Respondents under 62 years of age who reported age and some other form of discrimination remained in the sample. The reason is that, although respondents of all ages are covered by the law, its use is permitted in empirically derived scoring systems and only persons 62 or over are protected under the regulation.

**Due to multiple responses, total frequency is in excess of the number of purchasers perceiving discrimination.

or she had received less favorable treatment than others were thought to receive when applying for credit in at least one instance during the past two years.

Respondents who perceived discrimination were asked, "What do you think affected the way you were treated?" and, if an answer was given, "Anything else?" Age, sex, and marital status were most commonly cited as reasons for discrimination; race and nationality were reported by relatively few respondents (see Table IX-2). Reasons other than the six cited in the question accounted for about 36 percent of the responses, suggesting that respondents view discrimination more broadly than the law's coverage.

Another breakdown, reported in Table IX-3, considers the differences in perceived discrimination between respondents in classes intended to be protected by the ECOA and those in unprotected classes. A "protected" household is defined as one that is headed by a single female or single male, a minority group member, a person sixty-two years or older, an immigrant, or a person receiving public welfare payments. Approximately 14 percent of the protected class respondents perceived discrimination in obtaining credit, compared

TABLE IX-3 Perceptions of and Reasons for Credit Discrimination, Protected and Unprotected Households, Combined Sample, 1977

| | PROTECTED CLASSES* | | UNPROTECTED CLASSES | |
	Number	Percent	Number	Percent
Number of Respondents	417		428	
Perceived Discrimination ("Yes" or "Might have been")	60	14.4	31	7.2
Reason Reported				
Age	15	20.5	10	31.3
Sex	16	21.9	9	28.1
Marital status	20	27.4	1	3.1
Race	3	4.1	1	3.1
Nationality	1	1.4	0	0
Other	18	24.7	11	34.4
Total**	73	100.0	32	100.0

*A protected class household is defined as one that is headed by a single female or single male, a minority group member, a person 62 years or older, an immigrant, or a person receiving public welfare payments.
**Total includes more than one kind of discrimination reported by some respondents.

with 7 percent of unprotected respondents. Except for marital status, which was cited as the basis of perceived discrimination by a much larger proportion of protected class households, we find no important differences between the two groups in terms of the type of discrimination reported.

Although ECOA proponents can cite the law's effectiveness in achieving the moderate levels of perceived discrimination reported, the question that remained was whether or not reported levels would have been substantially higher prior to passage of the ECOA. This question applies more directly to discrimination based on sex and marital status than to the other bases for credit discrimination prohibited by an amendment enacted in March 1977. The survey question, asked in the fall of 1977, applied to instances of credit discrimination in the previous two years. The regulation covering sex and marital status had been in effect throughout that period, whereas the other bases of discrimination had been regulated for only six months. The fact that reported instances of credit discrimination were *higher* for sex and marital status than for the other bases, despite two years of regulation, suggests that the real preregulation problems lay with sex and marital status.

Many respondents fall into more than one protected class. For example, a sixty-two-year-old divorced Hispanic woman who was born in Cuba and receiving public assistance in the United States would fall in virtually all of the protected classes under ECOA. If she believed that she had received less favorable treatment than other applicants, she might have cited only one, or possibly two, of the prohibited bases for discriminatory treatment, or she might have offered reasons not covered by law. With this in mind, a review of the kinds of discrimination reported by respondents according to their sex, marital status, race, and age seems relevant.

Sex.   A greater proportion of women than men reported perceived discriminatory treatment in financing their purchases (12.3 percent versus 8.4 percent, see Table IX-4). One-third of the female respondents reported sex as the basis of discrimination, followed by marital status (24 percent) and age (20 percent). Women reported discriminatory treatment on the basis of sex or marital status more frequently than men. Male respondents cited age and various other reasons as the principal forms of discriminatory treatment.

Marital Status.   Table IX-4 also shows that unmarried respondents reported substantially higher perceptions of discriminatory treatment than married respondents. Divorced respondents reported the highest incidence of discriminatory treatment (23.2 percent), ascribing it predominantly to marital status or sex (or both). Separated and widowed respondents reported somewhat lesser levels (19.0 percent and 11.1 percent, respectively) and gave sex and marital status as the predominant reasons. The 20.5 percent of single respondents who perceived discriminatory treatment cited age as the predominant basis for discrimination.

Age.   Only four of the twenty-five respondents reporting perceived discriminatory treatment based on age were sixty-two years of age or older (see Table IX-4); the others were less than thirty years old.[23] Moreover, twenty-three respondents, predominantly those under thirty, were excluded from the tally because ECOA regulations primarily protect persons sixty-two or older (see the first note to Table IX-2). Thus, it is apparent that perceptions of discriminatory treatment among the young exceed those of other age groups. Even after screening out those respondents under sixty-two who reported age as the sole basis for discriminatory treatment, nearly one-half of

TABLE IX-4 Perceptions of and Reasons for Credit Discrimination, by Sex and Marital Status, Combined Sample, 1977

	WOMEN		MEN		MARRIED	
	Number	Percent	Number	Percent	Number	Percent
Number of Respondents	511		334		556	
Perceived Discrimination ("Yes" or "Might have been")	63	12.2	28	8.4	37	6.7
Reason Reported						
Age	15	20.3	10	32.3	4	11.1
Sex	25	33.8	0	0	10	27.8
Marital status	18	24.3	3	9.7	2	5.6
Race	2	2.7	2	6.5	4	11.1
Nationality	0	0	1	3.1	0	0
Other	14	18.9	15	48.4	16	44.4
Total*	74	100.0	31	100.0	36	100.0

	SINGLE		WIDOWED		SEPARATED		DIVORCED	
	Number	Percent	Number	Percent	Number	Percent	Number	Percent
Number of Respondents	146		63		21		56	
Perceived Discrimination ("Yes" or "Might have been")	30	20.5	7	11.1	4	19.0	13	23.2
Reason Reported								
Age	17	44.7	2	25.0	0	0	2	12.5
Sex	7	18.4	1	12.5	1	20.0	6	37.5
Marital status	2	5.3	4	50.0	4	80.0	7	43.7
Race	0	0	0	0	0	0	0	0
Nationality	1	2.6	0	0	0	0	0	0
Other	11	29.0	1	12.5	0	0	1	6.3
Total*	38	100.0	8	100.0	5	100.0	16	100.0

	UNDER 30		30–44		46–61	
	Number	Percent	Number	Percent	Number	Percent
Number of Respondents	252		293		256	
Perceived Discrimination ("Yes" or "Might have been")	45	17.9	29	9.9	8	3.1
Reason Reported						
Age**	21	34.4	0	0	0	0
Sex	14	23.0	9	33.4	2	25.0
Marital status	8	13.1	8	29.6	4	50.0
Race	2	3.3	2	7.4	0	0
Nationality	1	1.6	0	0	0	0
Other	15	24.6	8	29.6	2	25.0
Total*	61	100.0	27	100.0	8	100.0

	62 AND OVER		CAUCASIAN		MINORITY	
	Number	Percent	Number	Percent	Number	Percent
Number of Respondents	122		690		141	
Perceived Discrimination ("Yes" or "Might have been")	9	7.4	71	10.3	19	13.5
Reason Reported						
Age**	4	44.4	22	25.9	3	15.8
Sex	0	0	22	25.9	3	15.8
Marital status	1	11.2	19	22.4	2	10.5
Race	0	0	1	1.2	3	15.8
Nationality	0	0	0	0	1	5.3
Other	4	44.4	21	24.6	7	36.8
Total*	9	100.0	85	100.0	19	100.0

*Total includes more than one kind of discrimination reported by some respondents.
**These 21 respondents under 30 years of age reported some other reason, in addition to age, for their perceived discrimination.

the respondents under thirty who perceived discrimination believed that age was one of the most important reasons underlying their discriminatory treatment.

RACE.   The incidence of perceived discrimination among minority respondents (13.5 percent) was similar to that among nonminorities (10.3 percent). Table IX-4 also indicates that only three of the nineteen minority respondents reporting such treatment cited race as the reason for it.

CREDIT SOURCE.   Respondents reporting less favorable treatment were also asked: "What type of creditor was this [that treated you less favorably]?" In terms of simple frequency, banks and retail outlets accounted for three-fourths of the reported discrimination cases. In terms of the incidence of patronage at each source, banks, finance companies, and retailers had similar proportions of customers who cited discriminatory treatment in at least one instance (around 11.5 percent); the proportion for credit unions was markedly lower (around 2 percent).

In sum, consumer perceptions of discriminatory treatment over a two-year period were not extensive at the time of the survey. Although a 10 percent figure cannot be viewed as negligible, the responses indicate that consumers did not perceive widespread discrimination because of any one characteristic. Age was mentioned most frequently as the basis for perceived discrimination, but most of these instances were cited by respondents under thirty years of age, a group currently provided only limited protection under ECOA. With age group excepted, sex and marital status were the predominant reasons for discrimination reported among classes now protected by ECOA.

Credit Denials

Denial of credit, which is likely to be a reason for respondents to report discriminatory treatment, was examined in relation to perceptions of discriminatory treatment. To assess the incidence of credit denials, each respondent in the Shay-Brandt survey was asked: "In the past two years or so, have you ever been turned down for credit by a particular lender or creditor?" If an affirmative response was given, a question was asked to determine the type of lender who denied the credit and the reason given for the refusal.

TABLE IX-5 Reported Credit Denials and Reasons for Refusal, National and Combined Samples, 1977

	NATIONAL SAMPLE		COMBINED SAMPLE	
	Number	*Percent*	*Number*	*Percent*
Number of Respondents	813		967	
Credit Denied ("Yes")	100	12.3	135	14.0
Reason Reported				
No credit rating	19	20.2	26	21.3
Income	15	16.0	25	20.5
New job	14	14.9	18	14.8
Age	8	8.5	10	8.2
No collateral	6	6.4	7	5.7
Overindebted	6	6.4	6	4.9
Slow payer	5	5.3	5	4.1
Marital status	6	6.4	6	4.9
Mix-up	3	3.2	4	3.3
Bad credit risk	3	3.2	4	3.3
Moved recently	3	3.2	3	2.5
Sex	3	3.2	4	3.3
No cosigner	2	2.1	3	2.5
Other	1	1.0	1	.7
Total*	94	100.0	122	100.0

Some respondents reported more than one reason and others gave no reason.

The results, shown in Table IX-5, indicate that 12.3 percent of respondents in the national sample and 14 percent of the combined sample reported being denied credit within the past two years. Among the reasons given for denial, only 6.4 percent were attributable to marital status, 3.2 percent to sex, and 8.5 percent to age (mostly young age). The predominant reasons given for credit denials in the combined sample were no credit rating, income, new job, and age. Only a relatively small proportion (around 10 or 11 percent) of the reasons given for credit denials could be attributed to perceptions of discriminatory treatment covered by ECOA (excluding young age).

A cross-tabulation of reported credit denials and perceptions of discriminatory treatment suggests that one-third of those who were refused credit believed that discriminatory treatment might have been involved (see Table IX-6). Among those who were not denied credit, less than 5 percent acknowledged discrimination in some

TABLE IX-6 Reported Credit Denials and Perceptions of and Reasons Given for Credit Discrimination, Combined Sample, 1977

| | CREDIT DENIED | | CREDIT NOT DENIED | |
	Number	Percent	Number	Percent
Number of Respondents	135		829	
Perceived Discrimination ("Yes" or "Might Have Been")	47	34.8	39	4.7
Reason Reported				
Age	10	17.2	15	31.9
Sex	12	20.7	13	27.7
Marital status	16	27.6	5	10.6
Race	1	1.7	3	6.4
Nationality	1	1.7	0	0
Other	18	31.1	11	23.4
Total*	58	100.0	47	100.0

*Total includes more than one kind of discrimination reported by respondents.

form. Whether the perceived discriminatory treatment was, in fact, linked with the reported credit denial cannot be determined, but the evidence strongly suggests that some perceptions about discrimination were associated with credit denials. Marital status was the only ECOA-protected criterion that appeared to be associated with credit denial and perceived discrimination. All other reasons for discrimination were more commonly reported by respondents who were not denied credit than by those who were.

Multivariate Analysis of Discrimination in Consumer Credit Markets

The legal definition of discrimination states that certain consumers are treated less favorably than others. To investigate this issue more rigorously, we need to move beyond simple cross-tabulation, which considers one variable at a time. Multiple regression analysis allows us to address the question of discrimination in a way that takes into account differences in socioeconomic and demographic characteristics other than those prohibited by law. For example, were minorities more likely than whites to receive unfavorable treatment when possible differences in income, education, and family size were also considered?

In the analysis that follows, the discrimination issue is approached from three perspectives:

1. Are consumer perceptions of credit discrimination related to perceptions of *less* credit availability after differences in socioeconomic characteristics are taken into account?

2. Are perceptions of credit discrimination related to *less* use of nonmortgage debt after the same differences are considered?

3. Are these perceptions related to a *greater incidence* of credit denials when other factors are taken into account?

A subsequent question in each instance is whether respondents in protected groups have stronger associations with each dependent variable (perceptions of credit availability, use of nonmortgage debt, and credit denials) than respondents reporting perceptions of credit discrimination. If so, there may have been unperceived and/or unreported discrimination against respondents in groups protected by ECOA, suggesting that they did not recognize and/or report discriminatory treatment.

Perceptions of Credit Availability

To measure confidence in their ability to obtain credit, respondents were asked: "Now, let's suppose you wanted to make a large dollar purchase, like a color T.V. How difficult do you think it would be for you to borrow from a bank for an installment loan?" The answers ranged on a four-point scale from "extremely difficult" to "not at all difficult." The question was repeated for finance companies, credit unions, installment plans from a retail store, and a credit card from a department store.[24]

Regression analysis showed that perceptions of discrimination were significantly related to perceptions of less credit availability, even with differences in income, education, family size, age under thirty, and level of nonmortgage debt held constant. Among groups covered by ECOA in 1977, only single males and minorities held perceptions of less credit availability that were significantly different from consumers without these attributes. Female heads of household, senior citizens, welfare recipients, and immigrants did not show significant differences when variations in other socioeconomic characteristics were taken into account. It should be noted that the statistical test of discrimination as perceived by ECOA-protected groups is a stiff one, since it asks whether, after accounting for differences in credit worthiness (for example, income and debt level), respondents protected by ECOA or those reporting discriminatory behavior perceived that credit was less available. The statistical answer is affirmative for the group that reported discriminatory treatment. Among respondents protected by ECOA, only single males and minorities passed the statistical test.

Using the same statistical technique, it is possible to evaluate whether respondents reporting perceptions of discriminatory treatment or those covered by ECOA held higher or lower nonmortgage debt levels. The hypothesis in this instance is that those repondents who reported discriminatory treatment were unable to obtain as much credit as others, after differences in income, education, family size, and age under thirty were taken into account.

Considering only socioeconomic characteristics, family income, family size, and age were positively related with the level of nonmortgage debt. Respondents who perceived discriminatory treatment did not have significantly lower levels of nonmortgage debt relative to other respondents. This finding is critical, since it shows that perceptions of discrimination, whether based on fact or not, did not preclude those respondents from obtaining debt. In both instances, of course, we are referring to respondents with similar socioeconomic characteristics.

A comparison of protected and unprotected respondents indicated that the debt level was influenced only by age: respondents sixty-two years or older had significantly lower debt levels. Because this group did not perceive that credit was more difficult to obtain, it seems probable that the lower level of debt by senior citizens resulted from reduced demands for durable goods rather than from discriminatory constraints upon the supply of credit. The fact that other ECOA-protected classes did not have lower debt levels implies that these groups were able to obtain debt at a level consistent with their incomes (the only significant characteristic besides age).

These findings do not support a judgment that credit discrimination was nonexistent at the time of the survey. Rather, they indicate that where credit discrimination was perceived or where respondents in classes protected by ECOA were concerned, there were no statistically significant differences in debt levels, holding certain socioeconomic characteristics constant. In short, allowing for differences in these socioeconomic factors, the evidence suggests that credit discrimination since enactment of ECOA has not resulted in lower nonmortgage debt levels either for respondents perceiving discriminatory treatment or for those protected by ECOA. Whether these consumers were forced to borrow from higher cost sources or on less favorable contract terms, however, cannot be determined directly from these results. By assessing the incidence of credit denials among the same groups, we can draw other inferences about the discrimination process.

Credit Denials

The third test for discrimination was conducted using the credit denial question described above. When socioeconomic characteristics alone were regressed on the credit denial variable, family income showed a negative association, while nonmortgage debt levels and young families exhibited a positive linkage; that is, more denials are experienced when family incomes are lower, total debt is higher, and the head of the family is under thirty.

Respondents who perceived discriminatory treatment in the financing of their durable goods purchases reported more instances of credit denials during the past two years than those who did not, after consideration of the above socioeconomic characteristics. This finding supports the thesis that credit denials occurred among respondents perceiving discriminatory treatment, even after differences attributable to income, debt level, and other measures of credit worthiness were taken into account.

When this result is compared with the finding that debt levels of respondents reporting credit discrimination were no different from others, the two findings are consistent only if respondents perceiving discriminatory treatment went elsewhere to obtain the needed credit. For some, this may have meant obtaining credit from higher cost outlets.

Respondents who are minorities and/or female heads of families—two of the six characteristics protected by ECOA—reported a significantly higher incidence of credit denials than was dictated by the socioeconomic circumstances considered. It will be recalled that despite the fact of the significantly higher incidence of credit denials, both minorities and female heads of families were able to obtain nonmortgage debt levels consistent with the socioeconomic characteristics considered. However, the fact that minorities perceived that credit was more difficult to obtain further suggests that, in the past, these consumers might well have been denied credit because of race alone. Out of this experience could have evolved a perceptual set, based on reality, that credit was more difficult for them to obtain and that to borrow money they were best advised to start their search with higher cost sources, a finding supported by Day and Brandt.[25] These respondents did not search more or less widely than white respondents when other characteristics were taken into account.[26]

Perceptions of Credit Availability in 1970

In the 1970 survey of California consumers conducted by Day and Brandt for the National Commission on Consumer Finance, responses to questions similar to those asked in the 1977 Shay-Brandt survey were available for comparative analysis.[27] Although questions relating to perceptions of discriminatory treatment in financing purchases were not asked, comparable questions concerning perceptions of credit availability and nonmortage debt levels were asked.[28]

The socioeconomic characteristics held constant in this analysis were income; age under thirty; credit attitude (on a scale from one to seven, with higher digits denoting a more favorable attitude toward the use of credit); education; family size; and awareness of the annual percentage rate (APR). These variables are similar to those considered in 1977, with some additions (credit attitude and APR awareness) and one omission (nonmortgage debt level). The additions and omissions did not appear to affect the comparability of the results, however.

Income, credit attitude, heads of families under thirty, and APR awareness were all related to perceptions of credit availability. Credit attitude and income were also associated with the level of nonmortgage debt in a manner that was consistent with perceptions; that is, families with higher debt levels had higher incomes and more favorable attitudes toward credit. Young respondents, however, perceived more limited credit availability and had higher nonmortgage debt levels than their other socioeconomic characteristics would have predicted. Education, family size, and APR awareness showed no consistent coefficients at acceptable levels.

When these socioeconomic characteristics were taken into account, each of the classes later covered by ECOA, except for senior citizens (sixty-five and over), considered credit more difficult to obtain than did the unprotected groups. Given the strong relation between perceptions of credit discrimination and credit availability in the

1977 sample, this finding suggests that perceptions of credit discrimination may have been higher in 1970 as well, but this cannot be verified.

Looking at the level of nonmortgage debt among the protected classes, we find that only senior citizens and single, female family heads had significantly lower debt levels, but even here the coefficient for female family heads is only marginally significant at the 90 percent confidence level. Minorities, on the other hand, had significantly *higher* debt levels than would have been predicted by their socioeconomic circumstances. As was the case in 1977, the lower debt level for senior citizens was not accompanied by perceptions of less credit availability and can be attributed to a smaller demand for credit at this later stage of the life cycle. In short, only female family heads had perceptions at all consistent with differences in debt level.

Although the evidence from 1970 is fragmentary, it indicates that perceptions of restricted credit availability were more widely held among groups now protected by ECOA than was the case in 1977. It also suggests that female family heads (in California) were the only protected group that might have been forced to maintain a lower level of debt than others not now covered by that legislation.

Creditor Discrimination Under Empirically Derived Scoring Systems: Two Cases

To investigate the likelihood of discriminatory credit-granting practices by creditors, the analysis shifts from consumer perception and related outcomes to creditor practices that might reveal intended or unintended discriminatory results under empirically derived scoring systems. The samples of customer accounts used by two firms to set up statistically based credit-scoring systems in the early 1970s were point scored to ascertain whether empirically derived, statistically sound credit-scoring systems would have been affected by the passage of ECOA, as well as whether such systems contribute to discriminatory practices according to ECOA criteria. The two firms represent large creditors in two major segments of the consumer credit industry: retailers and finance company cash lenders. Retailers' customers have the broadest range of income, while finance companies cater primarily to the needs of lower middle income recipients.[29] Finance companies are typically allowed to charge higher rates than their cash-lending competitors;

they also assume greater risks of default and experience higher loss ratios than other lenders.[30]

All creditors attempt to minimize losses by extending credit to borrowers who can be expected to repay and by not granting credit to applicants who may not repay. Nevertheless, there is widespread agreement that many, if not most, causes of default on debt repayment are difficult to ascertain in advance. In 1970, five years before ECOA was enacted, finance company and retail executives cited unemployment, overextension, and illness as the most common reasons why debtors fail to meet contractual terms, followed by separation, divorce, family illness, family relocation, and lack of intention to repay. Among the reasons cited, separation and divorce became illegal bases for credit discrimination under the marital status criterion in ECOA.

Basic to our investigation of the impact of ECOA upon credit-granting systems is the distinction between a judgmentally based system and a statistically derived system. In some judgmental systems experienced credit department officers assign points based on criteria which in their experience separate applicants who will repay from those who will not. Empirically derived credit-scoring systems, on the other hand, base the assignment of points on criteria derived by processing a representative sample of accounts. The criteria that best classify "good" and "bad" accounts on the basis of whether they paid their debt in a satisfactory manner in the immediate past are assigned points, which are then aggregated to an applicant's score.

ECOA, as noted earlier, prohibits the use of certain types of information in credit applications. In our analyses of samples of applicants accepted and rejected by the two creditors we sought to determine:

1. whether applicants in the ECOA protected classes were rejected more frequently than other applicants both before and after differences in demographics, financial status, account references, and prior credit performance were considered;

2. whether the removal of the protected class criteria from a statistically derived credit-scoring system would have reduced the accuracy, and therefore the efficiency, of the credit screening process; and

3. whether other criteria could be utilized to compensate for the reduced accuracy, if any, caused by the removal of bases for discrimination under ECOA.

Methodology

Multiple regression and discrimination analysis were used to identify the criteria that best explained or predicted (1) acceptance versus rejection of applications by the creditor; and (2) the performance of accepted applicants, that is, whether the account was repaid in a satisfactory manner (a "good" credit) or whether it was repaid in an unsatisfactory manner or not repaid (a "bad" credit).

For each creditor, two samples were utilized: the accept-reject sample and the good-bad sample of customer accounts accepted by the creditor. Analysis of the accept-reject sample permits insight into the criteria used by the creditor in the credit-granting system *prior* to the time accounts were gathered to establish a statistically derived point-scoring system. Analysis of the good-bad sample of credit accounts permits identification of the criteria that, with hindsight, would have best predicted the performance of an account with information at hand (from the application and credit reporting agencies) at the time the application was made.

The information at hand for use in screening credit applications by the creditor(s) was divided into five groups:
1. Protected class information dealing with age, sex, and marital status.
2. Demographic information other than protected class criteria (family size, homeowner or renter, number of months at present address).
3. Financial status indicators (total monthly income, types of bank accounts, total amount owed).
4. References to credit or deposit accounts held by banks, savings and loan companies, finance company loans, department store or other credit card issuers.
5. Credit agency ratings (excellent, satisfactory, minor derogatories, major derogatories).

The data consisted of 4,705 customer accounts of the national retailer and 4,176 customer accounts of the large finance company. For the national retailer, our statistical requirement that all the information be available for each account reduced the accept-reject sample to 2,723 accounts, and the good-bad sample to 1,726 accounts (or 64 percent of the accept-reject sample). The finance company accept-reject sample was reduced to 2,470 accounts, and the good-bad sample to 1,244 accounts (or 52 percent of the accept-reject sample).

Both these samples were split into two subsamples to avoid the problem of statistical artifacts—findings unique to a given set of observations—since our goal was to extrapolate the findings with some degree of confidence. By splitting the sample in half, it was possible to perform the statistical analysis on the analysis sample, and thereafter validate to the results by replicating the analysis on the remaining data, known as the validation sample. The entire sample was sufficiently large that it could be split in half without causing problems of too few observations among the variables. The replication of results, with only a few exceptions, was successful. Where replication did provide significantly different findings, results from both the analysis and validation samples are presented.

Analysis of Retailer Data

The data for the customer accounts were first analyzed using the pre-ECOA model. When *only* the protected class varibles were used to predict credit performance, their predictive ability was quite weak. When all of the variables were used, however, their predictive power was relatively high. Of the protected class variables, only young age was statistically significant as a predictor. Thus, it is clear that all the variables other than the protected class variables provide the predictive power of the pre-ECOA model.

The pre-ECOA model assumed no interaction among the protected class variables. However, interaction may exist. For example, one might argue that, with respect to predicting credit performance, age may have a different effect for a male than for a female. To examine this possibility, a second pre-ECOA model was formulated in which all the protected class variables were specified in such a way as to allow estimation of interaction effects. Rather than employing separate variables, such as FEMALE, SINGLE, and LOWAGE, for example, composite variables were utilized, such as YNGFSING (young, female, single) and MIDMWID (middle-aged, male, widowed). Composite variables were defined for all combinations for which the samples sizes were sufficiently large. The definitions for variables other than those for the protected classes remained the same.

The results for the pre-ECOA model with interaction assumed are nearly identical to those for the pre-ECOA model without inter-action. Thus, for the retailer data, there are no statistical reasons to prefer the pre-ECOA model with interaction to the pre-ECOA model without interaction.

The parameters of a post-ECOA model were similarly estimated. Here, too, omission of the protected class variables had an imperceptible effect on prediction of credit performance, suggesting that it would not be useful for this retailer to employ the protected class variables in a credit-scoring system.

These findings were affirmed by an analysis using linear discriminant functions, estimated from the analysis sample for the pre-ECOA system (without and with the interaction assumption) and for the post-ECOA system. Aside from LOWAGE, the protected class variables displayed little predictive utility. Omitting the protected class variables decreased the percentage of cases correctly classified only from 72.71 percent of 72.47 percent.

The discriminant functions estimated from the analysis sample were used to create scores for each individual in the validation sample. These scores were then used to predict good and bad risks, and the pre- and post-ECOA models were compared for accuracy.

The relative accuracies of the pre- and post-ECOA models were assessed by determining the percentage of classification errors that would result were each applied to the validation sample applicants. A classification error occurred if an applicant was predicted to be a ''good'' risk (would pay the account in a satisfactory fashion) when in fact that applicant was a ''bad'' risk (did not pay the account in a satisfactory fashion) or when an applicant was predicted to be a bad risk and in fact was a good risk.

In practice, a simple credit-scoring system would classify an applicant as good if his or her discriminant score exceeded a particular cutoff value. To set the optimal cutoff value for a system, it is necessary to know the relative costs of the classification errors, namely, the cash cost of accepting what will be a bad account and the costs, in terms of opportunity and ill will, of rejecting what would be a good account. For the optimal cutoff point, one must also know the long-run chances that an applicant is either a good or bad risk.

Since such information was not available in this study, rather than establishing a single optimal cutoff value, several cutoff values were examined. For each value, the validation sample applicants were classified as predicted good risks and predicted bad risks. Each group was further divided into applicants who did and did not pay their accounts in a satisfactory manner. For example, for a cutoff value of 1 percent, the pre-ECOA model would predict 16.7 percent of the validation sample applicants to be good risks. Of those applicants, 15.1 percent actually were good accounts and 1.6 percent were bad.

The classification error percentage is the sum of the percentages for bad risks classified as good and good risks classified as bad. For a cutoff value of 1 percent with the pre-ECOA model, 46.5 percent (1.6 plus 44.9) of the validation sample applicants were misclassified.

The percentages of applicants misclassified are shown for several cutoff values in Table IX-7. These figures suggest that the pre- and post-ECOA models lead to similar overall levels of accuracy. In particular, the minimum percentage of classification errors appears to be in the neighborhood of 27 percent for each system. For the pre-ECOA system, the minimum seems to occur in the vicinity of a cutoff value of 0; for the post-ECOA system, the minimum appears to be near a cutoff value of -.5. The exact values for the minimum error percentages (and corresponding cutoff values) could be determined with a finer calibration of cutoff values than the .5 intervals employed in Table IX-7.

According to the Equal Credit Opportunity Act, not only are variables such as age, sex, and marital status proscribed in the credit-granting decision, but also variables that would have the same effect. For example, even if marital status were removed from the criteria used in a scoring system, other variables might be strongly associated with marital status and play its role in the post-ECOA system. Most of the pairwise correlations among the variables were below .10. However, to examine whether or not linear combinations of variables were associated with the protected class variables, factor analyses were performed.

For the retailer, after varimax rotation, eleven factors appeared to capture the variation in the data set. Of the protected class variables, FEMALE had a relatively high loading (.40 or more) in two factors—the same factors for which DIVSEP and WIDOWED showed a relatively high loading. In those two factors, no other independent variable had a high loading. HIGHAGE appeared in no factor. These results suggest that if these variables were deleted from the data base, no linear combinations of other variables would be likely to replace them in a regression or discriminant analysis.

TABLE IX-7 Comparison of Retailer Classification Errors, Pre- and Post-ECOA Model Discriminant Scores (Percentages of Validation Sample)

Cutoff Value	PRE-ECOA MODEL*					POST-ECOA MODEL				
	Predicted Good		Predicted Bad		Classification Errors	Predicted Good		Predicted Bad		Classification Errors
	Good	Bad	Good	Bad		Good	Bad	Good	Bad	
2.0	.7	.2	59.3	39.8	59.5	.9	.3	59.6	39.2	59.9
1.5	5.8	.7	54.2	39.3	54.9	6.0	.8	54.5	38.7	55.3
1.0	15.1	1.6	44.9	38.4	46.5	14.8	1.6	45.7	37.9	47.3
.5	29.1	4.0	30.9	36.0	34.9	29.2	4.6	31.3	34.9	35.9
.0	44.0	10.9	16.0	29.1	26.9	43.4	10.5	17.1	29.0	27.6
-.5	51.7	19.2	8.3	20.8	27.5	52.6	19.1	7.9	30.4	27.0
-1.0	55.9	27.0	4.1	13.0	31.1	56.6	26.8	3.9	12.7	30.7
-1.5	58.3	33.5	1.7	6.5	35.2	58.8	32.3	1.7	7.2	35.0
-2.0	59.4	37.4	.6	2.6	38.0	59.9	37.4	.6	2.5	38.0

*No interaction.

The variable SINGLE did not appear in the same factor as NODEP (no dependents)—an a priori reasonable result. However, when SINGLE was deleted in the regression analysis, the beta coefficient for NODEP (which was not statistically significant) changed from -.07 to -.04—a result favorable to applicants with no dependents. The results of other factor analyses that included the interaction forms of the protected class variables were consistent with these findings.

Given that this study attempted to construct a predictive system a firm would use, how similar was the system that was developed to those employed by firms such as this retailer? The system employed by the retailer was *not* known. However, it was possible to identify those variables that were highly associated with the retailer's acceptance or rejection of an application. Once again, the data were split into halves—an analysis sample and a validation sample.

According to analyses of these data, sex, marital status, and age did not appear to have been utilized by the retailer as criteria for accepting or rejecting applications. The retailer apparently did not give the protected class variables much, if any, weight in deciding who would receive credit, even when such information was available prior to passage of the ECOA. Compared to the previous analyses, the retailer seemed to give considerably more weight to the credit performance variables, such as number of excellent ratings or number of major derogatories, than to any other criteria available.

Analysis of Finance Company Data

Analysis of the finance company data followed the same steps as those used to analyze the retailer data. The observations were split into an analysis sample and a validation sample. Pre- and post-ECOA models were estimated from the analysis sample observations and their predictive accuracies compared by analyzing the validation sample.

Overall, the findings for the finance company resembled those for the retailer, although they were not quite so clear-cut. For the finance company, the protected class variables, as a group, were much less closely associated with credit performance than were variables concerned with family financial position and previous credit experience. However, among the protected class variables, both age and whether the applicant was divorced or separated were significantly associated with credit performance, other things equal.

For the finance company accounts, information was available for each of thirty-five independent variables. This list of variables is much the same as that for the retailer, although there were some minor differences in definition.

Compared to the retailer data, a greater proportion of finance company applicants were female (15 percent), single (13 percent), divorced or separated (16 percent), and between the ages of eighteen and twenty-five (30 percent). In particular, 7 percent of the finance company applicants were divorced or separated women between twenty-six and sixty-one, as compared to only 2 percent of the retailer applicants. Moreover, 40 percent of the finance company applicants were from households of one or two persons (only 7 percent of the retailer applicants reported no dependents). The finance company applicants had been at their current job fourteen fewer months on average than the retailer applicants and only a third had bank accounts (savings, checking, or both), compared to nearly nine out of ten retailer applicants.

Proportionately fewer of the finance company applicants had department store or credit card accounts, but more had obtained credit from finance companies previously. Finally, more than twice as many finance company applicants had experienced minor or major derogatories and had received a lower average number of excellent or satisfactory ratings than the retailer applicants.

Conclusions

On the basis of responses to our 1977 survey, we conclude that a significant proportion (about 12 percent) of individuals purchasing consumer durable goods perceive that they have been treated less fairly than others. Two-thirds of those responding in this way gave reasons covered by the Equal Credit Opportunity Act, while one-third gave other reasons. Mainly, the reasons given were attributed to age (young), sex, and marital status, despite the fact that sex and marital status had been illegal as bases for granting credit for the previous two years, while age had been prohibited by law for only six months. Respondents either did not believe race, religion, or national origin were the bases for their perceptions or did not wish to report them as reasons.

After allowing for deficiencies in income, education, and age (under thirty), respondents who perceived discriminatory treatment in the previous two years had been denied credit more than others, indicating that perceptions of discrimination were often related to applicants being denied credit. Despite the denials, there was no statistical evidence that those who perceived discrimination had less nonmortgage debt than those without such perceptions. This finding offers little support for the notion that self-discrimination is widespread—that individuals will not apply for credit elsewhere if they are rejected for reasons covered by law.

In addition, we find little evidence that empirically derived credit-scoring systems contain discriminatory biases. For the sample of pre-ECOA accounts of a national retailer, the only useful predictor of credit worthiness which would be incorporated with negative values in such a system was young age. Since Regulation B now permits age to be included in empirically derived systems, we found no likely impact of the imposition of ECOA on the practices of this firm. The pre-ECOA sample of accounts offered no evidence that any of the criteria prohibited by ECOA were used to accept or reject applicants.

In the case of the large finance company, our findings were similar but less clear-cut. The similarity is based on the fact that categories protected by ECOA were less useful predictors of satis-factory debt payment than categories reflecting family financial circumstances and previous credit performance. On the other hand, both age and whether the applicant was divorced or separated were significantly associated with differences in credit performance, other things being equal. As was the case with the national retailer, analysis of acceptances and rejections of applications revealed no evidence of credit discrimination based on age, sex, or marital status in the pre-ECOA period.

On balance, we conclude that discrimination is a fact of life which can be limited, but not eradicated, by the passage of laws. At the present time, most perceptions of discriminatory practices prohibited by law are based on marital status and sex. Under current laws, protection of young people is limited to judgmental systems of granting credit. It is also the case, however, that the young have a poorer record of paying their debts, possibly because of their limited experience in handling credit. If they were given the same access to credit as others, irrespective of age, the efficiency of empirically derived scoring systems would decline significantly.

Application of the effects test would not have affected either of the two scoring systems that was established. In the retailer sample there were no significant correlations between variables. Only the single person and small family size variables in the finance company sample were strongly interrelated. In neither case were the interrelated variables useful predictors of credit performance, indicating that they would not have been selected for use in either scoring system.

We offer no recommendation for changing the status quo of the Equal Credit Opportunity Law, other than to suggest that the 1976 amendments were not supported by perceptions that these forms of discriminatory practices were widespread.

NOTES

1. Public Law 88-352, Title VII, Sections 703, 705, 708. Stat. 225, 258, 42 U.S.C., Sec. 2000-e-4 (1976).
2. 15 U.S.C. Section 1601 et seq.
3. "Equal Credit Opportunity," *Federal Reserve Bulletin* (February 1977); 101.
4. Public Law 93-495, 1975, effective in October 1975.
5. Public Law 94-239, 1976, amendments effective in March 1977.
6. The 1978 decision of the U.S. Supreme Court in the *Bakke* case raises the question whether favored characteristics will be protected by ECOA, along with groups thought to be subjected to discriminatory treatment.
7. E. Furubotyn and S. Petrovitch, "Property Rights and Economic Theory: A Survey of Recent Literature," *Journal of Economic Literature* X, no. 4 (December 1972): 1137–1183.
8. See, for example, Table 7-7 in Thomas A. Durkin and Gregory Elliehausen, *The 1977 Consumer Credit Survey* (Washington, D.C.: Board of Governors of the Federal Reserve System, 1978).
9. Regulation B, part 202, Introduction.
10. "Equal Credit Opportunity."
11. 401 U.S. 424 (1071).
12. Regulation B, Section 202.6(a).
13. 422 U.S. 405 (1975); Senate Report to accompany H.R. 6516, No. 948-589, pp. 4-5; House Report to accompany H.R. 6516, No. 94-210, p. 5.
14. 45 U.S.L.W. 4031 (1976).
15. "Equal Credit Opportunity," p. 106.
16. Gary G. Chandler and David C. Ewert, "Discrimination on the Basis of Sex Under the Equal Credit Opportunity Act," Working Paper no. 8, Credit Research Center, Krannert School, Purdue University, 1976.
17. Bernard A. Shinkel, "The Effects of Limiting Information in the Granting of Credit," Ph.D. dissertation, Krannert School, Purdue University, pp. 176–177.

18. Regulation B, Section 202.2.

19. Ibid., Section 202.2 (t).

20. Durkin and Elliehausen, *The 1977 Consumer Credit Survey.*

21. See Robert P. Shay and William K. Brandt, "Public Regulation of Financial Services: The Truth-in-Lending Law," in *The Costs and Benefits of Public Regulation of Consumer Financial Services,* eds. Arnold A. Heggestad and John J. Mingo, Final Report to the National Science Foundation (Cambridge, Mass: Abt Associates Inc., 1978).

22. In the analysis that follows, reference to the national sample indicates that only the national probability sample was used, inner-city sample refers to the 100 interviews with inner-city respondents, and combined sample indicates the entire group of 967 households.

23. Twenty-three respondents who were less than sixty-two years of age and who reported age as the *only* kind of discrimination encountered were eliminated from the combined sample. The twenty-one respondents who were less than 30 years old and who reported age as a reason for being discriminated against also offered some *other* reason besides age for their perceived discrimination.

24. George S. Day and William K. Brandt, "A Study of Consumer Credit Decisions," National Commission on Consumer Finance, *Technical Studies,* vol. I, 1973, p. 76.

25. Shay and Brandt, "Public Regulation of Financial Services," Table 16.

26. A more detailed description of the sample and the questions asked is available in the Shay-Brandt technical paper, ibid.

27. The question concerning credit availability was: "Now, let's suppose you wanted to make a large dollar purchase, like a color T.V. How difficult do you think it would be for you to borrow from a bank for an installment loan? Do you think it would be extremely difficult, somewhat difficult, not too difficult, or not at all difficult to obtain this type of loan for this color T.V.?" The question was repeated using appropriate wording for a finance company, retail store, credit union, or credit card.

   The question to ascertain nonmortgage debt level was: "Now let's talk about another aspect of credit for a moment. I'd like to get an idea of *all* the money you *owe except* for your mortgage. Consider *all* the money you owe different places and people, such as loans to pay off furniture or cars, doctor bills, charge accounts, and everything else you owe. About how much money do you think it would take to pay off the entire amount? Would it be over or under $1,500?" If under, "Would it be under $500 or over $500 but less than $1,500?" If over $1,500, "Would it be $1,500 but less than $3,000; $3,000 but less than $5,000, or $5,000 or over?"

28. R.P. Shay and M. Schober, "Consumer Awareness of Annual Percen-

tage Rates of Charge in Consumer Installment Loans: Before and After Truth-in-Lending Became Effective,'' National Commission on Consumer Finance, *Technical Studies,* vol. I, 1973.

29. Paul Smith, *Consumer Credit Costs* (Princeton, N.J.: National Bureau of Economic Research, Princeton University Press, 1964).

30. National Commission on Consumer Finance, *Consumer Credit in the United States* (Washington, D.C.: U.S. Government Printing Office, December 1972), chapter 3.

TEN
Discrimination in
Consumer Credit
John M. Marshall*

Introduction

The Equal Credit Opportunity Act (ECOA) of
1975 prohibits certain kinds of discrimination. The basic requirement of Regulation B, the instrument by which the Federal Reserve
enforces these prohibitions, is: "A creditor shall not refuse to grant
an individual account to a creditworthy applicant on the basis of
sex, marital status, or any other prohibited basis."[1] Here "individual account" includes ordinary loans, and the bases prohibited
include race, color, religion, national origin, age, and receipt of
public assistance. The rule also prohibits discrimination against
those who exercise their rights under the Consumer Protection Act
of 1968. Sections of Regulation B are directed at abuses in application procedures. This paper examines whether certain suppliers of
consumer credit complied with the rule quoted above either before
or after enactment of ECOA.

Causes of discrimination may be social and cultural. The

*The author acknowledges the contributions of Aileen Reynolds, who
supervised preparation of the data, and John S. Greenlees, who performed
many of the computations.

phenomenon itself is frequently economic, and there is a considerable literature concerning economic discrimination, offering conflicting interpretations of discrimination and alternative ways in which to study it. The research reported here relies upon the definition of discrimination used in Regulation B, which is most closely related to E.S. Phelps's notion of statistical discrimination.[2]

Statistical Discrimination

Phelps's paradigm of economic discrimination involves jobs, but it is readily adapted to the credit market. Suppose that each applicant for credit has a true quality of credit worthiness. The lender employs a credit-scoring system that produces an estimate of quality for each applicant. The estimates are unbiased; that is, on the average they are accurate. However, any individual may by chance be underrated or overrated.

Lenders have another bit of information: applicants come from two classes, and one class is known to have a lower average quality than the other. Given an applicant's credit score and his class, the lender can form a new unbiased estimate of the quality of the applicant. Given a fixed credit score, the information that an applicant is in the high-quality class produces a greater predicted quality than the information that the applicant is in the low-quality class. This provides a logical reason for treating applicants with equal credit scores differently. Phelps calls this statistical discrimination and points out that it is completely rational. A consequence, which Phelps does not stress, is that a firm discriminating on this basis is following the only policy consistent with its survival in a market where competitive equilibrium exists among many similar firms.

The concept of statistical discrimination is relevant in interpreting Regulation B. The regulation specifies that certain items, such as credit scores, may be used in evaluating credit applicants, while other items, such as membership in protected classes, may not be used. Thus, Regulation B forbids certain kinds of statistical discrimination.

Interpreting ECOA and Regulation B based on the model of statistical discrimination entails certain abstractions. In reality, several factors related to credit worthiness are admissible in the process of evaluating applicants, some of which are used in constructing credit scores. However, these scores are not ordinarily the sole factors involved in credit decisions. Ideally, the credit score represents the use of all admissible factors in making a decision to grant or deny credit.

Regulation B also governs aspects of behavior that are not accounted for in the theory of statistical discrimination. The theory assumes that a lender's behavior would be purely rational in the absence of regulation. However, real firms rely to some extent on guesswork, custom, and rules of thumb. Regulation B requires that these irrationalities not work unfairly against protected classes. Some examples may help clarify this aspect of Regulation B, which is often overlooked or misunderstood. A lender who irrationally grants credit to men who undertake unwise financial speculations must also grant credit to women who undertake similar speculations. A lender who irrationally refuses credit to all clergymen, priests, and rabbis may also refuse credit to women in similar vocations.

Definitions of Discrimination

Under ECOA and Regulation B, lenders may not use membership in a protected class in estimating credit worthiness. This situation creates two potentially conflicting definitions of discrimination. Suppose provisionally that membership in protected classes does furnish information that significantly affects the estimate of credit worthiness. ECOA and Regulation B require lenders to behave as if the best available estimate of the credit quality of applicants ignores their membership in protected classes. The lender has profit incentives to employ such information, but under Regulation B, that would be discrimination because it would treat applicants with the same scores on admissible variables differently. However, one might argue that the behavior is not discriminatory because membership in a protected class is valuable in predicting credit worthiness. According to the definition of discrimination underlying this argument, discrimination exists only if applicants with equal estimated quality, based upon both class and admissable variables, are treated differently.

In studying compliance with Regulation B there is no alternative to accepting its definition of discrimination. Moreover, there is good reason why this definition is acceptable. First, membership in a protected class has never been shown to be a useful predictor of credit worthiness in the presence of admissible variables that also predict credit worthiness. In Chapter Nine Shay, Brandt, and Sexton examined this question directly and concluded that the protected class information has no value in one case and minimal value in a second case. The practical usefulness of protected class information is thus very much in doubt. While future research might alter this conclusion, it is important in the absence of such findings to adhere to the definition of discrimination implied in Regulation B.

An important subsidiary reason for using the Regulation B definition is that it encourages the disclosure of facts concerning the value of protected class information. Lenders objecting to the Regulation B definition of discrimination can advance their case by producing statistics showing that their use of protected class information is proper because such information has a significant, independent effect upon credit worthiness.

Caution is needed in evaluating evidence that protected class information is valuable in predicting the credit worthiness of applicants. If an admissible objective factor is omitted from the set of variables used by a lender a protected class may differ from other groups in having a different average value for that factor. It will then appear that protected class membership is important in predicting quality when in fact the omitted variable is the important factor. Sufficient evidence of the predictive importance of protected class membership can be produced only in the presence of a full set of other explanatory variables.

Statistical Methods

The data to be reported here consist of applications for credit that were either approved or denied. The frequency of approval can be estimated as a function of applicants' characteristics, including admissible variables and membership in protected classes. If the lender discriminates, the frequency of approval will depend upon protected class information, as well as upon the admissible variables. Thus, the test for noncompliance with Regulation B is a test of the significance of the variables identifying protected class.

In principle all admissible variables might be used in explaining the frequency of approval, but in practice only the statistically significant variables are used. The insignificant variables are typically quite numerous relative to sample size, and their inclusion would tend to disguise discrimination by masking the explanatory power of protected class variables.

This method has a valuable by-product. The credit score used by the lender is in each case highly significant in explaining frequency of approval. The credit-scoring system is the best measure of the lender's evaluation of credit worthiness, and Regulation B requires that it be based on a statistically sound analysis of the lender's experience. Suppose that a lender is found to discriminate relative to a set of admissible variables, which includes the lender's own credit score. Then the lender is discriminating relative to its own evaluation of credit worthiness. In effect, this method uses a definition of discrimination that is based upon the lender's own policies, thus providing a fair means of judging the lender, and that agrees with the formally superior definition of discrimination already developed. The method was used to analyze the lending practices of two finance companies before and after the passage of the ECOA in 1975. The empirical findings concerning compliance with Regulation B are reported in the following two sections.

Analysis of Axial Finance Company

Axial Finance Company has offices throughout the country and is one of the nation's larger suppliers of consumer credit.[3] Large size is important because smaller chains of finance suppliers are known to be less likely to comply with the Truth in Lending Law and may also differ in their tendencies to discriminate illegally. Large size makes a reasonably large sample of data possible, although in this case Axial supplied information on only 200 applications for credit from the period before the October 1975 enactment of ECOA and on 200 applications thereafter. These data were drawn from a tape prepared for internal use by the company. The only variable identifying a protected class is age; other protected classes could not be recovered. Since all the Axial data are from the period before amendments extended ECOA to protect the old, any difference in the treatment of the old between the two periods must be interpreted as resulting from anticipation of future law or heightened sensitivity to unfair credit discrimination. This particular data set lacks many variables of potential interest, but its simplicity permits a clear exposition of the method of analysis, and the results are unambiguous.

Descriptive Statistics

The overall character of the data is summarized in

Table X-1. Observe that the total numbers of approvals and denials are the same in both periods. This reflects the sampling procedure: Since the company's average denial rate is 30 percent, the sample reflects a 30 percent rate of denial in each period.

The experience of young applicants (those under twenty-five years of age) seems to be about the same in the two periods. Their overall approval probability of .57 is consistent with both subsets of observations. It is somewhat worse than the approval probability for all groups, but this difference is accounted for by differences in credit score. Old applicants (fifty-five and over) were more frequently granted credit than those who were not old. They appear to have done better in the period after ECOA, although this difference or a greater one in sample proportions might be expected to occur about one time in five, even if there were no difference in population proportions. These observations are, of course, not conclusive without examining whether the older applicants in the two periods had approximately the same qualifications and whether they fared better or worse than applicants who were not old but otherwise had comparable qualifications.

Table X-2 breaks down the data by the credit score assigned. To simplify the presentation, young and middle-aged applicants are grouped together. The totals are slightly different from those in Table X-1 because some credit scores are missing. The credit scores of the old tend to be high in both periods, and the distributions do not seem to differ. Any difference in approval rates is therefore not readily attributable to differences in qualifications.

Empirical Findings

The effect of age on decisions to grant credit was examined statistically.[4] Prior to enactment of the ECOA, the old appeared to be victims of discrimination relative to credit score. The old also had a higher average credit score (285.4 versus 242.0 for those who were not old) in this period, perhaps indicating a higher population mean. Axial Finance's scoring system did not add or subtract points for age, although it could legally do so under ECOA, provided that the scoring of age had a statistical basis. On the other hand, age was positively correlated with important credit-scoring variables, such as time on the job (.46) and time at address (.43). In a linear regression of credit score on other applicant characteristics, the presence of age, which was not a credit-scoring variable, reduced the influence of time at address and time on the job and actually made the latter insignificant.

This credit-scoring system may overrate the old. Suppose that age does not itself increase credit worthiness. Consider items such as time at address and time on the job as signals that can be purchased by applicants for credit. Older individuals find these signals cheaper to purchase and are more likely to possess them at any given level of true credit worthiness. Thus, ten years at a single job or at an address is not as remarkable a credential for an older person as for a younger one and does not denote equally high quality as a credit risk. This argument does not settle matters, however, because age itself may increase credit worthiness. The credit-scoring system used by Monumental Finance, which is discussed below, does give points for age.

Analysis of Monumental Finance Company

Monumental is another large, national finance company.[5] The Monumental data differ from those for Axial Finance chiefly in the depth of coverage of individual applicants. The Monumental data were taken from original applications, on which names and street addresses had been blocked out to perserve confidentiality.

The Monumental data also differ from those of Axial in having a clear interpretation of before and after samples. The sampling periods span both the enactment and amendment of ECOA. Sex and marital status are identifiable in the sample, as well as age. However, there are very few married women among the applicants. The main focus in this section will therefore be on women as a group, with the understanding that these are chiefly single women.

Credit Scoring

The Monumental Finance Company credit-scoring system underwent an alteration between June 1975 and June 1977, the dates of the two subsamples. The alteration is complicated to describe because different versions of the system, which will be referred to as A, B, and C, were used in three different geographic areas. The instructions given to credit officers for interpreting the scores, however, did not differ geographically. Thus, the system was coordinated in the sense that a numerical score had the same mean-

TABLE X-1 Loan Applications Approved and Denied by Axial Finance Company

	BEFORE ECOA			AFTER ECOA			BOTH PERIODS
	Number Approved	*Number Denied*	*Proportion Approved*	*Number Approved*	*Number Denied*	*Proportion Approved*	*Proportion Approved*
Young (under 25)	12	12	.5	16	9	.64	.571
Old (55 and over)	18	7	.72	15	1	.938	.805
Other	110	41	.728	109	50	.686	.706
Total	140	60	.7	140	60	.7	.7

TABLE X-2 Axial Finance Company Credit Approvals, by Credit Score*

Credit Score	Before ECOA		After ECOA	
	Number of Applications	Proportion Approved	Number of Applications	Proportion Approved
20	0	-	1	1
120	0	-	2	1
130	0	-	1	1
140	1	0	0	-
150	1	0	1	0
160	1	0	3(1)	.333(1)
170	2	0	3	.333
180	8	.125	4	0
190	3	0	6	0
200	11	.273	10	.5
210	5	.2	16	.562
220	17	.647	19	.684
230	23(1)	.87 (0)	14(1)	.786(1)
240	23(1)	.826(1)	20(1)	.8 (1)
250	16(1)	.688(1)	25	.8
260	27(1)	.963(1)	19	.79
270	16(4)	.812(.75)	17(3)	.706(1)
280	9(5)	.778(.8)	12(1)	.667(1)
290	15(2)	.867(.5)	10(3)	1 (1)
300	6(3)	.667(.667)	6	1
310	6(2)	.833(1)	5(2)	1 (1)
320	6(3)	.833(.667)	5(4)	.8 (.75)
330	1(1)	1.000(1.000)	0	-
Total	197(24)	.711(.75)	199(16)	.704(.938)

Numbers in parentheses refer to applicants over the age of 55.

ing in the three versions, even though it was calculated differently.

The alteration of the system was a direct consequence of the passage of ECOA. It consisted mainly of deleting the word "housewife" wherever it had previously appeared. This change does not affect our study, for the few married women in the study were all employed. In version A of the system housewives received points for years on the job in 1975 but did not in 1977. In version B the housewife category was removed from the employer category, but because the points given for housewife in 1975 were the minimum possible in that section—the same as the points given in both years for being unemployed—there was no effective change here. In version C the housewife category was removed from the occupation and employer categories, but housewives were presumably grouped with "all other" in 1977, which earned the same number of points as being a housewife previously had earned. Women might have been nominally affected by the disappearance of the no-spouse category under spouse's occupation. However, the points earned by no spouse in 1975 equaled those earned by "all other" in 1977. In summary, these changes did not affect the scoring of women in our samples.

Men were nominally affected by the change because the category "housewife" vanishes under the heading for spouse occupation in version C. Since "unemployed" earned the same score as "housewife" here, again, the change was apparently purely cosmetic.

Several changes were made in the guidelines for evaluating credit scores. The changes appear to give credit officers more freedom to exercise judgment. In 1975, 200 was the critical point in credit scoring, but in 1977 risk was considered to improve from 181 upwards. From 165 to 180 the credit manager could approve if the trend was favorable, where "favorable trend" presumably meant that the applicant had prospects of an improved credit standing in the future. The change in the nominal cutoff from 200 to 180 or 164 is not as important as it might at first seem because there were numerous exceptions and special classes, which underwent little change from one year to another. Judging only from the instructions, one would guess that relatively few applicants were affected by these changes.

Descriptive Statistics

Table X-3 presents a breakdown of credit approvals and denials by sex. Women were more numerous among the accepted applicants after ECOA, and the difference between proportions before and after ECOA (.14 versus .197) is statistically significant at the 10 percent level. A breakdown by credit score and sex is presented in Table X-4. There may appear to be a difference in the company's response to female applicants, for six of those accepted in 1977 had scores below 206, while none of those accepted in 1975 had such low scores. However, the median score among female applicants granted loans is in the 256–260 range in both cases, and statistical tests show that the difference in distributions is not more than would be expected to occur by chance.[6]

TABLE X-3 Monumental Finance Applications Approved and
Denied, by Sex

| | BEFORE ECOA | | AFTER ECOA | |
	Approved	Denied	Approved	Denied
Female	32	38	55	37
Male	196	146	224	144
Proportion	.140	.206	.197	.204

New Applicants and Old Customers

An important feature of these data is that they
represent two populations: old customers and new applicants. These
groups differ in age, credit score, and acceptance rate, as shown in
Table X-5. The difference in acceptance rates is in part accounted
for by differences in credit scores and other variables. In 1975
women were a larger percentage of the new applicant group than of
the old customer group.

There are also differences in the behavior of the company toward
the two groups. Given credit score and other characteristics,
previous customers were much more likely to be approved for credit,
which is not surprising, since the previous customers were a select
group. At some time in the past they had all qualified for credit at
Monumental, whereas only a percentage of the new applicants
would do so.

The sources of differences between new applicants and previous
customers in the 1975 data are interesting. Credit was less likely to
be granted to old customers if the amount requested was large,
while for new applicants the opposite relation is reversed. The influence of a high nonmortgage debt level was unfavorable for the old
customer group but favorable for first-timers. The relationships in
the old customer group are those that would be expected, given that
the credit score measures the inherent quality of the borrower as a
credit risk: the greater the payment size, the greater the chance of
delinquency or default. For new customers, the amount requested
and existing debt were apparently correlated with factors observable
to loan officers but not recorded in our data, which indicate higher
quality of the applicant.

Discrimination Against Women

Presupposing that present and former customers are a different population from new applicants, one should examine possible discrimination against women in each group separately. The immediately interesting question is whether a variable identifying females has a significant negative coefficient, as the variable identifying the old has. Statistical tests show that this is not the case; women are not singled out in this fashion. Moreover, this is a robust result of the data; it does not depend upon the specification used.

The sense in which discrimination is lacking deserves emphasis. Since the credit score is regarded as an independent variable in this analysis, there is no implication that the credit score either is or is not as fair an indicator of credit worthiness for women as it is for men. Similarly, previous experience is taken as a given. However, in the earlier period women seemed to be underrepresented among the ranks of previous customers. This certainly hurt their chances for receiving credit and may have been a result of past discrimination. The result found here is that, given credit score and previous business with the company, there is no discrimination against women relative to men with the same credentials. Thus, in both periods Monumental complied with Regulation B's prohibition of discrimination against women.

Conclusions

The purpose of this study was to evaluate the effects of ECOA upon two finance companies. No effort was made to examine the overall effectiveness of ECOA or even the specific clause of Regulation B that defines discrimination as it is examined here. Both companies discriminated against the old, either before or after ECOA. Such discrimination can perhaps be explained by the tendency of scoring systems to overrate the old, which is probably true of most credit-scoring systems in use. If so, the phenomenon may be general among suppliers of consumer credit. Hence, there are interpretative problems with discrimination against the old which cannot be resolved without direct examination of credit-scoring systems to determine if they account for age fairly.

Monumental Finance Company did not discriminate against women, according to the Regulation B definition of discrimination,

TABLE X-4 Monumental Finance Applications Approved and Denied, by Credit Score and Sex

| | BEFORE ECOA | | | | AFTER ECOA | | | |
| | MALE | | FEMALE | | MALE | | FEMALE | |
Credit Score	Approved	Denied	Approved	Denied	Approved	Denied	Approved	Denied
82–180	2	39	0	14	9	35	2	12
181–185	5	6	0	2	1	9	-	-
186–190	0	4	-	-	5	9	2	0
191–195	1	3	0	1	2	5	2	3
196–200	2	5	0	3	4	4	0	2
201–205	5	2	0	1	9	3	0	3
206–210	7	4	2	0	4	5	2	3
211–215	1	1	-	-	5	5	2	1
216–220	6	2	4	1	8	2	-	-
221–225	5	3	0	3	5	4	1	0

Credit Score	Before ECOA				After ECOA			
	Male		Female		Male		Female	
	Approved	Denied	Approved	Denied	Approved	Denied	Approved	Denied
226–230	5	1	3	0	15	4	1	1
231–235	8	5	1	0	7	1	1	0
236–240	5	2	0	1	13	7	2	0
241–145	2	6	1	0	8	4	0	2
246–250	2	0	2	0	11	3	6	1
251–255	8	1	1	0	3	4	3	0
256–260	6	1	1	1	4	6	4	2
261–265	4	5	1	0	9	3	3	0
266–270	9	2	1	0	5	0	3	0
271–275	7	3	2	0	7	3	1	1
276–280	5	0	1	2	6	1	2	0
281–285	9	0	-	-	8	1	3	0
286–290	7	2	2	1	4	0	-	-
291–372	47	3	7	0	48	5	12	1
Total	158	100	29	30	200	123	52	32

TABLE X-5 Average Characteristic of Old Customers and New Applicants at Monumental Finance Company

Customer Characteristic	OLD CUSTOMERS			NEW APPLICANTS		
	1975	1977	Both Yrs.	1975	1977	Both Yrs.
Age	39.9	39.1	39.5	30.5	32.0	31.2
Amount requested ($)	810	750	779	982	1293	1140
Credit score	258	255	256	196	208	202
Income 1975 ($1,000)	11.5	-	-	10.0	-	-
Income 1977 ($1,000)	-	10.2	-	-	11.1	-
Nonmortgage debt in monthly payments ($)	162	174	168	112	189	151
Percent women	13.1	19.0	16.2	25.6	20.0	22.8
Percent accepted	81.9	82.1	82.0	20.7	37.6	29.3
Total	160	168	328	82	85	167

either before or after ECOA. Whether other finance companies also comply with Regulation B remains to be seen.

Finance companies occupy a relatively competitive sector of the consumer credit market. Economic theory suggests that competition will reduce certain kinds of discrimination. This provides a possible explanation for the behavior of Monumental, namely, that a firm that discriminated could not survive in competition with sheerly rational firms. In comparison to finance companies, banks tend to be sheltered from competitive forces by regulation of banking operations and by licensing laws. These regulations have many purposes and various desirable consequences. However, it is possible that as a result of extensive regulation, competition may not work as effectively against credit discrimination by banks as it may do in other sectors. Thus, some banks may not comply with Regulation B as fully as Monumental Finance does. This argument is by its nature speculative and is noted here to suggest areas for further research.

The methods used in this study could be used to study other suppliers of consumer credit. The major difficulty in pursuing such studies will be the inability to identify the protected classes. A credit officer knows by direct observation the color of the applicant's skin, but he or she is neither required nor permitted to record race as part of the application. Consequently, neither regulators, researchers, nor even the management of the firm can recover the information needed to reveal whether the credit officer discriminates. Since under ECOA designation of Mr., Mrs., or Miss is voluntary, a similar situation exists with respect to sex. In this study, the sex of applicants had to be inferred from a variety of sources, rather than being directly reported. The rules concerning such information are intended to inhibit discrimination, but they also inhibit investigations of compliance with the law.

NOTES

1. Regulation B, Section 202.7 (a).
2. Edmund S. Phelps, "The Statistical Theory of Racism and Sexism," *American Economic Review* 62, no. 4 (September 1972).
3. Axial Finance Company is a pseudonym.
4. The statistical methods employed are fully described in Arnold A. Heggestad and John J. Mingo, eds., *The Costs and Benefits of Public Regulation of Consumer Financial Services*, Final Report to the National Science Foundation (Cambridge, Mass.: Abt Associates Inc., 1978).
5. Monumental Finance Company is a pseudonym.
6. The test employed was the Kolmogorov-Smirnov.

INDEX